THE BIG
TWITCH

THE BIG
TWITCH

SEAN DOOLEY

ONE MAN,
ONE CONTINENT,
A RACE AGAINST TIME
– A TRUE STORY ABOUT
BIRDWATCHING

ALLEN&UNWIN

First published in Australia 2005

Copyright text © Sean Dooley 2005

Allen & Unwin Pty Ltd
83 Alexander Street
Crows Nest NSW 2065
Australia
Phone: (61 2) 8425 0100
Fax: (61 2) 9906 2218
Email: info@allenandunwin.com
Web: www.allenandunwin.com

National Library of Australia
Cataloguing-in-publication entry:
      Dooley, Sean, 1968-
      The big twitch : one man, one continent a race against
      time – a true story about birdwatching.

      ISBN 1 74114 528 7.

      1. Dooley, Sean, 1968- . 2. Bird watchers - Australia.
      3. Bird watching - Australia. I. Title.

      598.072340994

Cover design: Cheryl Collins Design
Text design: Phil Campbell
Typesetting: Prowling Tiger Press
Author photo (front cover): Greg Elms
Bird photos (front cover): in hand, Rohan Clarke; top, Chris Tzaros
Author photo (back cover): Mike Carter
Printed in Australia by Griffin Press
10 9 8 7 6 5 4 3 2 1

To Diane and Barry Dooley
For their love, for their example and for giving me the
opportunity to piss an inheritance up against a wall.

Contents

A Foreword for Birders

White-bellied Cuckoo-shrike. Red-necked Phalarope. Forty-spotted Pardalote. There, now that the non-birdwatchers have lost interest and have skipped to the first page containing a description of an outback sunset, I can have a little chat. This is the story of my quest to break the Australian birdwatching record and as such is concerned primarily with birds. In order to keep the dude non-birdwatching readers interested, however, occasionally I have had to divert from a purely birding focus. I would love nothing more than to write a book solely dedicated to each and every bird I saw during my big year, but I fear that I would lose the non-birding audience if I attempted to outline such things as the morphological differences between the New Zealand and Australian races of Shy Albatross. Please bear with me at these times as I try and placate those weird non-birdo readers.

To my many wonderful birding friends throughout the Australian ornithological community – an advance apology. You must remember that for most people, birdwatching seems a particularly unfathomable pastime. For their benefit I have at times exaggerated our behaviour for comic effect. If you feel you recognise yourself in these pages please remember that no malice is intended and it is all meant in good humour. I hope that I can still look forward to your friendly greetings in the swamps, scrubs and sewage farms around the country for many years to come.

Thanks for taking the time to read this, and if you do know a non-birder, let's just keep this bit between ourselves shall we?

A Foreword for Non-birders

Feelings. Relationships. Social interaction. Now that the birdwatchers have lost interest and have skipped to the first page containing a description of an immature Zitting Cisticola I can have a little chat. This is the story of my quest to break the Australian birdwatching record and is concerned primarily with birds, which keeps the nerdy birdwatching readers interested. Happily for everyone else there are plenty of non-birding diversions. I would love to have written more extensively about the landscape I travelled through, the characters I met and the emotions I felt during my big year but I fear that I would lose the birdy-nerdy audience if I didn't occasionally lapse into outlining something technical like the morphological differences between the Australian and New Zealand races of Shy Albatross. Please bear with me at these times as I try and placate those weird birdo readers.

I have many wonderful birding friends throughout the Australian ornithological community, but I feel I must apologise for them in advance because we are a particularly unfathomable lot. You may think I have exaggerated the behaviour of these birdy nerdies for comic effect, but in all honesty I dare only scratch the surface of this bizarre world lest they recognise themselves in these pages and fail to see the humour. Remember; I have to contend with these freaks out on the swamps, scrubs and sewage farms around the country for years to come.

Thanks for taking the time to read this, and if you do know a birder, let's just keep this bit between ourselves shall we?

Glossowary

A guide to a few of the more specialist terms in the book

Glossowary: Glossary combined with cassowary, Australia's second largest bird. The last stupid bird pun of the book. I promise. Well, almost the last one.

Twitch: The act of chasing after a rare bird. Can be both a verb: 'I tried to twitch the Grey Falcon', and a noun: 'I dipped when I was on the Grey Falcon Twitch'.

Grey Falcon: A mythical bird that doesn't exist.

Dip/dip out: The most depressing term in birdwatching. To miss out on seeing a bird.

Birder/birdwatcher/birdo: Someone who watches birds. All are fairly interchangeable and fluid terms. I tend to describe myself as a birder as I think it is the least daggy of the three. Kind of like saying you choose cyanide as your favourite poison because it is the least deadly.

Twitcher: An extremely dangerous creature with a nasty reputation. Essentially a birder who indulges in the act of twitching. Doesn't have quite the same negative connotation in Australia as it does in places like Britain. In fact most birders here would admit to occasionally indulging in a little of bit of twitching behaviour and if they don't they are most probably dirty rotten liars or total dudes.

Dude: A non-birdwatcher. Often used as a term of derision especially when applied to someone who is actually a birder.

Tick: What a twitcher does to a bird: reduce its beauty, majesty and wonder to a mere tick in a checklist.

Stringer: The greatest villain of the birding world. Someone who makes claims of non-existent birds (the act of stringing). Not to be confused with simply making a mistake of identification. Rarely done deliberately (one hopes), stringing usually occurs when a birder doesn't see a bird well enough, jumps to the wrong conclusion and is either too proud or stubborn to back down. To be labelled a stringer is to lose all credibility.

Lifer: A bird a twitcher has never seen in their life before. Also what many birders would like to turn a stringer into for their crimes.

Grip off: Not as grubby as it sounds but still an unpleasant experience. When one birder teases another after having seen a bird the other one hasn't.

Pelagic: a) Oceanic. b) a type of oceanic seabird. Note: Pelagic seabird is not a tautology as some species of seabird are usually found in coastal waters such as Pacific Gull and Black-faced Cormorant while others such as albatross are almost exclusively oceanic. c) Boat trips organised to go out to look for pelagic seabirds.

Seabirders: Birders who pay money to go out to sea in tiny boats in the middle of the ocean in order to get a closer look at pelagic species such as albatross. Idiots in other words.

Chum/berley: The fish guts and offal that seabirders cut up and throw overboard to attract seabirds to the back of the boat. See I told you they were idiots.

Bins: Binoculars. Also the receptacle that your housemate makes you throw the dead birds you've been keeping in your freezer into.

Jizz: The intangible essence of a bird that helps to identify it.

Jezz: An old school friend who first makes an appearance in Chapter 19.

Jazz: A form of music that I am sure many birdos are into.

Jozz: Now I'm just being stupid.

Breeding/non-breeding plumage: Some birds grow a distinct set of feathers during the breeding season to attract a mate. The bird can look totally different in each plumage, the avian equivalent of Pamela Anderson without her make-up.

Twitchathon: A birdwatching race where teams of twitchers try to see as many birds as possible in 24 hours. The crack cocaine of birding.

Flush: What you do with your crack cocaine if you are busted by the cops. Also what you do when you make a bird fly from where it has been standing.

Bird hide: What rare birds usually do when I am looking for them. Also the structures that birders use to hide in so as to observe birds without flushing them.

Pash: Kissing passionately. Something about as common as Night Parrot sightings when you spend a year twitching.

Night Parrot: A rare desert species that has not been authenticated alive in the wild for almost a hundred years.

Collingwood/The Magpies/The Pies: A Melbourne based Aussie Rules football team with a tendency to break the hearts of their supporters.

Pill: Another name for a football. What a twitcher soon becomes if they don't get to see the bird they are looking for.

PROLOGUE

13 December 2004, St Kilda, Victoria:
721 species, 0 girlfriends

The date was going well. A good choice of restaurant. I hadn't made a goose of myself while ordering the wine. She had beautiful, soft blue eyes and was laughing in all the right places. We had discovered a mutual appreciation for saganaki, that artery busting, salt laden, fried goat's cheese. I really liked this girl. Then she asked me the question.

'So, Sean, what do you do in your spare time?'

'Um...'

'What do you do for fun?'

Oh dear.

When I was ten, birdwatching seemed cool. I grew up in a fairly rough area – the local high school regularly featured on current affairs programs throughout the seventies as the toughest in the state – yet bizarrely enough being the best birdwatcher at primary school gave me a big man on campus status. Now that I am in my thirties, however, I kind of know that unlike my bogan primary school chums, most people don't actually think that birdwatching is cool. They think it's weird. Some people think it's a cute weird in a quirky way, some a creepy weird in a stalkerish, he's hiding bodies in a barrel way. But they all think it is weird.

This had been thumped into me from my first day at high school (not the scary 'as-seen-on-TV' school, but an exclusive private establishment that my parents had made me sit a scholarship for). I didn't know a soul at this new school and stupidly, on the enrolment form where it asked for your hobbies, did I put footy or cricket or petty vandalism like all the other kids? No, I put down birdwatching. And the sadist of a form teacher on the first day when he was introducing me to the class said, 'And you've got a special hobby haven't you Sean?'

'No.'

'Yes you have. Sean's a birdwatcher, everybody.'

Thirty pairs of scathing schoolboy eyes bore into me as the whispered cry, 'Poofter!' wafted through the agonisingly silent class-room. That was it. I was stained with a stigma that would take me the rest of school to shake for this was Homophobe High, where any difference was immediately stomped upon by that most conservative of bodies – the teenage peer group. I shared a locker with a guy who went on to play a few games of AFL footy and a couple of months later as we were packing our things away at home-time he turned to me and said, 'You know, Dooley, when you first came to this school, we all thought you was a poofter. But you know what, you're not, you're a good bloke.' And with that he gave me an affectionate dead arm. It was his way of saying I was accepted – just don't mention that weirdarse birdwatching thing again.

Birdwatching was not an attempt to be weird. I just liked doing it. It was fun. It got me outdoors, got me interested in the wider world. What's so weird about that? I was (and still am) into a lot of other things – sport, politics, music, culture. I spent a lot of time at the racetrack. I did a lot of theatre, particularly comedy, and ended up making a living out of writing for TV comedy shows. I even managed to squeeze in a law degree and did honours in English lit. Yet because over the years birdwatching was one of the things I'd most enjoyed doing, my date's simple question put me on the back foot, feeling like I had an awful lot of ground to make up just to prove that I was not a weirdo.

'Really, you're a birdwatcher? Like one of those twitchers?'

Her eyes had widened when I mentioned the birdwatching thing but I still thought I was in with a chance. And what amazing eyes – the same soft blue as the undertail coverts of a Bourke's Parrot.

'So are you like one of those anorak wearing trainspotter types?'

'No… well I do have an anorak, but I only wear it when it's pour-ing with rain or when I'm on a boat trip.'

'You're into fishing too?'

'No, I go on fishing boats out to the continental shelf to look for seabirds like albatross.'

'That's a long way to go just to see a bird.'

'I guess so, but it's about the only way I can see a new bird these days. Unless some vagrant species turns up somewhere like Broome or Darwin, then I'd have to fly up there to see it.'

'And you've done that? Just for a bird?'

I was drowning here. Yes I had done that, just for a bird. Earlier in the year I'd flown to Townsville for a day; an eight-hour return flight just to look for a seagull that had turned up from Japan. I didn't see it.

A couple of months later I was on another last minute flight across the country to look for Australia's first Rosy Starling when it turned up in Broome. That time I saw it and while it was a gorgeous pink and black creature, it wasn't so much the aesthetics of the bird but the thrill of the chase that appealed. That's not weird, just having a bit of fun doing something that I enjoyed. It wasn't like birdwatching ever got in the way of my functioning as a normal human being. Well sure, the day before I had my first law exam I had skived off studying to drive three hours south of Melbourne to see my first Arctic Tern. And yes, I spent my twenty-first birthday by myself, getting lost in the Mallee trying to rediscover a colony of Black-eared Miners. And I lost my first job as a bartender because I had missed the vital New Year's Eve shift when I'd rushed off to Adelaide to twitch the Hudsonian Godwit. But I wasn't one of those obsessive birdwatching freaks. I was just having a bit of harmless fun. If only I could have convinced my date.

'So even though I go birdwatching I don't really think of myself as a birdwatcher as such. I mean, they're generally very nice people, but they're just a bit too obsessive for my liking.'

I scanned her face to see whether she was buying it. Actually, her eyes were more silvery blue, like you'd find on a Red-winged Fairy-wren.

'So you don't have any birdwatching friends then?'

'Well, I guess there's only two birders that I'd consider I was good mates with. We actually do things together outside of bird-watching, like seeing bands and going to the footy. In fact we hardly ever go out birding these days. Except for the Twitchathon.'

'The what?'

Oh God. Why had I mentioned the Twitchathon? A birdwatching race in which teams of twitchers roam the countryside trying to see as many birds as possible in a 24-hour period. Even to me it seemed a bit weird. But with the Twitchathon I always had the excuse that it was for fundraising purposes – you'd get people to sponsor you a certain amount for every bird you saw, and the money raised would go to conservation projects. Still, that didn't explain how much I actually enjoyed cramming myself into a car laden with a bunch of birders and their assorted gear and driving around the state for twenty-four hours of nonstop birdwatching action. We wouldn't sleep, we wouldn't stop for food or even toilet breaks as we needed every spare moment for birdwatching. Or more precisely, driving to the places where we try and find the birds. We figured that the optimal way to see the most species was to drive to as many different habitats as possible and tick off the different birds in each of them rather than sticking to just a couple of areas and trying to see every bird that was there. The price for this strategy was that we spent more time in the car driving between sites than we actually did birding. This usually meant driving fourteen hundred kilometres or so in that one twenty-four hour period.

'Sounds like you're really into it.'

'Oh no, it's only a once a year thing,' I tried to reassure her. 'It's kind of like the Grand Final of birdwatching.'

'But to get to the Grand Final you have to play through the whole season, don't you?'

This girl was onto me. I'd have to explain how I would spend much of the weeks leading up to the Twitchathon sussing out where the birds actually were because they moved around so much in any particular year. Then that would lead on to how often I would go out birdwatching in general; the interstate and overseas trips, the mad dashes where I would fly or drive overnight because a rare bird had turned up somewhere and I didn't want to miss seeing it. Basically I would have to fess up to the whole twitching thing.

To be honest, the older I get the less I actually care if people think I'm weird. Maybe the older you get, the quirkier you are allowed to be. By the time I'd reached my thirties I was no longer as embarrassed to admit to my birdwatching habit. In fact I began to notice that rather than turn people away, the whole birdwatching thing began to fascinate them. To most people I think I appear fairly normal. Rather nondescript probably. Certainly I don't match the archetype most associate with birdwatching. I'm not a grey-haired old lady or a retired colonel. I don't wear glasses; I'm not bandy legged, and I don't talk like Jerry Lewis or wear daggy, oversized bermuda shorts. So when people find out that I am a birdwatcher, I get quite a positive, if somewhat surprised reaction. In fact once, at a restaurant not a million miles from this one, a similar girl once sat across from me at a similar looking table and announced she wanted to break up with me. Desperate for something to salvage my shattered pride I asked her why she had even gone out with dull old Dooley in the first place. I was hoping she would say something ego bolstering like, 'You're such a spunk,' or 'You've got a hot body.' She paused for a while, looking thoughtful and concluded, 'Because you were a birdwatcher.'

Apparently what I considered to be my nerdiest feature was actually my most attractive asset. At first I was shattered, but then I thought, 'Well stuff it.' And now I am happy to proclaim that yes, I am a birdwatcher, and what's more, I am a twitcher, which is at the serious end of birdwatching addiction. I am happy to say that.

Just not on a first date. I didn't mind being considered weird, but admitting straight up that you were into birdwatching put you a long, long way back in the credibility stakes. Second dates could be hard to procure if you hit them with that bombshell before they got to know the charming, funny, NORMAL Sean first. I couldn't get over how lustrous those eyes were – more dazzling than the blue shoulder patch of a Rainbow Pitta. But it was looking more and more unlikely that I'd ever have a chance to gaze into them again. Especially when she asked the killer question.

'So what's the longest time you've ever been birdwatching?'

I shifted uncomfortably, desperately trying to feign casualness.

'Oh, a year.'

'A year? You went birdwatching for a whole year? Why?'

'I was trying to break a record.'

'What? A birdwatching record? How?'

Maybe I should order another drink. This could take a while.

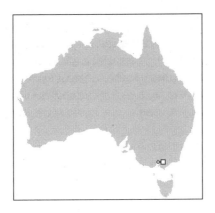

CHAPTER 1

New Year's Eve 2001, Bunyip State Park, Victoria:
0 species

Like many of my generation I spent New Year's Eve 2001 surrounded by a writhing mass of grooving hippies, overwhelmed by the incessant throbbing of electronic dance music of a rave party. The difference for me was that I was in the middle of a forest, spotlight in hand, trying to see a rare species of owl.

As I'd locked the door of my inner city terrace house a few hours earlier, hippies were the last thing on my mind. I was busy loading the car with binoculars, spotlights and a bottle of beer in case I had cause for celebration. My last act before leaving was to send a message to Birding-Aus an Internet birdwatching site which read in part:

As the clock winds down on 2001 I am preparing to head out to the wet forests east of Melbourne to look for, on the stroke of midnight, Sooty Owl.

If I see it, then Sooty Owl will be the first bird on my year list, and more importantly, take number one spot for the 'Big Twitch'.

The 'Big Twitch' was the culmination of a twenty-year dream – to break the Australian birdwatching record by seeing more than 700 species in a year. Sure, it may not seem all that impressive as far as dreams go, but it was my dream and I was finally going for it; committing myself wholeheartedly for an entire year, focused solely on the pursuit of birds. This was it. It was really happening.

The front gate swung shut. The street seemed eerily quiet, especially for New Year's Eve, so the sound of the diesel engine rumbling to life startled me out of my melancholic reverie. I put the 4WD drive in gear and headed off. Yet as I drove through the sprawling eastern suburbs of Melbourne that seem to stretch endlessly towards the mountains, I was not feeling exultant, or even nervous, but rather, resigned, as if it was the pre-dawn moment before the start of a crucial battle. Five minutes from home as I swung onto the Eastern Freeway I got a call on the mobile from two of my oldest and dearest friends. If I had been behaving as normal people do I would have been seeing in the New Year with them. I noted sadly that like everyone I was close to, I would barely see them over the forthcoming year. They didn't greet me with a 'Happy New Year' or wish me good luck on my quest. They just made hooting noises like an owl. Maybe a whole year away from my friends wouldn't be long enough. And they got the species wrong.

For I was after a Sooty Owl, one of the rarest and most difficult to see of Australia's ten species of owl. Actually three or four of the others were pretty bloody tricky to get onto as well, but I decided I was going to try for the Sooty as first bird on my 'Big Twitch' list. I could have started off my year list with a more mundane bird – a grungy inner city sparrow or pigeon, but I really wanted to kick things off with a bit of style.

And one of the best places I know to find a Sooty Owl is in the magnificent forests of the Bunyip State Park, an hour's drive east of Melbourne. Massive, straight-trunked eucalypts strain skywards: Messmate, Mountain Grey Gum, and on the higher slopes Mountain Ash, the tallest flowering plant in the world, tower majestically above exuberant fern gullies. Like much of the Australian bush, these forests do burn, and phenomenally fiercely – the Mountain

Ash has evolved to germinate only following the holocaust of a bushfire – but for the most part, even at the height of the unrelentingly hot Aussie summer, they emanate a tantalising coolness reminiscent of a Northern Hemisphere woodland glade.

Bunyip is the southern outlier of an almost contiguous block of forest that clothes the flanks of the Great Dividing Range. If you were to start here, you could virtually walk all the way to the northern tip of the continent without leaving a forest or woodland of some type. These forests stand as a testament to the majesty and indomitableness of nature. Sure, since the coming of humanity, both black and more particularly white, they have been burnt, cleared, logged, exploited and generally harassed, yet still they endure.

As do the creatures that dwell within them. Though in the case of the Sooty Owl, only just. They still manage to hang on despite their habitat being disturbed over pretty much their entire range. Interestingly, Sooty Owls occur in greatest densities in unlogged, or lightly logged, areas. Crucial for a large owl's survival are large trees old enough to have developed hollows in which they and their major prey species breed and shelter. And Bunyip has enough old growth trees to make this a prime Sooty Owl habitat.

And it was into this habitat, at about 11.30 pm, that I drove, having passed more than forty kilometres of suburban celebrations – people gathered in parks around a barbie or bonfire; premature fireworks displays for the kids to enjoy before bedtime; hoons in souped-up cars cruising the highway in packs, impatiently waiting for midnight to have a crack at becoming the first road fatality of the New Year. Entering the state park, I turned my back on civilisation and headed into the darkened forest alone.

Or so I thought.

The bush tracks were wet, but the skies seemed to be clearing as I stepped out of the car and waited to be greeted by the call of the owl. Instead I was assaulted by the disturbingly familiar 'doof doof doof' of electronic dance music. Somewhere further up the valley a bunch of hippies were getting back to nature by loading up on mind altering chemicals and overwhelming their senses with five million decibels of digital bass and jungle beats. They could have been miles away, but in the stillness of a mountain night they sounded as if they were around the next bend. As on any birdwatching occasion, I knew I wasn't guaranteed of seeing my target species: the bird might be foraging in another part of its range; it might be sitting tight on a nest; it might be there but not giving itself away; the weather might not be conducive; or the wind; or the phases of the moon; you might be struck down with blindness. All these permutations I had factored in to my calculations. But a techno dance party in the middle of the forest?

Eleven forty and my ears began to distinguish natural sounds from the 160 beats per minute of the rave music. No Sooty Owl but the unmistakable deep double 'whoo whoo' of the Powerful Owl drifted in from further up the gully. In the opposite direction their smaller cousin, the Southern Boobook gave its eponymous cheery call. Even if I dipped out on the Sooty Owl these other two would be ample compensation. But by eleven fifty the Boobook stopped 'boo-booking' and five minutes later the Powerful Owl also shut up. By eleven fifty-nine the forest had fallen completely silent.

Talk about the calm before the storm. On the stroke of midnight the ravers on the hill let off a cacophony of fire crackers as they ramped up the doof doof even louder. I spent the first minutes of the New Year walking disconsolately along the sodden track, heart sinking. This was not the brilliant start to the year I had hoped for. Encouraged by a successful reconnaissance mission only three nights earlier, my plan had been to arrive in the closing moments of 2001, line up a Sooty Owl, tick it off on the stroke of midnight and be home snuggled in bed by two. It seemed almost too easy.

After about fifteen minutes the Powerful Owl started calling again – bless its little cotton talons – and the Big Twitch was back in business. I walked along the gully towards the bird. As soon as I arrived it shut up and another (or the same bird) started calling from where I had just come. For the next half-hour I traipsed up and down the length of the gully, being led a merry dance by the nebulous hooting that always stopped as I drew near.

Then the rain started to bucket down. There was even a touch of hail. On the bright side it muffled the techno beats from up on the mountain. On the other hand, the owls fell silent and even if they were calling, the rain was so thick my spotlight beam wouldn't have been able to pierce its sheeting effect. I retreated to the car, musing on the irony that in the middle of a drought, I chose to venture into the forest on the one night it decided to rain. I cracked open my one bottle of beer and toasted myself and my venture. What a dill, what an absolute dill. I thought of all the people out there having a good time, in the company of their loved ones. Everybody seemed to have somebody to see in the New Year with yet I had chosen to turn my back on all that for the sake of an owl, a bloody owl, and even that wouldn't come to the party.

Sometime after one thirty, I ventured out into the black, dripping forest. The rain was gentler now, more intermittent, but it seemed to have driven all the creatures of the night into hiding. My spotlight beam revealed nothing. By two o'clock I'd had it. As had my spotlight battery. From now on, if I wanted to use the spotlight, it would have to be plugged in to the car. I left the sodden hippies dancing obliviously up on the hillside and started to drive the lonely road back to Carlton, crawling along in first gear, window wound down and arm out training the spotlight into the treetops.

The key to good spotlighting is to hold the beam as directly in front of your eyes as possible, enabling you to pick up the reflective eye-shine of any creature staring back at you. This means you see an awful lot of spiders (probably more than most people wish to know are out there) as they have a surprisingly vivid eye-shine. Finally I saw two glowing orbs staring back at me. My moment of exhilaration faded pretty quickly when I realised the eyes belonged not to a bird but to a Greater Glider, the largest of the gliding possums, a gorgeous, fluffy, teddy bear-like marsupial. It was also a prey species of the Powerful Owl, but for tonight this little fella was safe. Perhaps the owls had moved up the hill and were feasting on the carrion of exhausted hippies who'd danced themselves to death. One can only hope.

At the very last patch of suitable habitat for Sooty Owl, where the tall forested gully gave way to the more heathy woodland of the broader valley, I stopped the car for one last forlorn listen. As the engine cut out I heard the cry of a Sooty Owl. I jumped out of the car, hopes suddenly raised. For five excruciating minutes all was silent. I resorted to doing something I loathed to do – play a tape of the call to try and lure the bird in. My qualms about the taped call disrupting the bird's foraging patterns were unfounded as the tape had absolutely no effect. The bush remained totally quiet. Desperate, I tried out my pathetic impersonation of a Sooty Owl. Heard up close, the main territorial call of the Sooty Owl sounded disconcertingly like the high-pitched scream of a petrified woman. From a distance the same call sounded like the whistling of a falling bomb.

I pursed my lips and gave a wavering, descending whistle. There was no way any self-respecting Sooty Owl would dignify this pathetic attempt with a response. Instantly my whistle was answered by the shrill scream of a bird coming in closer. So unenthused at my prospects had I been that I hadn't even bothered to have the spotlight at the ready and had to scramble about for it on the front seat. Once the beam was turned on, there on a branch about ten metres away was a male Sooty Owl going absolutely spare at me with a manic series of trills sounding more like crazy electronic feedback than any call you'd expect an owl to make. The hippies would have loved it.

I certainly did. To see an owl at night was always a thrill, and the Sooty was simply a gorgeous bird. The critter going nuts at me, probably berating me for my attempted mimicry – 'That's not a Sooty Owl, this is a Sooty Owl' – was a foot long, stunning sooty grey nugget of an owl. The spotlight made the plumage shine almost like pewter. This is a bird that is very rarely seen so to have it as my first bird for the year was utterly exhilarating. Where ten minutes ago I had been totally despondent, now as I started the long haul back to the city I was pumping my fists in triumph.

Sooty Owl. Bird number one. Six hundred and ninety-nine to go.

CHAPTER 2

15 July 1980, Nicholas Hall, Lonsdale Street, Melbourne, Victoria:
545 species

So what the hell is the Australian birdwatching record and why would anyone bother trying to break it? The latter part of the question was something I was to ask myself an awful lot throughout the coming year; the first part is relatively straightforward.

Put simply, the Australian birdwatching record I was concerned with was about seeing the greatest number of species of bird in Australia in the one year. As records go, there's not much pomp and ceremony attached. There is no trophy, no official presentation and quite frankly very few people, even in the birdwatching world, knew or particularly cared that it existed. In terms of world-shattering significance, it is barely a notch above the record a couple of kids might have for hitting a tennis ball on a racquet a consecutive number of times in their backyard. But it was the only record I've ever been interested in breaking. Or more precisely, the only record that I was interested in and actually capable of breaking, having at the age of thirty-three finally come to terms with the fact that I was unlikely to kick the winning goal in the Grand Final or take the greatest number of test wickets or have the highest selling rock album in history. No, if I ever wanted to break a record, birdwatching it had to be.

And the Australian birdwatching record had been an obsession for many, many years. And for that I blame a humble postie more than sixty years older than me. His name was Roy Wheeler, a legendary figure in Australian birdwatching. In 1979 at the age of seventy-four he did something that was to have a profound effect on the rest of my life – he attempted to see the greatest number of Australian birds in a year, a quest articulated in a piece he wrote for *The Bird Observer*, the newsletter of the Bird Observers' Club of Australia (BOCA) entitled 'Chasing a Record'. As a young birdwatcher I avidly soaked up every word detailing Roy's quest. Re-reading 'Chasing a Record' today, I realise it is little more than an unrelenting list of places visited and birds seen. Hardly Tolkien, but to my eleven-year-old imagination this opened up a world every bit as magical as Middle Earth.

I was hooked. I immediately set about compiling my first list, counting up all the birds I had seen to that point in 1980. Roy's article coalesced my passion for birds with my near autistic obsession for list making. I had been into birds for about a year, but now it dawned on me that I could order the birds I'd seen in all sorts of ways – year lists, life lists, state lists, day lists. The possibilities were endless.

OK. It's at this point I have to stop the story to address a certain issue. For those of you who were tempted to titter at the phrase 'I had been into birds for about a year' it's time to clear some things up. Yes, 'birds' is a classic sniggering euphemism for women. And guess what? You're not the first to make that connection. And it is not only in English that the joke applies. For some reason birds serve as double entendre in many languages. Apparently the German word for bird, *vogeln*, is the same as their slang word for having sex. In Australia we tend to use the word 'root'. Makes you wonder what that says about our respective cultures; they associate the act of making love with winged creatures that soar above this earthly realm, we with a bit of wood that stays stuck in the ground, away from the light and covered in dirt.

From the very first moments I began birding I was assaulted with these 'fnar fnar' style comparisons – I'm sure you can imagine the sort of thing: 'Birdwatching, hey? I'm a bit of a birdwatcher myself. Nudge-nudge, wink-wink.' My dad was particularly fond of that one. Coming home from work one night, he told me that he'd seen a couple of interesting birds out of his office window in Queen Street, Melbourne. This was possibly the first time he had taken much interest in my new hobby so my ears pricked up and, eager to make a connection and solve his identification problem, I naïvely asked him to go into more detail. I still didn't twig when he started talking about these birds' long legs, and it was only when he got to the stage of saying one was a blonde that the penny finally dropped. Since then I've put up with those kinds of jokes countless times, and you know what? It hasn't got any funnier.

I've actually got used to the jibes in the same way, I guess, someone with the surname Treblecock or Sidebottom lets people have a bit of a snigger and then move on. But there is one thing I just can't let go, and that is when someone I've been introduced to says, 'Birdwatching, hey? What, the two legged kind?'

Now let's stop for a moment and consider this. Never mind the dubious nature of the humour, focus rather on the fact that both an Albatross and Kylie Minogue have got two legs. So unless the speaker is specifically referring to Paul McCartney's second wife, the joke makes no sense. If you feel compelled to make this kind of witty remark, for accuracy's sake it should go something like this.

'Hi, my name's Sean and I'm a birdwatcher.'

'Birdwatching? What, the feathered kind!?'

It won't win you many marks for originality but at least it will be biologically correct. No wonder I call myself a twitcher...actually that has an entirely new set of connotations.

But getting back to Roy. In his article he stated that he saw a total of 545 species, breaking the previous record held by Darwin's John McKean by ten species (and almost 400 ahead of my ultimate 1980 total). Until this time very few people would even have seen this many species in Australia in their lifetime, let alone in the one year. Birdwatching has been around since the First Fleet, but for much of the two centuries of European occupation, the opportunity to look at birds on a continental scale was rather limited. The 730-odd species that had been found to that time were spread across the entire continent. The only place you could ever hope to see a Golden-shouldered Parrot, for instance, was on Cape York Peninsula; to get onto a Red-capped Parrot would require a trip to the opposite end of the continent, to the southwest of Western Australia. In a country where the main highway between the two major cities of Sydney and Melbourne had only been fully sealed in the 1960s, the opportunity for the average punter to travel these vast distances was severely limited. Birdwatchers tended to be either enthusiastic amateurs who were generally limited to looking at the birds of their local regions, or they were professional ornithologists such as the legendary John Gould, who had the opportunity to study birds from all over the country, though usually dead and laid out on a museum table.

By the turn of the last century, some birders began to put down their shotguns and pick up their field glasses, contenting themselves to merely look at the birds rather than obliterating them. The first bird clubs began to form, such as the Royal Australasian Ornithological Union (now known as Birds Australia) in 1901, BOCA in 1905 and the South Australian Ornithological Association in 1899. The exchange of information about birds began to flow more freely and with the development of good optical and photographic equipment, field guides, and improved communication and transport, a more comprehensive picture of Australian birdlife began to emerge. By the 1970s strong networks of birdwatchers had become well established and news of rare and interesting birds spread like wildfire. Predating the Internet, the birding grapevine could disseminate information faster than anything previously known to man.

I've had first hand experience of this. In 1998 I found a Bridled Tern by the lake outside my parents' house, probably the rarest bird I've ever personally found. In terms of worldwide rarity, the Bridled Tern is a long way from Dodo status. There are millions of them in the tropical seas of the world. The thing is, until that fateful December day there had never been any in the state of Victoria. The bird I saw had been blown in by the same ferocious storm that had killed a number of Sydney to Hobart sailors in that year's yacht race. This wind was so fierce that my Bridled Tern may have been blown in from its nearest breeding grounds – about four thousand kilometres away in Western Australia.

Knowing it was a first for the state I immediately tapped into my portal into the birders' matrix. Sadly the Bridled Tern only stayed long enough for three other birders to see it, but over the next day many others turned up, including, within two hours of the bird being sighted, a birdwatcher from Britain whom I had never met. Now I am not saying that he managed the 13 000 kilometre trip from England in supersonic time just for this Victorian rarity – most likely he'd been birding locally when he bumped into someone who'd mentioned a Bridled Tern had shown up nearby – but the lengths to which birders will go to see a new bird can be quite surprising.

Such birders are known as twitchers. Twitchers are the hard core of the birdwatching world. If you were likening birdwatching to extreme sports, your kindly little old lady who puts out a few crumbs for the pigeons would rate at about the same level as a game of coits, whereas twitching would be more akin to parasailing off a Himalayan cliff-face whilst blindfolded, drunk and wrestling a shark. Put simply, twitching is actively chasing after birds to add them to your list. Very early on in your birdwatching career, this may entail a simple walk to your local park. But once you've seen all the common birds in your area, you have to search further afield in order to see new ones. Eventually there will come a point when you'll have seen nearly everything there is to see. This is when twitching comes into its own. If you've seen nearly every bird in Australia, whenever a new one turns up you simply have to go see it, no matter if it is in Tasmania or Townsville, Broome or Bermagui. It is not unknown for a twitcher to fly from Sydney to Darwin for the day just to see a vagrant Asian duck.

The word twitching itself suggests action, liveliness, as opposed to the more static form of bird*watching*. The term originated in England in the late 1950s. Amongst the first birders there to get into this new form of birdwatching were two blokes from Norfolk. Upon hearing of a rarity, they would jump on their pillion passenger motorbike and burl across the countryside in pursuit. Being Britain, of course, it meant that they would often arrive at their destination frozen stiff, shivering massively – twitching, if you will – from the cold. Amongst their friends they became known as 'the Twitchers' and thereafter their birding excursions as 'being on a twitch'. The term caught on, apparently much to their eternal embarrassment.

Roy Wheeler was probably not much of a twitcher as such. It's pretty hard to dash off after every rarity when you are in your seventies and reliant on somebody to drive you everywhere. But after sixty plus years of birdwatching Roy had travelled a fair deal and seen an awful lot of birds. All he had to do was to put all that knowledge together and call in a few favours to get people to take him out to the best birdwatching sites. Over his lifetime Roy had met countless numbers of birdwatchers from around the country and there were plenty of people more than happy to oblige. By all accounts, Roy was an extremely generous, enthusiastic and engaging fellow. So by the end of the year, a lifetime of goodwill had netted him the record. Perhaps not the greatest adventure in the world, but try telling that to me as an eleven year old sitting in a draughty old hall in Melbourne listening to Roy speak of his travels.

I learnt a lot that night. Not merely about the birds of Australia and where they occur and how to see them, but also about the politics of the birdwatching community. Before Roy's talk the secretary of the birdwatching club called for any reports of interesting sightings from the audience. As the old ladies around me reported on the various birdies spotted in their gardens, I got swept up in the moment and stuck my young hand up.

'Glossy Ibis at Seaford Swamp.'

The secretary paused briefly and then shot back, 'Are you sure it wasn't a young Straw-necked Ibis?'

Of course I was sure. You'd have to be an idiot to mix up a Glossy and a young Straw-necked. Oh…that was her way of saying she thought I was most probably an idiot. I should let the grown-ups get on with their business. Shut up and I might learn something.

But I was a slow learner. A few minutes later, the secretary was calling for people to report on any sightings of the Spiny-cheeked

Honeyeater, a common desert bird that sometimes appeared in the suburbs of Melbourne during the winter. Again, all around me blue-haired ladies and balding gentlemen were divulging observations of a Spiny-cheeked at Montmorency in April, another at Beaumaris in June. Each contribution was greeted by a little cooing of approbation by the crowd. Down at my patch at Seaford we'd been seeing heaps of Spiny-cheeks that winter. Foolishly I raised my hand again.

'There's been quite a few at Seaford this year.'

'Yes, well they *are* quite common on the peninsula,' she snapped in reply.

She was partially correct. They were common along the southern coastal areas of the Mornington Peninsula, where there was an isolated population. Seaford, which wasn't technically even on the peninsula, was almost fifty kilometres from the nearest of these birds. It was only fifteen kilometres from Beaumaris, where apparently a Spiny-cheeked Honeyeater was colossal news, yet my sighting had been summarily dismissed. It was kind of humiliating for an eleven-year-old kid making his first foray into the adult world, but I learnt an invaluable lesson that night. In the world of bird-watching, reputation was everything. If Roy Wheeler had claimed those birds, no problem – he had decades of experience to back him up. I was just a kid, I had no reputation. Why should they believe me? Actually, I bear no grudges from that moment for it indelibly imprinted on me the notion that before I claimed to have seen any bird I had to be damned sure about it as humiliation was only one condescending cluck away.

Interestingly, I didn't have to defend my sightings to Roy. On meeting him after his talk he asked me about the Glossy Ibis, saying he hadn't seen it at Seaford before but had seen a flock of them once in a nearby swamp. He asked me to describe the bird and when I had he said with a twinkle, 'It must have been pretty exciting to see it.' Who knows if he really believed me, but to be taken seriously for that moment by such a figure meant the world to me. I was glad Roy had the record.

But he didn't have it for long. In 1982, one of the new generation of twitching birdwatchers, Kevin Bartram, smashed Roy's record and saw an unprecedented 607 species in the one year. It was only a few years earlier that the first birders had reached six hundred in their entire lifetimes. And yet here was an unemployed, hard-core music fan (Kevin's other obsession is punk music – he even hosts his own garage and hard-core show on a Melbourne public radio station under the moniker 'Kev Lobotomi'), often bedecked in ripped jeans and t-shirt, hitching his way around the country birdwatching. Kev's strategy was different to Roy's in that, plugged into the emerging twitching network, he made sure he chased after as many rarities as possible snaring, on top of the birds Roy saw, such unusual vagrants as Black-tailed Gull, Oriental Reed-Warbler and Buff-breasted Sandpiper, ensuring he passed the magic six hundred barrier. The birding world was agog. Surely this record would take some beating. For almost a decade no Australian birder was able to surpass Kev's feat. It would take an interloper to snare the record.

Mike Entwhistle was an English twitcher of the new generation. Rather than content himself with chasing after the latest rarity to turn up amongst the relatively depauperate bird populations (species wise) in the British Isles, he had sought to see as many of the world's ten thousand species as possible. As part of his world birding quest he set up camp in Australia during 1989 and managed to travel so extensively that by year's end he had seen a record 633 species. I don't think Mike actually intended to break the record rather, like most dedicated twitchers, he just wanted to see as many birds as possible.

I'm unable to ask Mike about his intentions or anything else associated with his record year, because after Australia he moved on to South America where he was killed in Peru by Shining Path guerrillas. You may have thought I was jesting when I likened twitching to an extreme sport, but twitchers seem to place themselves in life-threatening situations in the pursuit of birds with alarming regularity. The area where Mike and his birding companion, Tim Andrews, were killed was in territory so dangerous even the CIA were reluctant to send in operatives. But despite warnings from the locals, the lure of potential new ticks for their world lists proved far greater than common sense. Most people would say it is not worth risking your life to see a bird. Plenty of twitchers would disagree.

And so the record stood. Nobody seemed to be much concerned with it, unlike in Britain or the States where Big Years are hotly contested amongst twitchers. In Australia, it seemed no-one could really be bothered. The distances were too vast, the potential cost too enormous, the absurdity too great. Why bust a gut spending a year seeing all the stuff you'd seen before when you could be pooling your resources to go for birds that you hadn't ever seen? A Big Year remained a very low priority for Australian twitchers. And to top it off, the precedents set by the record holders were rather off-putting as by 2000 the champs were all dead. Mike as outlined above; Roy in 1988 after illness had confined him to a nursing home for several years; John McKean unexpectedly from a heart attack in 1995, and though Kevin is still very much alive and kicking, he does work in public radio, which is kind of like being dead. Only joking, Kev – I'll have to take out a subscription to his show to make up for that one.

But for me, the record remained a Holy Grail. Throughout my teenage years in those idle, daydreaming moments when I wasn't thinking of kicking that winning Grand Final goal or pondering how I could strike up a conversation with Naomi Stephens on the school bus on the way home, I would contemplate how you could break the birdwatching record. Where would I go? Should I make two trips to the Top End, one in the dry season, another in the wet? How many boat trips would I need to take? How was I going to find a Night Parrot? Though I never admitted this to anyone, the primary reason I took a year off between school and university in 1987 was to have a crack at the record. Well, that's an exaggeration, as I didn't feel I was worthy enough to be the record holder. I still had so much to learn about birds. But I was determined to become the youngest person to have seen 600 birds, whether in the same year or not.

My plans were railroaded somewhat by a bout of unexplained nausea that lasted three months. I also got my first girlfriend, which made it really hard to drag my sorry, lovesick carcass away from Melbourne, and not having any money didn't help, nor did being hopelessly inefficient in general. It wasn't until the next year, after a trip to Kakadu, that I even passed the five hundred mark and it took me until early 2001 to get to six hundred. It wasn't that I'd stopped birding – in fact the older I got, the more important birdwatching became to me. It went from just a hobby to being fundamental to my sense of self and a vital component in maintaining my mental health. Birds became my access point to something larger than the problems of a gawky, law student-cum-comedian. Birding gave me the excuse to get out into the bush, to lose myself in the wider world of nature, detox my mind of everything that was going on. Without birdwatching who knows what sort of basket case I might have ended up? My God, I could even have become a lawyer.

Luckily (more for my potential clients than anything else) I didn't become a lawyer but managed, somehow, to earn a living for a few years as a television comedy writer. By 2001, however, every show that I had ever worked on had been cancelled due to poor ratings and I think television producers around the land were beginning to twig that it might have been me that was the common factor. My employment prospects for the coming year were not looking good. With no work on the horizon I had to assess my options. By now, at thirty-three, I was beginning to grow up and be a bit more far sighted in my life – sure, I was only thinking of the upcoming twelve months, but for someone who was reluctant to commit to Friday night drinks more than an hour out from the event, twelve months was a big improvement. I could try and get a real job, perhaps even return to law or I could, of course, always try for the record…

It was a daunting prospect but I was far better positioned to go for it than I had been as a callow eighteen year old. While I was still hopelessly inefficient, at least I'd shaken those bouts of nausea. I no longer had a girlfriend to worry about leaving behind, having only months before successfully buggered up yet another relationship. And despite the lack of a job I didn't have money troubles this time thanks to the really crap genetic hand my parents were dealt, both dying of cancer within two years of each other.

The money I inherited was not a huge fortune, but it was enough to buy a comfortable house in the outer suburbs of Melbourne, as my brother had done. My Dad in particular had been very keen for this money to help set us up in the real estate market so that he could rest easy knowing that at least we wouldn't have to worry about a roof over our heads. The trouble was, I didn't know where I wanted to live. Their deaths were sobering not merely because of the searingly unbearable wrench of losing those two wonderful people, but because it left me exposed as rudderless. I had lived most of my life in my head, never attaching to the corporeal tangibles of the world. I had no sense of my place within the world. The idea of putting down roots was so disorienting to me because I still didn't know where I belonged. A year after receiving my inheritance I still had absolutely no idea what I was going to do with it.

For almost as long as I could remember, I'd fantasised about running away – hitting the road and losing myself in the wider world. Not that I had anything to run away from, quite the opposite, for I had a fantastic childhood, but the idea of engaging with the world, being completely free to go wherever I chose, do whatever I wanted, was intoxicating. I was always way too responsible for such nonsense, however, and those thoughts remained the stuff of musings to drift off to sleep to. Suddenly, there was no impediment to following that dream. No family, no job, no ties. I was in the rare position where I could run away without leaving behind an unresolved mess. The record beckoned. I might never have this sort of opportunity again in my life, at least not until I retired and by then would I have the energy to bother? For so many years going for the record had seemed a sensational thing to do, yet when faced with it as a palpable option, I was daunted to the point of inertia. 'Be careful what you pray for, you just might get it.' The idea of actually pursuing a dream, the prospect of going after something I'd always wanted to do, in fact filled me with the direst dread.

The matter was decided for me in one of those embarrassing moments when you say something that you desperately wish you could just take back. I was returning to Melbourne with a birding friend after a trip to central Victoria. The long conversations about birds had finally petered out and we had moved on to talking about our personal lives. I started rabbiting on about my predicament and found myself uttering the words, 'Sometimes having money is a curse.' What a dick. My friend was planning to start a family, was worried about being able to pay off his mortgage and raise a child, and here was I wallowing in self-pity because I didn't know how to spend my cash. It was like someone complaining about the cost of a manicure to a double amputee.

I couldn't believe I'd said something like that. This was not who I was. Perhaps my inertia sprang from the fact that my inheritance was a last link with my parents, perhaps I was frightened to waste it on a mad scheme they wouldn't have approved of. I would have given anything for my parents to still be alive so that I didn't have to deal with their money, but that was not going to happen. This inheritance had been their last gift to me and I know that they intended for it to make my life better, help me make my dreams come true. Owning a home had never been a dream of mine. So rather than putting a deposit down on a funky inner city pad, I bought a four-wheel drive, a new atlas and began planning. And on the last night of 2001 I left a message on the Internet declaring to the world my intention to break the Australian birdwatching record. There, it was public now, no going back.

In a cemetery in suburban Melbourne, an odd spinning noise could be heard coming from the graves of Barry and Diane Dooley.

CHAPTER 3

3 June 1996, Collingwood, Victoria:
19 species

Tell a birder that you are trying to break a birdwatching record and their first question will be something like 'Where do you plan to get Buff-breasted Button-quail?' Confide to a non-birder and they invariably ask, 'How can you prove it?' I guess technically there was nothing to stop me from staying home all year, and pretending I saw a whole stack of birds other than the fact it would be a really stupid and pointless thing to do – unlike chasing after birds for a year which is, of course, not stupid or pointless in the slightest. Actually, I think that is part of the appeal of birdwatching for me – you come away from an encounter with a bird with absolutely nothing tangible to show for it other than the memory of the experience and maybe a tick in your notebook. You indulge in the experience merely for the nature of the experience. It is conquering without violence, hunting without the kill. There are no trophies in birdwatching. Well, one birder I know of makes up a little commemorative plaque for himself every time he discovers a bird not previously seen in Australia, but generally the rewards of birdwatching are far more esoteric. What I am particularly charmed by is not only the encounter with what is inevitably a beautiful creature but also that every correct identification is like uncovering a little kernel of truth. Every bird that you see has to belong to some species and there is immense satisfaction in working out exactly which species that is.

Not that you could always convince others of that. And with the task I had set myself I would somehow have to find a way to prove the truth of my convictions on 633-plus occasions. One obvious way would be to photograph each species I saw. While I would have a camera with me on my travels, it was hard enough just seeing the buggers in the first place, let alone getting close enough for long enough to focus a nicely framed shot. Some, like the aforementioned Buff-breasted Button-quail, have never been photographed in the wild. To take a happy snap of every species I intended to see would have taken considerably longer than a single year.

For every bird I couldn't photograph I could always try to ensure that I had another credible observer along with me to verify each sighting. That would entail spending the entire year in the company of at least one other birdwatcher. I go birdwatching for the birds, not the birdwatchers. The thought of spending a year in close company with twitchers chilled me to the core. Not that I have anything against them, I am terribly fond of the members of the tribe, it is just that basically, they are a bunch of obsessive freaks.

There is a form of autism known as Asperger's Syndrome in which the sufferer, most often male, becomes so fixated on one particular subject that everything else is excluded, especially normal social interactions. Often the only way they can interact with others is through the medium of the obsession that consumes them. Some argue it is nothing more than an extreme form of maleness, coming from the same part of the brain that enables a bloke to sit totally absorbed in a game of football, oblivious to everything around him. The argument goes that such a narrow focus on the one subject was an essential skill for our early ancestors when on the hunt. People with Asperger's are simply unable to switch off this trait.

In Britain Asperger's is sometimes known as the 'trainspotters' disease', but it could just as easily apply to birders. I've known some twitchers for twenty years and still have no idea about their family life or what they do for a living. All I know about them is whether they have seen the Blue Rock Thrush, or if they can identify a White-winged Black Tern in non-breeding plumage. In Mark Cocker's excellent and illuminating book, *Birders*, he describes a classic example of a birder's inability to communicate on any level other than birds. America's most famous bird watcher, Roger Tory Peterson, was in England with a party of pre-eminent birders. Cocker writes: 'Lord Alanbrooke, keen birder and Chief of Imperial General Staff during the Second World War, was expanding on his relations with Sir Winston Churchill. But in the midst of the Field-Marshal's historical monologue, Tory Peterson turned to the group and said, "I guess oystercatchers will eat most any kind of mollusk".'

Having spent years associating with birders I find this anecdote amusing but totally unsurprising. Just after my mother died I received a call from a birder friend. He had enough awareness of the forms of social intercourse to greet me with a perfunctory inquiry as to how I was. I told him that in fact I wasn't all that great as Mum had just passed away. There was an uncomfortable silence at the other end of the line. After about twenty seconds he managed, 'There's a Broad-billed Sandpiper at Werribee Sewage Farm.'

If my only option for verifying my record was to spend a year constantly in the company of these people, then I thought I'd rather not bother, for while I'll put my hand up and admit to certain Asperger's tendencies, even I have my limits – they usually kick in after the first half-hour of intense discussion of wing moult sequences in wading birds.

Not that I would be able to have a twitcher chaperone me at all times even if I wanted to. I couldn't find any takers to accompany me on my New Year's Eve owl quest. What a depressing thought – all the tragic Asperger's cases had somewhere more interesting to spend the evening. Even my two closest birding friends, Puke and Groober, turned me down. Puke's real name is Paul Peake and with a propensity to be sick every time we go out on a boat, it's easy to see why he's been saddled with that nickname. I'm not quite sure why we call

Groober Groober, we just do. A couple of years older than me but with a similar sense of humour (not necessarily a free flowing commodity amongst what is often a very earnest group) they are about the only birders with whom I have a relationship that extends beyond birding matters. In fact apart from our annual Twitchathon pilgrimages, I rarely even get out birding with them anymore. So I thought they would have jumped at the chance but no, it seemed they had actual lives that involved going out and being with people on New Year's Eve. Freaks.

I soon realised I could never have my total officially verified. There was no official body to monitor the verification anyway. To try and give my quest some credibility in the eyes of others I would have to rely on my reputation. In the birding world, reputation is everything. And like virginity, reputation can only be lost once – well, maybe twice in the right circumstances. As far as I knew my reputation was still intact in the sense that I had no dodgy records in my past that other birders questioned. Every rare bird I had ever seen had been above reproach, usually backed up by a photograph or somebody else confirming the sighting. But that didn't mean that I had much of a reputation amongst the upper echelons of the twitching world as a good birder, more that I didn't have a reputation for being a stringer, someone who makes spurious claims about which birds they have seen. To be honest, though I had been on the fringes of the birding scene for the past twenty years and knew many of the main players, I was probably regarded as little more than a twitching dilettante. Even if I'd had the gravitas Roy Wheeler used to have, there was still no practicable way I could verify my sightings.

It all came down to a matter of honour. People would either have to believe me or not believe me. Ultimately I didn't really care who believed me as long as I was happy with the sighting. To this end I took it upon myself to set some kind of parameters for my task so that I could be satisfied within myself that I really had seen each species. And besides, it gave me the opportunity to make another list. I liked lists. So here were the five basic rules I developed for the Big Twitch.

1 Only actual birds that are wild and free flying can be counted.
2 All birds must be seen within a calendar year.
3 All birds must be seen within Australian Territory.
4 A species can only be counted in accordance with the official Australian Bird Checklist.
5 All species have to be seen well enough to establish their identity.

Simple enough, I thought. But each category raised a veritable Hydra's head of questions and dilemmas as a quick exploration of each of the rules demonstrates.

1 Only actual birds that are wild and free flying can be counted
This may seem rather self-evident but some birders do in fact keep a list of birds they have seen on television or in movies or on the Internet. Even to me this seems a bit odd. Sure there might be a bit of skill involved in working out which bird is calling out in the background of that Tarzan movie but, really, what was the point of such a list? (By the way, the birds you most often hear in old Tarzan movies are Australian kookaburras and Indian peacocks, which seems rather incongruous considering the loin-clothed one is supposedly barrelling around the African jungle.) As surprising as it may seem, there are circumstances where the temptation might exist to tick off a video image. For example, if there was a camera set up on a feeding station at the breeding grounds of the endangered Orange-bellied Parrot in Tasmania, I could have tuned in via a webcast to see the actual birds live in real time without ever visiting Tasmania. This rule knocked that possibility out. It also stipulated a very basic criterion that each species must be an actual bird. Not the nest of a bird, or even an egg. Questions of when life begins don't enter into the equation here, for although there may be a bird inside the eggshell, we couldn't see it yet. In twitching it doesn't matter which comes first, the chicken or the egg, because the egg doesn't count. Yes, you could x-ray the egg to see the bird inside but rule number one stipulated that you must see the *actual* bird with your own eyes.

The wild and free-flying clause ensured that I just didn't head down to the local museum and tick off a number of stuffed and mounted specimens. It also meant that any bird I found dead I couldn't count. But what exactly qualified as dead? I know one very reputable birder who for years had Masked Owl on his list because one night he found a freshly road-killed specimen. He swears that as he picked it up the owl blinked – proof, he said, that the bird was still alive for that split second and therefore countable. Made me wonder whether I should invest in a portable MRI unit to monitor birds about to join the choir invisible for any signs of brain activity.

This rule also voided any birds seen in captivity. So visits to zoos generally wouldn't be that useful to me although sometimes, especially in the case of waterfowl, it is very hard to pick which are the wild birds and which are part of the collection. Generally there are subtle differences that can distinguish a domestic bird from a genuine wild bird: they may have bands or other identifying marks. The domestic bird may have had its wings clipped. And if it flies onto your shoulder and asks for a cracker, chances are it is not a wild bird. Similarly, work for the dole kids dressed in chicken costumes advertising inner city carparks don't count either.

The term free-flying didn't preclude flightless birds such as emus or penguins or even lazy ducks who just couldn't be bothered with the whole flying thing. It simply meant that the wild bird must be unrestrained. You could count an injured bird that couldn't fly so long as you found it and it hadn't been brought to you by someone else. How to determine what was free-flying could actually be quite difficult. The rule of thumb is that for a species to be countable it has to be part of a wild and self-sustaining population that has existed for more than ten years. Ostrich is on the Australian list, having escaped from failed ostrich farms at the turn of last century, but I was assured by an expert that these birds have never been truly wild and in the eighties the last supposedly wild population was rounded up and corralled for a while. So I didn't even bother looking for this one remaining population. I found out later that many people disagree with this expert's view and most twitchers include Ostrich on their list. I may have cost myself a tick before I'd even started. Damn those rules; it was supposed to be birdwatching, not moral philosophy.

2 All birds must be seen within a calendar year

I guess there was nothing stopping me from choosing my year to run from 27 May to 26 May, but it seemed so much easier to confine my efforts to a calendar year. I guess if I'd chosen 27 May and then didn't see as much as I'd hoped I could then delay the starting date until I got a good run of sightings. And so on and so on. There would be a very real risk that I would never actually get started and this thing could go on forever. I refused to allow myself to be a freak for more than one year so for the sake of convenience, simplicity and my own sanity, my big year would be the calendar year 2002, not a day before and not a day after. Having decided on this rule late in 2001, it didn't give me much time to prepare.

3 All birds must be seen within Australian territory

Mike Entwhistle's record of 633 was seen on the Australian mainland but the official 1994 checklist includes the birds seen in Australia's external territories – Norfolk, Lord Howe, Christmas, Cocos-Keeling, Macquarie and Heard islands, though not Australia's Antarctic Territory. Why Antarctica doesn't cop a guernsey I don't know but as I was not planning on going down there the point was moot. By convention most twitchers also include the external territories when they tally up their Aussie lists so who was I to argue with convention? Especially when it took the number of potential species up to over 830, at least thirty more than for the mainland alone.

Not that all those juicy Southern Ocean seabirds that nest on Heard and Macquarie islands were much use to me as I had no way of getting there. A tourist boat does call in at Macquarie but by the time I made inquiries the only cruise available for the year was already booked out. And as the cheapest berth cost around US $8000, which, given the exchange rate at the time, translated to something like nineteen million Australian dollars, I wasn't too sorry to have missed out. It meant I would have to take a heap of boat trips within the 200 mile limit in order to see some of the ocean going birds.

4 A species can only be counted in accordance with the official Australian Bird Checklist

In 1994 the RAOU published what is considered to be the official checklist of Australian birds. There is no more controversial issue amongst birdwatchers than taxonomy. Even what constitutes a full species is a matter for hot debate. Passions are so aroused that some people have barely spoken a civil word for years over the issue of albatross taxonomy. The 1994 checklist created disquiet because some species of bird were deemed to no longer officially exist in their own right as a species, being regarded as only a race or form of another species, a process known as lumping. (The reverse process where a bird hitherto thought of as a race is given full status is known as splitting.) In general a twitcher is in favour of splitting as it gives them more species they can tick off on their lists but I figured, what did I know about taxonomy and genetics so I'd go along with what the experts said. At least it meant I was singing from the same songbook and people could compare like against like when comparing my list with others.

The trouble was that as soon as the 1994 checklist was published there was a revolution in genetics thanks to new DNA techniques that turned much of the previous taxonomic orthodoxy on its ear. A new checklist incorporating these changes was promised as early as 1995. By late 2001 there was still no sign of it coming out so in a sense I was operating in the dark. I had an idea of what the changes were but nobody was really sure. This might mean that I waste vast amounts of time searching for a species only to find that it no longer counted when the new regime is in place. All that effort spent backing the wrong horse. Conversely it meant that there were birds that were currently considered subspecies that might well one day be classified as fully-fledged ticks. So as well as trying to find as many species as I could I would now also have to put an effort in for as many races of species just to cover me for future taxonomic changes. As there were some hundreds of different races of the 830 current species, I had my work cut out for me.

5 All species have to be seen well enough to establish their identity
Not that I am privileging sight above hearing. Hearing is one of my all-time favourite senses – certainly in the top five, at least. I know

that under the American Big Year rules and even in our Twitchathons, hearing a bird counts as much as seeing it. In many cases this makes sense because a bird's call is often every bit as distinctive as its looks. About the only way to tell a Chirruping Wedgebill from a Chiming Wedgebill without taking a slice of its DNA is to listen to it sing. The Chirruping sounds like a happy sparrow, the Chiming's call is reminiscent of a musicalised squeaky bicycle wheel. There is also the fact that I trust my eyes more than my ears. When you see a bird, unless you've dropped some acid you can be sure that what you are looking at is a bird. Things I've mistaken for bird calls in the past include dogs, cats, babies, mobile phones; even the rumbling stomach of a birding companion. Put simply you never can be sure just what is making a particular noise until you see it making the actual noise, as illustrated by the cautionary tale of Puke and Groober on Mount Lewis.

The rainforests of Mount Lewis in North Queensland are a well-known haunt for Lesser Sooty Owls, the smaller, tropical cousin of the Sooty Owl. Groober and Puke were up on the mountain one night trying to spotlight them. To aid them they had a tape of owl calls. They were having no luck. Puke wandered down the track in one direction, Groober in the other. After another unsuccessful playback session, Groober forgot to turn the tape off. The next call on the tape was a Barking Owl. These birds do actually make a barking noise. It's normally a bird of open woodlands, so Groober was surprised to hear one respond from across the dense rainforest gully. He played the tape again and was immediately answered. So ensued a tense duet as Groober moved toward the sound that was getting closer by the second. Eventually the call was so close it was coming from just around the bend. Groober jumped out with his spotlight only to have another spotlight shone into his face. The Barking Owl was actually Puke imitating the call he was hearing from Groober's tape. For ten minutes they had been stalking each other, drawing one another closer with their fake barks.

When it comes down to it, just hearing a bird is not the same experience as when you see it, particularly when you see it well. To see some birds I would have to travel hundreds, even thousands of kilometres and expend a great deal of time and energy. A fleeting glimpse or hearing a snatch of a call is not exactly what I was after. I wanted the total experience of seeing a bird and that meant being able to recognise what the hell it was I was looking at. If I am walking through a gorge in the Kakadu National Park and a large, dark pigeon flies off, there will be little doubt the bird is anything but a Chestnut-quilled Rock-Pigeon. But if all I see is a brown blur, well it's hardly a valid experience of the essence of the bird, of what makes it a unique creature. I won't be satisfied putting it on my list until, at the very least, I have seen the diagnostic feature of the chestnut wing patch that makes it a Chestnut-quilled Rock-Pigeon. This will help me stand up to anyone who doubts I saw a Chestnut-quilled Rock-Pigeon but, more importantly, it means that I will be happy within myself that I truly experienced the bird. And ultimately, for me, that's what counts.

With those parameters ironed out it was time to turn my attention to more practical matters. A year may seem like a long time but there was an awful lot of territory to cover. Australia is a bloody big place. It has mountains, oceans, rainforest, deserts and everything in between. Birds have adapted to every one of these habitats. Some were specialists found in only one habitat; others were jacks of all trades who will find a niche almost anywhere. I had to work out a route that covered the diverse territory that all these different species occupied.

Complicating matters was the tendency of some birds to use their wings to full effect and not stay in the one place. Like Peter Allen, about a hundred thousand Sharp-tailed Sandpipers call Australia home and, like the flamboyant singer, they spend much of their time in more exotic climes, though not in this case, Rio; along with almost fifty other wader species, they go to Siberia. Look for a Sharpie in Australia in the middle of June and you'd be hard pressed to find a single bird. Conversely, most species of albatross come up from Antarctic waters when they start to freeze and are most easily seen off the Australian coast during the winter months. So in order to see everything, I needed to work out a schedule where I visited not only all parts of the country but all parts of the country at the right time. For instance, the best time of year to see many rarer Asian migrants is in our summer when a few overshoot their South East Asian wintering grounds and make it to the fringes of northern Australia. This also happens to be the peak time for visitors from New Guinea to come down along the east coast to breed. How to cover two ends of the continent at the same time?

Other permanent residents are less predictable, moving about the country in response to rain and good conditions. The Letter-winged Kite is a bird of prey that for the most part sticks to a core range in the backblocks of the channel country in Western Queensland. Following a good season their main prey, the Long-haired Rat, has a population explosion and the kites have a baby boom of their own and soon spread out across much of the country. They will appear in a district in huge numbers, hang around for a while and then disappear again, not to return for decades. There is often no pattern to such movements and in a year such as 2002 when much of the country was suffering the worst drought in recorded history, the movements were all the more erratic. Still others, like the Red-lored Whistler, remain almost invisible for much of the year and only emerged during the whirlwind of the mating season.

It was like a giant jigsaw puzzle with over 830 pieces to fit together. With twenty years' experience I felt I had a handle on recognising the pieces and knowing where most of them should go but I had never been particularly good at fitting jigsaws together, especially under pressure. A year may seem a long time but as I sat down to work out my strategy it seemed alarmingly restrictive.

In the past I hadn't exactly been the most successful twitcher. When a Hudsonian Godwit turned up at Werribee Sewage Farm I went out looking for it five times and never found it. Everybody else seemed to. A New Zealand species, the South Island Pied Oystercatcher, appeared in Australia for the first time on a beach in northern New South Wales. Every twitcher worth their salt went up and twitched it, no worries. Every twitcher but me. I walked up and down that goddamned beach for two whole days and didn't see a thing. That same trip would have to go down as the greatest dipping fest in Australian birding history. I had five target species and never saw one, despite spending a week looking for them.

With that track record, I knew it wouldn't be a case of simply turning up and instantly ticking off the required species. I had to try and estimate how much time I could afford for each one. There was no point spending five days looking for one species if it was going to cost me five others in the process. To this end I crossed one species off my list of potentials. The Princess Parrot lives in the remotest deserts and is only ever regularly seen in one place along the Canning Stock Route, which is about as far from anywhere that you can go and still be on Earth. Just getting there and back from Alice Springs is almost a week's round trip and that doesn't include any time spent searching for the birds. There was nothing else on the Canning that I couldn't see elsewhere so I ruled out an expedition there. As much as I would have loved to see a Princess Parrot, for they are as beautiful as they are rare, I simply couldn't afford to take that much time out of my schedule for just one bird.

The first logistical task was to decide exactly how many birds I realistically had a chance of seeing. Of the 830-odd birds that have been recorded in Australia and its territories, quite a few have been one-off sightings. When I eliminated such extreme vagrants it still came out at around 710. That didn't seem right. No-one could possibly see seven hundred birds in Australia in the one year. The record was only 633.

I decided I needed expert advice on this to see whether my assessment was realistic. I sent my proposed schedule to Puke and Groober. I trusted their judgement and knew that we were close enough for them to say to me, 'Get your hand off it Dooley, you're dreaming.' They assessed my itinerary, ruled out a couple of species, pointing out that at least one of the birds I had listed was actually extinct, but in general were as surprised as me to find that it was theoretically possible to see 705 species in a year. Possible in theory. Whether it was possible for me to do it was another question entirely. Off the top of my head I could think of at least twenty birders who were far better at the caper than me. This was a job for a 'real' birdwatcher.

A real birdwatcher is someone who dedicates their entire lives to studying birds. They are the sort of person who gets out at every possible opportunity and when they can't they spend every spare moment reading about birds, studying them in minute detail. Real birders know all the birds and all the parts of the birds. They know what each feather is called and how it should look for every bird. They can look at a particular bird and not just recognise what species it is but what sex, age and how many feathers are missing from its wing. In other words they are freaks. A real birder possesses an encyclopedic knowledge of the subject as well as a phenomenal eye. Not only can they look out over an open expanse of ocean and see a bird from a distance of a couple of kilometres, they can immediately pick it out as a Soft-plumaged Petrel and be proven correct ninety-nine times out of a hundred. The most impressive example of this skill I'd ever witnessed was on Stradbroke Island in Queensland. I was walking through the bush with a birder named Chris Corben, when he stopped and casually said, 'Look, there's a frog.' I couldn't see anything. Chris pointed to a tree about thirty metres away. Sure enough, when we walked over, there was a small camouflaged tree frog the size of a ten-cent piece sitting frozen on a leaf. And to top it off, he had correctly named the species from that distance. Next to guys like this I am an absolute duffer.

But most importantly, the real birder has a single-minded tenacity. That's why they are freaks. That's why they are so damned good at what they do. These are the sort of people whose very sense of self revolves around their ability to separate a Wandering Tattler from a Grey-tailed Tattler by being able to spot its longer nasal groove at a distance of two hundred paces. The sort of person who has virtually constructed their moral universe around how good someone is at identifying birds. I have actually heard comments such as, 'Bruce is a nice bloke but he couldn't tell a Phylloscopus warbler from his elbow,' in such a tone that brings into question Bruce's legitimacy as a fellow human being. When your entire world revolves around one thing, to master that thing is to invite a certain arrogance. It's good to be the king. Even if the kingdom is rather small. It is amazing how often really good birders are borderline megalomaniacs. Because with birdwatching you are, in a sense, mastering nature itself. By identifying and listing a thing you are satisfying that deep-seated psychological need to impose some order on an otherwise chaotic and baffling universe. It gives people who probably don't have much control in other aspects of their lives at least some illusion of control. There is nobody more frightening than a nerd in total control – think Hitler…kind of nerdy; very scary. Cool people don't bother becoming dictators; they're too busy getting laid.

If I was to go after 700 I had to want it, had to become one of those people I had always found daunting yet amusing. Was I one of those people? I seriously doubted it. But then I began thinking. For twenty years I'd stuck to birdwatching despite the embarrassment and risk of social stigmatisation. My bedtime reading usually consisted of bird books. After two weeks without getting out birdwatching I start to get a little bit ratty. And of all the hard-core twitchers I knew I was the only one who kept a daily bird diary, writing down every bird I saw every day. It had become a compulsion.

Opening an old bird diary at random, Monday 3 June 1996, I noted that I saw nineteen species that day in Collingwood and Yarra Bend. Just from the fact that I saw Red-rumped Parrot and White-browed Scrubwren evoked in me a fairly strong picture of what that day was like. It was cold but clearing. I spent the day working from home desperately trying to come up with some comedy ideas. I was working at my first TV job on a show called *Full Frontal* and I was floundering. I hadn't got a sketch to air for something like six weeks and if I didn't improve my strike rate this would probably also be my last television gig. I'd gone for a walk across to Yarra Bend Park to clear my head and seek some inspiration. I was pretty sure that was the day I'd almost walked over a couple fornicating under a blanket. I didn't know what connection that triggered in my mind but I remembered coming back from the park with an idea for a sketch. Jason Donovan, fresh from his River Phoenix tribute collapse outside the Viper Room, had just landed the part of Frank'n'Furter in a revival of *The Rocky Horror Show*. I thought it might be a neat idea to have Jason sing a parody of 'Time Warp' with a chorus that included the line 'Jase hit the sidewalk again!' The producer went with it and my flailing career had a revival of its own. I remembered all that from a date and a list of nineteen birds. My whole life seen through the prism of birdwatching. Calling Dr Asperger!

But there was still the question of how the real twitchers would regard my effort. Would they see through the facade and pick me as a fraud? Puke and Groober thought my plan was doable but I decided I should spread my net further. I went right to the top and took my proposal to my birding mentor, Mike Carter, the man who has seen more birds in Australia than anyone else. I figured if anyone was going to have an objection it would be him, for even though he didn't bother with year lists I might be stealing his thunder just a little bit. To my relief Mike was very supportive about my plans, even enthusiastic. He warned me against aiming as high as seven hundred as he thought it an unreachable target and that even if I fell only one short what would be a great achievement would always be tinged with disappointment for me. He told me that he was organising a boat trip to the Torres Strait at the end of August and another on the same boat out to Ashmore Reef in the Indian Ocean in October and reserved a place for me on both trips. Having those to anchor my plans around, my agenda began to take shape.

Within a week I had been contacted by Chris Lester, who organises the boat trips off Port Fairy, asking me which months I wanted to book. Chris didn't believe I could see seven hundred either but he was certainly willing to help me try. Soon I had similar trips booked on boats off Brisbane, Wollongong, Tasmania and Perth. I was taken aback at how nearly all of the 'real' twitchers were more than happy to support my endeavour. Sceptical they may be but they were not hostile and many adopted me for the year, making it a special project to help me out whenever they could. It was really quite overwhelming and I almost regretted calling them megalomaniacs and freaks. Almost.

And so the wheels were set in motion. I even gave the project a name, the 'Big Twitch'. The plan of attack was fairly straightforward. As I still had much to organise I would spend the first half of the year based in my home in Melbourne trying to see as many species as close to home as possible so that when I did head farther afield I wouldn't have to waste my time on the more common stuff and could focus exclusively on the harder to see birds. Any major trips I did in this period would be no longer than a week or ten days to allow for maximum flexibility if I needed to alter plans so I could go chasing after vagrants as they turned up. From July onwards I planned to be on the road till the end of the year, essentially circum-navigating the country twice. The biggest risk in this strategy was that I had planned only one crack at the majority of northern Australia, towards the end of the year. There was a chance the mon-soon may start early, stymieing my access to species that would have been easier to see earlier in the year during the dry season. It was not ideal but it seemed to be the most workable solution to a myriad of permutations.

So on that last night of 2001 I headed out into the darkness and steeled myself to becoming a total birdy nerdy – but only for a year mind you, just one year.

CHAPTER 4

1 January 2002, Melbourne General Cemetery, Victoria:
25 species

New Year's Day is one of my favourite days of the year. Not New Year's Eve, which I invariably find anticlimactic, for no matter where you end up, you always feel like you'd be having more fun if you'd gone to that other party. Certainly for much of the night during those owl-less hours when the rain was teeming, I would have preferred to be anywhere else, even those appalling teenage New Year's parties of my youth where everyone threw up from a lethal mixture of rocket fuel and cough mixture. For me the thrill of the first day of every year was that each bird I saw, no matter how common, was a new tick for my year list. Everyday birds in the back garden that I would pretty much ignore the rest of the year, such as starlings and blackbirds became interesting again, at least for one brief moment, as they take up their positions on the list.

A twitcher's list is very democratic. Each bird counts as one tick. There are no extra points for beauty or rarity. The humble sparrow counts just as much as a Wedge-tailed Eagle or a Paradise Parrot. Sure, encountering a Wedgie can be an exhilarating experience and seeing a Paradise Parrot would be somewhat mind-blowing considering it has been extinct for eighty years, but in terms of the list these factors do not privilege them above the House Sparrow – they are all worth just one tick. If I wanted to break the record it was as essential that I saw every common garden bird as it was that I saw every rarity.

So it was to the gardens of Melbourne that I turned to get the year list kicking along. It might not be the most exotic of locales, but you had to start somewhere. One of the attractions of birdwatching is that you can see birds no matter where you are, from the edge of the polar icecaps to the middle of a teeming concrete metropolis. Aside from the odd rodent scuttling out of sight as we enter the kitchen, the modern human rarely encounters a wild mammal in our daily lives but birds seem to be everywhere. City birds may often seem pretty lacklustre but even the most familiar can fill me with a sense of wonder. I have a soft spot for the Spotted Turtle-dove which was bird number five for the year, seen feeding in my tiny backyard. A very common species, introduced from Asia in the nineteenth century, the Spotted Turtle-dove is quite a handsome bird on close examination. Possessing the sweet, innocent features of a dove with a wonderfully subtle pink hue across the breast, this was also the first bird I remembered tracking down to identify.

I was around four years old and was woken one morning by the incessant cooing of a turtle-dove. Thinking it might be an owl hooting I had jumped out of bed and, in my pyjamas, followed the sound down the street to a large tree in the yard of the house on the corner. I remembered being disappointed that it wasn't an owl calling but I did have the satisfaction of making that discovery for myself. And my mother had the joy of entering my room and discovering her son missing from his bed, the first of many bird-induced disappearances she was to have to get used to over the coming years.

Just as I would get used to seeing Spotted Turtle-doves. In bird-watching terms, familiarity can breed contempt and birds that once delighted and fascinated can become easily overlooked. But each bird is unique. They all have a story, even common city trash birds.

Most introduced species were deliberate releases designed to make Australia feel more like 'home' (i.e. England). Introduced species come in for quite a panning from birders – they are often referred to as 'plastics', meaning they're not as authentic as the home-grown item. Some twitchers don't even count them on their lists. I am generally sympathetic to this line of birding apartheid but at times can't help but feeling that this view is just a tad overzealous. Introduced species are bad news, no question about it. They don't belong here and can create rampant havoc when let loose upon local ecosystems, the Cane Toad and the Prickly Pear being two infamous non-bird examples. But there is very little of a 'natural' ecosystem left in the cities. If all the introduced species were somehow miraculously removed, I seriously doubt whether many native species would be able to fill their niche and our cities would fall silent of birdcalls – lyrebirds aren't really into feeding on human refuse.

The real trouble occurs when the introduced birds build up in such numbers that they break out into surrounding habitats. A classic example of this is the Common Myna. Introduced to Melbourne from India in the 1860s, for most of the next century it remained relatively uncommon, confined to small pockets of suburbia and industrial areas. But Common Mynas are canny opportunists well adapted to living with humans and as the tentacles of suburbia spread, so did their opportunities. Over the last thirty years they seem to have reached a critical mass in the cities and have begun spilling over into the surrounding countryside, utilising the emerging freeway system as a…well, freeway system. Fuelled by the phenomenal waste produced by our throwaway society, the Common Myna has muscled its way into the bush fringes where it competes with hollow-nesting natives such as rosellas and other parrots. It took a hundred years to reach the western fringes of Melbourne, but only a decade or so to leapfrog to the outskirts of Ballarat along the recently upgraded Western Freeway. Locals in the small northern Victorian town of Chiltern are talking about forming myna vigilante posses to keep them from invading. It will be a battle on two fronts as the mynas inexorably wend their way along the Hume Highway corridor, from Sydney and Canberra in the north and Melbourne in the south.

But it is not only introduced species that are to be found in the inner city; a surprising number of natives still persist here. Some even thrive in what you would expect to be a biological desert. But if you think about it, the resources of the countryside all funnel into the cities and are then spat out again by the consumer society creating a bonanza of riches for an opportunistic bird. It is not only Common Mynas that thrive in such circumstances. Native species such as ibis, currawongs and ravens do a roaring trade, not to mention the Silver Gull. Back in the 1950s there were a few Silver Gulls nesting on Mud Islands, a group of small sand heaps at the southern end of Port Phillip Bay, about fifty kilometres from Melbourne as the gull flies. Fifty years later that colony has grown to over a hundred thousand; a phenomenal population explosion fuelled by the rise of the takeaway society. There are a cluster of small islands off Wollongong piled high with the bones of thousands of birds...mainly leg and wing bones, because the source of this birding graveyard is the local KFC outlet on the mainland opposite. Silver Gulls breed here and the parent birds take the remnants of thousands of family meal deals across to feed their voracious young, resulting in an upsizing of their population.

Yet you don't have to be a scavenger to do well in the cities, though being aggressive is certainly an advantage. Thanks to the cultural shift that occurred in the Australian consciousness from the 1960s onwards, when we stopped trying to turn our homes into little patches of England and began planting indigenous species, many native nectar-feeders have returned to the suburbs – the White-plumed Honeyeater, Noisy Miner and the Red and Little Wattlebirds. But they are all aggressive little buggers and none more so than the magnificent Rainbow Lorikeet, a stunning burst of colour that now wheels about most Australian cities in raucous flocks. I have seen a British twitcher fresh off the plane weep at the beauty and abundance of these birds. They are now back in such numbers that even in the inner city they are giving the Common Mynas a run for their money.

It's amazing just where birds can thrive in the city. I headed to Melbourne General Cemetery to see a few extra native species.

Death may never take a holiday, but funeral directors occasionally did and luckily for me there were no burials being conducted on New Year's Day. When birding there in the past, I have more than once stumbled out from a tangle of headstones, slap bang into a funeral party lowering their loved one into the ground. Everyone mourns in their own way but I was pretty sure that having someone with binoculars barging into the middle of Aunt Louise's funeral didn't figure in most people's bereavement itineraries.

In fact birdwatching anywhere in the urban area can be fraught with such potentially awkward moments. Binoculars make bird-watching so much easier, but they also make you look like a pervert, especially when combined with the sort of camouflage gear that birders tend to go in for. People just don't expect birds to be in the city and they certainly don't expect birdwatchers to be chasing after them. My suburban birding activities have attracted the attention of the police several times and I have freaked out joggers by emerging unexpectedly from the undergrowth on many occasions. But where it gets really awkward is when a patch of useful habitat coincides with a homosexual beat, which happens more frequently than one would expect. I guess the same attributes that attract birds – quiet, leafy, out of the way spots with lots of hiding places – also attract those looking for discreet encounters. In places as diverse as Melbourne, Canberra and Paris I've stumbled onto such places and found myself having to convince eager cruisers that I really was there just for the birds.

In a wooded glade in Madrid's Parque del Retiro I garnered quite a collection of men trying to pick me up. Quite flattering, I suppose, but I didn't have the requisite Spanish to tell them I wasn't interested so I made a big exaggerated show of trying to look for birds through my binoculars. Trouble was, any birds had been scared off by the fruity conga line trailing behind me, so to them it must have seemed as if I was putting on some kind of floorshow for their viewing pleasure. Fearful my admirers might turn nasty when I didn't finish off with a bang, I thought it would be best if I removed myself from the scene and so, like some adult version of the Pied Piper, led a merry band across the park to the exit.

Luckily there were very few members of the public for me to spook as I wandered about the cemetery grounds looking for a few additions to the list before the sun went down on the first day of my quest. Melbourne Cemetery is a surprisingly good place for birds, especially when they let the weeds grow amongst the headstones. There were plenty of hiding places for small birds to shelter and lots of feeding opportunities in what was, for wildlife, an oasis in the middle of a busy city. I loved coming here to birdwatch as oddly enough I felt a great sense of calm as I wandered amongst the grave-stones and there was something delicious in the notion that so many birds are living on top of humanity's graveyard when, for them, the rest of the city was a graveyard. They say the best revenge is to live well, and in the cemetery this day I spied birds such as the Red-rumped Parrot, Silvereye, Superb Fairy-wren, and Yellow-rumped Thornbill all doing a splendid job of living it up amongst the bones of the society that wreaked such havoc on their ancestors.

By day's end my list stood at twenty-five. Not a particularly awe-some figure, especially when I heard later that Keith and Lindsay Fisher from Cairns saw a lazy 160 species on New Year's Day, but as I have said, you had to start somewhere. And if I could keep adding 25 species per day I would have broken the record by Australia Day (26 January), but of course, things are never that easy.

CHAPTER 5

4 January, Seaford Swamp, Victoria:
92 species

Imagine you are standing on a small rise at the southern end of a large plain. To the east are three wooded hills. Distant forest-clad mountain ranges mirror each other in the northeast and southwest. To the northwest are lower, drier escarpments. The whole area is in fact a giant basin, collecting water from the surrounding highlands. Herds of animals graze amongst the grassy woodlands by the lazy river that meanders through the centre of the plain. Though not heavily populated, small family groups make a comfortable living from the plain's bounty. Here they live, love and make stories.

Around ten thousand years ago – give or take a few minutes – the basin filled with water through a gap to the south as the great polar icecap thawed, creating what is now called Port Phillip Bay. By the time the first Europeans sailed into the bay, the territory of one people, the Bunarong, straddled much of the coastal strip around the almost landlocked body of water, suggesting that perhaps these areas were the fringes of their original territory, to which they had to seek refuge as the plain was inundated. Part of their jurisdiction took in the flat country on the easternmost arc of the bay. Over the centuries as sea levels have risen and fallen, the sea and land have done battle, each skirmish leaving a scar on the land in the form of a residual sand dune. These dunes act to block the waters draining from the northeastern mountains (which we now call the Dandenongs) and a vast swamp known as the Carrum-Carrum formed behind the sand barrier.

Here the Bunarong people continue to live. Their stories now tell of the abundant game attracted by the sweet waters of the Carrum-Carrum. Among them is a new tale about the spirit of a recently dead warrior who returns in the form of a white-skinned man with the odd name of 'William Buckley'. Thirty years later more white men arrive and claim Buckley as one of their own – an escapee from a failed convict settlement who, on the run, had picked up the spear of a recently buried warrior leading to a case of mistaken identity. The return of Buckley's mob signals the end of the stories of the Bunarong, for unlike Buckley the new arrivals are incapable of sharing the land. The last of the original Bunarong clan, Jimmy Dunbar, dies in 1878, a mere forty years after permanent white settlement. The Carrum-Carrum dies with him for in 1879 the Patterson River channel is completed, draining the swamp into the sea.

New stories emerge. Small fishing settlements transform into beachside holiday destinations once they are connected to the new settlement of Melbourne by the railway. Market gardens and dairies are established, the fertile soil of the former swamp now feeds the population of the growing city. The mighty Phar Lap builds up strength on the lush grasses of the former wetland in preparation for his successful 1930 Melbourne Cup campaign. And in 1953 at a local youth group badminton night a skinny young larrikin of Irish Catholic origins meets a demure girl whose strict family of Protestant matriarchs has moved from the city into their bayside holiday house. Between smashing the shuttlecock smack bang into the faces of his 'proddo' opponents, the freckle-faced young bloke takes a shine to the tall, quiet girl, declaring that one day he will marry her. She thinks he's an uncouth yobbo and won't have a bar of him. Twelve years later he finally wears her and her cabal of misanthropic aunts down and they marry in a small fibro church on the edge of the old swamp. They build a house in the coastal scrub of the old dunes where their eldest son begins to ramble and splash his way through Seaford Swamp, one of the last remnants of the Carrum-Carrum. And so the stories continue.

Seaford Swamp was where the Big Twitch really began: not just because it was the first day of proper birding that I put in for the year, but because this suburban patch of wetland had been as important in shaping my story as any single person or event. Even by most other birdwatchers, Seaford isn't regarded with huge amounts of affection. As a wilderness experience it pales in comparison to the Amazon or the Serengeti, being only a hundred-odd hectares of mainly thick, tangled reed beds broken by the occasional open body of shallow, stagnant water. It's hard going just to get through; a typical foray leaves you with scratches, spikes and boots full of the foulest black muddy water. But even though it is hemmed in on three sides by urban development, even though at times it can be seemingly devoid of birds, Seaford Swamp does it for me like nowhere else.

In this country we tend to ignore landscape as a factor in developing our character. You will hear people banging on about how the boundless frontier forged the American sense of optimism, how the Mediterranean sun fuels the passions of those who live under its blazing influence, yet in Australia it's as though we are ashamed of our landscape. Rather than embrace it we have for the most part of our short history denied the reality of the landscape like a shameful family secret, expending an awful amount of energy in European makeovers or simply willfully ignoring its existence altogether.

For me, the impact of landscape has been as pivotal to my sense of identity as have my parents, my education or any other aspect of my life. Rather than deny it, I am proud to proclaim that the landscape has forged me. I see the fact that I grew up alongside Seaford Swamp as critical to my personal development. I am a product of that landscape and it manifests in my personality. Thank you, Seaford Swamp, for making me what I am today – flat, featureless, a bit soggy below the surface, with the occasional malodorous whiff.

Actually, Seaford Swamp's greatest impact on my life is that it made me a birdwatcher. That and my grade five teacher. Well, that and the fact that I was a little suck who was petrified of getting the strap from my grade five teacher. My first school, Seaford North Primary, was perched right on the edge of the swamp. The swamp figured large in my primary school imaginings. It was the source of much drama. In summer we had bushfires, tiger snakes and the occasional flasher. In winter we would have floods on the oval, infestations of frogs in biblical proportions, and the occasional flasher. It was a generator of local childhood myth. No-one knew what was hidden in its depths, but there were stories of secret stashes of everything a kid would ever want to get his hands on – money, slingshots, nudie pictures, canoes; there was even supposed to be a 'graveyard of the cows' lurking within the depths of this mystical realm. And like all mystical places there had to be a resident troll.

Peter Jackson was his name. Part teacher, part bunyip, he looked like a straighter version of beat poet Allen Ginsberg, sporting a bushy beard, thick, tinted prescription glasses and oftentimes a daggy green bush hat. 'Jacko' was the first birdwatcher I knew. He was also the first vegan, the first Mazda driver and, as one of the few male teachers in the school, Jacko was allowed to deal out corporal punishment, which was then still legal. According to the lore of the schoolyard, Jacko wielded the strap with particular relish. As with all legends, there was only a small kernel of truth at its heart but I fully expected to be getting the strap on a regular basis in his class, unless, I thought, I could get on his good side. I knew he was a science and nature nut, particularly when it came to birds…maybe if I was into birds, Jacko wouldn't be into me with the strap.

So the week before school started, armed with the *Gould League Book of Urban Birds*, given to me by the last of my mother's surviving aunts, I started crawling around the local park trying to identify the common birds in my neighbourhood. I was able to identify Red and Little Wattlebirds, a New Holland Honeyeater and that Spotted Turtle-dove. There was even a bird not in the book – a Black-faced Cuckoo-shrike, the first even slightly exotic looking bird I ever found. Today I would hardly give this handsome blue-grey bird (that is neither a cuckoo nor a shrike) a second glance, but when you first start out birdwatching, nearly everything takes on the glossy sheen of novelty.

I think it was that thrill of discovery that made birdwatching so attractive for me. From the first I had been passionately interested in nature. Long after I had developed a taste for exotic sugary breakfast cereals like Coco Pops and Fruit Loops I would eschew such treats in favour of plain old Weet-Bix because each box contained an African wildlife card. But wildlife always seemed to be elsewhere. There were no giraffes in Larool Crescent, no rhinos charging unsuspecting riders down at the motorbike tracks. My attempts to dig up our gravel front drive in search of fossils were halted not so much because my parents told me not to, but because they explained there were no dinosaurs to be found in the suburbs. Birdwatching, however, was a window into an entirely new world that existed right under your nose. Even in dull, suburban Seaford you could find moorhens along the creek, wrens decked out in brilliant blue amongst the blackberry tangles of vacant blocks, stunning fire-breasted Flame Robin in the cow paddocks. It was magic: a world that brought you out of yourself. Even if your stupid football team (Collingwood) lost another Grand Final, even if you had an after-school fight scheduled with Leigh Bayliss over who loved Vicki Bleazby the most, this other world was always there, and something was always happening. It was endlessly fascinating.

Within a week all fears of the strap were banished. Rather than being an ogre, Jacko turned out to be inspirational. He had turned his classroom into a menagerie with fish, mice, turtles and lizards competing with prescribed Education Department texts for our attention. He'd bought thirty pairs of binoculars, one for each class member, and would, at the drop of a bush-hat, declare it to be science time and take us off to the edge of the swamp to see what birds were there. Within a few weeks some mates and I were spending most of our lunchtimes patrolling the fence-line next to the swamp recording all the birds we saw. Sure, we'd occasionally be distracted by the odd game of footy or British bulldog, and I did allow myself to be 'caught' by Deidre Campbell in a game of kiss chasey (I'd moved on from Vicki Bleazby), but in general you could always find me down by the swamp looking for birds.

And twenty-three years later I was doing the same thing.

That day I was joined by Groober who I'd birded with more often than anyone. I was with him at Seaford in 1994 when we found the exceedingly rare Cox's Sandpiper. He was there with me when I saw my first Little Bittern. Unfortunately he was unsighted when it flushed from the reeds in front of me, and missed out on seeing it, something I remind him of every chance I get. But I think our friendship will survive because although he dipped on the bittern, he's seen Fluttering Shearwater (a type of pelagic seabird) at the swamp and I haven't. But then again I was there when a Spotted Redshank turned up and he wasn't. And so it goes. We will keep on gripping each other off like this until we are in our dotage. And before you get all hot and bothered, I'd just like to point out that, in twitching parlance, 'gripping someone off' simply means stirring someone, giving them a bit of grief when they've dipped out on a bird that you've seen. I suspect that some twitchers are motivated as much by the desire to avoid being gripped off as they are by the desire to actually see the bird in question. I tend to only actively grip off friends (get your mind out of the gutter) who can take a bit of ribbing (oh, grow up) because I know how awful it can be to be thoroughly gripped off. (Right, that's it, back to the main story. You are so juvenile.)

Groober shared not just a passion for birds (settle), but also a love of Seaford. In 1994, when I first started out doing monthly bird surveys of Seaford for Melbourne Water (the managing body for the swamp), I approached the local Friends of the Wetlands group to see if anyone wanted to assist. I got one taker, Helen, a woman approaching middle age who wanted to know more about the birds of the swamp. The trouble was, even on a dull day when there were no birds around, it took a minimum of two and a half hours to cover the entirety of the swamp. On a good day it could take up to six. And it was not an easy stroll. To get to where the birds were often required a great deal of bashing through choking reeds, getting spiked by needle-sharp rushes and sloshing your way through stinking sludge. The day Helen came out with me it was about 35 degrees, we hardly saw anything of interest and still the survey took over four hours. Helen never volunteered again.

Groober has been the only person idiotic enough to be roped into joining me at Seaford more than once. Our friendship was in fact cemented whilst birding Seaford together back in its halcyon days in the early eighties when, during a major drought, the water levels were kept artificially high. The resulting numbers of birds were spectacular, but it almost spelled the demise of Seaford as a viable habitat. The water filling the swamp originated from the Frankston Sewage Farm. It wasn't the actual raw sewage itself, but there were still enough nutrients in the water to lead to an absolute explosion of *Phragmites* reeds, which proceeded to choke the life out of the formerly open water. Coupled with this, the drain that delivered this nutrient bonanza was connected to Eel Race Drain, which was connected to Patterson Lakes, which were connected to Patterson River, which was connected to Port Phillip Bay. End result: a massive salt injection turning the freshwater swamp into a dead brackish write-off, and the huge numbers of birds moved off elsewhere.

But with better management, conditions had begun to improve and that day we managed to see a very respectable 68 species, nineteen of which were new for the year, including good numbers of wading birds such as Red-necked Avocet, Sharp-tailed Sandpiper, and only the second record of Caspian Tern for the swamp. We'd timed our visit to perfection. The open water had started to recede, exposing muddy edges loaded with invertebrate goodies that waders like the Sharpie love to feast upon. Pretty soon the swamp would have dried out too much and the birds would go. In most years this peak time only seemed to occur during a two-week window so I was lucky it had lasted into the New Year as it got me 19 species for my year list. This enshrined Seaford Swamp a rightful place in the pantheon of Big Twitch hot spots, for this was a game of diminishing returns and already, after only four days, the opportunity to add nineteen birds to the list at the one time, in the one place, was drastically reduced.

I should have been able to add twenty more birds at Seaford had I not the previous day driven down to Port Fairy (about three hours southwest of Melbourne) on a film shoot of sorts where I'd ticked off several species I had been expecting to see at Seaford. I say 'of sorts' because I was making a short teaser film designed to entice investors into funding a fully fledged documentary of the Big Twitch. I had this crazy notion that I might be able to interest somebody in paying me to film myself chasing the record. The trouble with making a film about birdwatching is that birds make very uncooperative subjects. They tend to fly away. Unless you are a David Attenborough backed by the resources of the BBC who can afford to send someone to sit in a hide for a year waiting for that perfect shot of frogmouths mating, most films about birdwatching would involve some dude driving to a spot in a car, getting out, looking at a distant dot, ticking it off, getting back in the car and driving off. A totally riveting subject.

Hardly surprising, then, that no-one wanted to invest in my documentary idea. Undaunted I went out and bought a ten thousand dollar broadcast quality digital video camera in the vain hope that I might be able to film enough interesting footage to cobble together something watchable. For the rest of the year I was to lug my camera equipment around the country, filming where I could. The end result was forty hours of largely unusable footage of me shakily holding the camera, saying, 'Here I am looking for the Rufous Scrub-bird' (or Hooded Parrot or Chestnut-breasted Whiteface) and then not being able to actually show the viewer the bird even if I saw it. I think as much as anything I was looking for something to justify my year. Saying I was taking a year off to make a documentary seemed easier than saying I was spending a year birdwatching. In this society being a wanker is socially unacceptable. Filming your-self while being a wanker, however, seems perfectly legitimate.

If I was to make a film, Werribee Sewage Farm would feature prominently. If Seaford is my personal birdwatching mecca, then Werribee (or Western Treatment Plant, to give it its sanitised title) would surely hold that revered status for a majority of Melbourne's birders. My first visit to Werribee took my breath away – no pun intended – for although 'the Farm' is so vast that most foul odours dissipate easily, there is always a slight whiff at Werribee, which I actually find most pleasant as I associate the smell with the excitement of seeing rare birds. And I'm not the only one. Probably one of the prime reasons birdwatchers are viewed as worryingly eccentric is that they get so excited about sewage farms, but the reason most people turn up their noses at the thought of sewage farms is the exact reason why wildlife finds them so attractive. All that nutrient concentrated in the one area provides a bonanza rarely found in nature. Birds love it. They come to feed on the little critters that come to feed on what we flush down the toilet.

Stretching for over twenty kilometres along the coast southwest of Melbourne, Werribee is on the opposite side of the bay to Seaford. It is similarly flat but, unlike the Carrum-Carrum, the wetland area has actually been expanded since the coming of white settlement. Alongside its mudflats, saltmarsh and freshwater wetlands have been added vast settling and filtration ponds. The largest of these is Lake Borrie. Apart from being home to thousands of wildfowl, Borrie has, in Melbourne at least, come to be known as a euphemism for pooh. Unfortunate for the family of EF Borrie, a civil servant whose vision for town planning in the fifties enabled Melbourne to become the livable city it is today, but I must admit the schoolboy in me does occasionally titter when I hear phrases such as 'I'm just going down to Borrie to see what turns up.'

Make no mistake, a trip to Werribee is one of the most spectacular wildlife experiences this country has to offer. Almost three hundred species of bird have been recorded on the Farm itself, but even more impressive is their sheer abundance. Especially during a drought year, tens of thousands of waterfowl are drawn to the permanent waters of the Farm. As they wheel about the lagoons in fluid yet cohesive flocks one is reminded of the accounts of early explorers who wrote of birds in such numbers that they darkened the skies. With the granite pyramids of the You Yang hills framing the background, the view from the shore of Lake Borrie on a still day is simply awesome.

I was here specifically that day chasing up a report of Red-chested Button-quail. These enigmatic little critters are one of those birds that I would have to see if I was to have any chance of getting anywhere near seven hundred for the year. It was a bird I knew very little about, not only never having seen it before but also not knowing any reliable sites for it. Even up north where they are more common they are particularly elusive. To be honest I was buggered if I knew where to find one. It was one of the few species I had no real plan for; to have them virtually on my doorstep was a bonus indeed.

I was joined again by Groober, who had seen Red-chesteds before, but never in Victoria. Both he and I are avid state listers. In fact I was more proud of having seen four hundred species in Victoria than I was of having reached the six hundred mark for the whole of Australia. Though not an easy task by any means, any decent birder should be able to reach six hundred Australian birds, simply by going on enough trips to enough different areas. To see four hundred birds in Victoria means that you not only have to go to all corners of the state but that you have to keep at it for a decent slab of time in order to see all the vagrant species that turn up over time. It took me twenty years, but my Vic list now stood at 403. Groober was about twenty ahead of that and if he wanted to catch up to Mike Carter, the Vic list champ who was about twenty ahead of him, he needed to get every new bird he could. And I'm sure if truth be told he probably couldn't bear it if I got one up on him.

Not that we had any luck. As is often the case, the birds were no longer there when we were. We had no reason to doubt the sighting but human nature being what it was, and twitchers' natures being at the extreme end of that spectrum, doubts crept in. I had been burnt before with Red-chested Button-quail. I failed to follow up a previous report of this species in Victoria because the location seemed so incongruous. When somebody claimed to have seen several in the woodlands of Gunbower Island along the Murray River, I thought that the observer must finally have lost the plot – surely in that habitat they would have been Painted Button-quail. I didn't bother chasing it up. Then more and more people kept seeing them and by the time I headed up there I'd missed the boat. Going on a wild-goose chase for a nonexistent bird is an annoying waste of time, but it is nothing compared to the earth shattering despair felt when you don't chase something up and it turns out to be bona fide.

As consolation there was the rest of the Farm. A quick two-hour scoot around the major birding areas yielded over seventy species for the day, including eighteen for the year list. Highlights were the massive numbers of waterfowl, refugees from the crippling drought inland: Pink-eared Ducks, Australasian Shovelers, Hardheads, and nineteen of Australia's rarest waterfowl, the Freckled Duck, a curious bird with a pointy head and plain brown-grey body that reminded me of the chocolate sprinkles on the top of a cappuccino. Many of the birds I added that day were more typical of inland areas. Normally, Black-tailed Native-hen, Red-kneed Dotterel and Wood Sandpiper would all be hanging around the billabongs of the out-back. Yet there they were on the southern coast – a reminder that in a drought year birds' normal patterns are disrupted and many of my plans may have to be altered to accommodate this fact.

By the end of the day I had my first major dip of the year but my total now stood at 110 species – over one-seventh of the way to the magical 700 mark. Sure, I could be further along, but it was still a start worth celebrating, so at night I headed out with a non-birding friend for a few drinks. The bartender didn't seem to share my enthusiasm, and nor did the girls at the bar. For some reason, 'I had a Freckled Duck today' never seems to work as a pick-up line.

CHAPTER 6

13 January, Chiltern, Victoria:
160 Species

Many people proclaim the Hume Highway to be one of the most boring stretches of road in the country. I couldn't agree less. Every time I begin the journey northwards on this main link from Melbourne to Sydney I feel like I am driving into history, driving into the heart of the country. Essentially following the route of the explorers Hume and Hovell, it hugs the boundary between the hills of the Great Divide and the endless plains of the inland. To me the Hume is a four-lane songline with a burger stop every couple of hours, that sings of geological history, ice ages, Aborigines, explorers, bushrangers, politicians, disasters, courage and, especially, birds. Man, am I going to be an annoying dad, pointing out to my long-suffering kids so much boring crap that they will seriously consider throwing themselves out of the car before we've even reached Kalkallo.

My excitement was compounded by the fact that on 11 January with my list on 129, I headed off on my first major foray outside Melbourne. It was one of those petulantly hot days where the fierce north wind kicked up the dust in a final act of defiance before it finally met up with the cool change sweeping in from the south. Everything was bothered and unsettled. Everyone you met was shitty because they hadn't had a good night's sleep due to the heat. I loved days like this. I never feel more invigorated than during episodes of extreme weather, even my very discomfort was a visceral reminder that I was alive. And there were few better destinations for a birder to be alive in than the little town of Chiltern. Surrounded by one of the finest examples of Box-Ironbark forest in the country, Chiltern is home to a suite of sensational birds. Over the next few days I added such corkers as Rainbow Bee-eater, Diamond Firetail, Black-chinned Honeyeater, Crested Shrike-tit and Speckled Warbler. I also got onto one of Chiltern's specialties, the Turquoise Parrot, a magnificent small, grass-green parrot, with blue face and wings, the male sporting a rich velvet-red shoulder patch. Once thought extinct, the Turquoise Parrot has bounced back and while nowhere near common, was a regular sight in the Box-Ironbark at Chiltern.

Box-Ironbark is a type of dry woodland. It occurs in a transition zone between the wetter forests of the Great Dividing Range and the scrubs and grassland of the vast inland plains. Some people may find the Box-Ironbark pretty ho-hum. There are no towering forest giants reaching to the skies, no luxuriant ferny glades shading clear, burbling streams. The understorey is so open that in order to have some privacy when answering the call of nature you have to walk for ages to ensure that when you squat down your camping companions don't cop an eyeful. But I love the Box-Ironbark. It has a stately, dignified, almost melancholic beauty all its own. Dominated by flaky-barked Box trees and Ironbarks with their dark, deeply fissured trunks this is a uniquely Australian landscape. It is the country of the gold rush. It is the country of the bushranger. It is country that has all but gone.

In 1996 the then Victorian State Government declared the former Chiltern State Park a national park. Its official title was to be *The* Box-Ironbark National Park, a name intended to placate the small but growing surge of voices demanding this habitat be saved. 'Protect the Box Ironbark? Of course we have. Look at that dot on the map. "*The* Box-Ironbark National Park". There, problem solved – it's protected. Now, who wants tickets to the Grand Prix?' The trouble is, especially in nature, things are rarely that simple. The Box-Ironbark once covered millions of hectares; the reserve at Chiltern comprises around four thousand. It is like proclaiming you have protected the works of Leonardo Da Vinci when all you have is one of the fingernails off the *Mona Lisa*. But as far as the government was concerned, the matter had been resolved and no amount of whingeing from those ratbag Greenies could change that. The Premier Jeff Kennett strode supreme on the political stage in Victoria, his authority unassailable. The decision had been made, the issue of the Box-Ironbark was settled, no further correspondence would be entered into. Jeff backed down for nobody. But then he hadn't met Eileen Collins.

Now approaching seventy, and a woman of slight frame, I would, however, not wish to be the subject of Eileen's disapproval. The Premier was on ABC radio, talking about the casino or the new Andrew Lloyd Webber musical in town or the new Lloyd Webber to be performed in the casino...on ice, whatever the topic, he certainly was not talking about the environment. He was more than happy to take a call from Eileen of Chiltern, a town in his coalition's heartland. She challenged him about the naming of the new national park. He was dismissive. She fired up. For possibly the first time in the history of his government, Jeff backed down and by the end of the week the signs for the new *Chiltern* Box-Ironbark National Park were going up. (Perhaps Eileen's encounter with Jeff Kennett was the first chink in his previously impervious armour, for within three years of their tete-a-tete the electorate gave his government the boot.)

I met up with Eileen out at the remnants of the Magenta Gold Mine in the middle of her park. It is not only that she had such a pivotal hand in its naming that I call it her park, but since Eileen moved to Chiltern with her fellow schoolteacher husband Roy in the late sixties, she has probably spent almost every day out in the forest in some capacity. No one knows the forest better than Eileen. I got the impression that upon arriving at Chiltern, each bird's first port of call was to drop in at Eileen's place to report for duty, as she seemed to know the whereabouts of every bird in the forest. I dreamt that one day I would be able to tell her of a bird at Chiltern that she didn't already know about. We checked out the area in the hope that the exceedingly rare Regent Honeyeater might have turned up. Chiltern is the last stronghold in Victoria for this enigmatic species and by stronghold I mean in a good year as many as ten birds can be found in the forest, usually about nine more than anywhere else in the state. But not that day. It was still too early in the year for the trees those nectar lovers feed on to have started to put out any blossom and Eileen pointed out that with things so dry, it was likely to be a very poor year for flowering which translated to a diabolical year for the Regent Honeyeater. But I knew that if any turned up they would not escape Eileen's vigilant gaze and I should be able to tick this rarity off on my list without too much trouble.

I'm not sure that Eileen's self-appointed policeman's role has necessarily made her all that popular with Chiltern people over the years – she doesn't seem to mind who she offends if she thinks they have been out of line when it comes to her forest. This is despite the fact that her standing up for the town in her encounter with the Premier has led to a small economic boom for Chiltern. The declaration of the national park has put it on the Australian eco-tourism map becoming for many birders a must-visit destination on an Australian birdwatching tour. It is a long, slow process but over the years I have felt the antipathy amongst locals towards interlopers with environmental sympathies softening. I hate wearing my binoculars in public. It singles you out as an unmitigated dork. Even Keith Richards would not look cool with a pair of bins around his neck. And to wear them in a country town invites hostility as people think you are either a rabid Greenie or a pervert. Or both. But I kept forcing myself to wear them at Chiltern to visibly demonstrate to the locals that I was here for what the forest has to offer. After years of incredulous looks and sneers I was for the first time recently greeted with a cheerful, 'Going birdwatching are you? The forest is great at the moment.'

After bidding Eileen farewell I headed back to my block. I wasn't kidding when I said I was passionate about Chiltern. So passionate I even invested here. Not necessarily in a financial sense as the block I bought is primarily for conservation purposes but if the property boom ever reaches Chiltern I may, unintentionally be sitting on quite a good investment. I bought the land from a conservation organisation called Trust for Nature who run what they call a Revolving Fund where the money they make from selling the property to me goes to buy the next block of important bush that comes up for private sale. I am yet to build and may never get round to it, but thanks to council rates I have one of the most expensive camping grounds in the country at my disposal. People always told me that owning property was a big turn-on for many women – a sign that a bloke has got it going on financially – but they don't seem so keen when I ask them if they want to come back to my place and we have to drive three hours and pitch a tent.

None of the locals I met could understand why I hadn't immediately built on the land, the mentality being that if you weren't putting your land to any discernible economic use then it was wasted land. Forget about aesthetics, forget about environmental values, unless you were running something on it, ploughing something into it or extracting something from it, then it was just a waste of space. When I was in the process of purchasing my land the block next door was also for sale. I rang the local real estate agent who was handling that block. Bear in mind that it was a couple of hectares smaller, and had no tree cover on it whatsoever. As one local commented to me about the cleared land, 'It's barely big enough to keep a horse starved. Wouldn't kill the horse, but it would keep it starved.' So using it as a hobby farm was out of the question.

Both blocks were being offered as 'lifestyle' properties. So assuming that you were buying it for a nice place in the country, which block seemed to offer the better lifestyle? For someone from the city I could guarantee it would be the block with shady trees, lots of wildflowers, birds calling throughout and even your own mob of kangaroos wandering about, not the bare paddocks on that ridge exposed to the unrelenting sun. But the agent didn't seem to see it that way. Pretending I was an interested buyer in the lot next door I found out that it was actually going for $20,000 more than mine despite its smaller size and grimmer outlook. I casually asked if there were any other bush properties available in Chiltern and he said he didn't know of any. Then he remembered one.

'Actually, right next door. Some nature mob has got it up for sale.'
'Really?'
'Yeah. But it's got all these bloody trees on it. You'd have to be a
fair dinkum Greenie, into birdies and trees and that crap to want to
buy a joint like that,' he snorted contemptuously down the line.
'Yeah, I guess you would mate, I guess you would.'
I bought the property that afternoon.

Just up the road from me, on the edge of the forest, I visited
Chiltern's last viable population of Grey-crowned Babblers. I often
get asked what my favourite bird is. I usually say the next new one I
am about to see. But if pressed I always plump for the Grey-crowned
Babbler. They are fascinating birds, a bit bigger than a blackbird, full
of beans, always bouncing around, thick tails half-cocked. They live
in family groups of up to a dozen, and are always in constant contact
with their weird array of yabbering chatter. I guess in a way they are
the most human of birds. Not the grim humans who struggle clench-
jawed into work each day, more like a boisterous bunch of
mini-humans let loose in a child's playground – free, rambunctious,
just happy to be alive and in the moment. I have a particular soft
spot for them as a colony inhabited my high school (one of the last
colonies in Southern Victoria) and I would try and follow them
around the school grounds at lunchtime – no easy task as they are
pretty active and I had to disguise my interest somewhat so that I
didn't give the other kids fuel for another barrage of 'poofter' taunts.

That colony has now gone. Not just moved up the road gone
but disappeared off the face of the Earth gone. Even though they are
still quite common in woodland across northern Australia, down
south they are rapidly going the way of the birds from my schoolyard. A bird of open woodlands, they seemed to survive the initial
impact of settlement reasonably well but the colonies became isolated in often marginal habitat. They persisted at places like Chiltern
for many decades and did quite well. Eileen remembers up to thirty
colonies in the district just after she first arrived in the early
Seventies. Now there are only a couple left and they are reaching
critically low numbers where the colony cannot sustain itself and
though the individual adults may live on for years, they lose the

capacity to successfully rear young and the population is doomed to extinction. This is a process called extinction debt, where the birds are essentially a kind of zombie, still existing in this world, but effectively the walking (or flying) dead. One event such as a fire or a predator like a fox can wipe out even just one or two of the last survivors and with no recruitment possible from anywhere else, they cannot successfully breed and are lost forever.

Chiltern has had its fair share of these flying dead. Bush Stone-curlew, Hooded Robin, Gilbert's Whistler, Southern Whiteface; they are all species that are on their way out at Chiltern, all species that I would have to travel further afield to see. For so many years we have had the mentality that no matter what we do to the country there will be always somewhere else for things to go. We have reached that time in our history where the eternal frontier is at an end and for many creatures there is nowhere left, no refuge to which to retreat and hold the fort.

I might have known this in the abstract previously but in my travels over the year time and again I saw evidence of these processes. Birdwatchers for the most part are a conservative, placid bunch. You rarely see gangs of drunken birders tearing up a resort town on one of their 'Birdies Week' rampages. But they are one of the few groups of people who regularly get out into the bush and are confronted with the reality of what is happening. Even twitchers who are supposedly meant to care more about the numbers game than the birds themselves make the connection that without habitat there are no birds to see. It is enough to turn the most docile bird-watcher radical, and birdwatchers were amongst the many who supported the campaign by green groups to properly protect the remnants of the Box-Ironbark.

Leading the campaign were two friends of mine, Chiltern residents, Susie Duncan and Barry Traill. I have known BJ (as Barry is universally known) since the eighties when he was a self-proclaimed rabid anti-twitcher so it was ironic that he and Susie took me out to the Barambogie Ranges that overlook Chiltern to try and find a couple of species, Peregrine Falcon and Barking Owl, for my list. Though not purely Box-Ironbark the Barambogies share many of the same species that are found in Chiltern and are actually the best place in Victoria for the Barking Owl. Part of their campaign was to have the Barambogies incorporated into the national park. Lining up against them was a loose coalition of interests groups who claimed that Ironbarks needed to be harvested like wheat. They claimed that after around eighty years (the timber harvesting cycle) the trees of the Box-Ironbark reached senescence and began to die. The idea that an Ironbark tree took hundred of years to mature was entirely a Greenie fiction and no such colossal trees ever existed, they argued.

In one sense they are correct. No such trees exist in the forest because they were all taken out long ago and any replacements were logged before they could reach their full potential size. But BJ and Susie took me to a roadside just outside the forest that the timber cutters were never able to access. Standing there was a gargantuan Ironbark tree, several times larger and broader than the regenerating trees a hundred metres away in the forest. BJ explained that this tree was estimated to be at least three hundred years old. I'm not sure how the existence of this tree was ever explained. All I know is that studies of the flowering capacity of these giants show that even when they are only twice as big they produce up to five times the nectar of their smaller cousins when they flower. If there were a few more of these trees there would be a few more Regent Honeyeaters.

We failed to find either the owls or the Peregrines and typical of the perversity of human nature, I left Chiltern after four days not thinking about the thirty-five birds I had added to the list, but the ones I had dipped out on. There would be plenty of other opportunities to see all of these species. I was beginning to worry though that if I was setting this trend of missing out on stuff this early, how would I go later in the year when I had little time for a second crack at anything? Only two weeks in and already I was doubting whether I could pull this thing off. If I kept dipping at this rate over the next few weeks I would have to seriously contemplate abandoning the whole thing.

CHAPTER 7

19 January, Bunyip State Park, Victoria: *175 species*

I first heard that maniacal cackle back on a hot summer's night in December 1983. A series of whoops that get quicker and higher pitched as they go along, this laugh could easily have made it onto Pink Floyd's *Dark Side of The Moon*. But it didn't belong to some stoned roadie; it was the property of a mysterious night bird, the White-throated Nightjar. Many times since I've heard that cackle, but I had yet to see the actual bird from which it issues. I've seen them in silhouette, I've even had a pair lined up in the car headlights, but at the crucial moment I turned to make sure my companion, a novice birdwatcher, had also seen them. He had and was getting crippling views of them at that very moment. First rule of twitching – like the oxygen mask dropping from the ceiling, make sure you see to your own needs first. By the time I turned back to raise my binoculars, the White-throated Nightjars had flown. I heard them calling in the first few hours of the Big Twitch, and one had flown past me in the dark at Cyanide Dam in Chiltern, before I had a chance to get my spotlight onto it. This is what is known in the caper as a bogey bird.

But not for much longer. All that was going to change for 17 January was the day I would finally get this bogey off my back. I was heading back out to Bunyip for another crack and joining me was Stuart Cooney and my old partner in crime, Groober. Groobs was with me back in 1983 at the beginning of my nightjar-mare, but Stu was a relative newcomer to the birdwatching scene. Though around my age, he had only started birding a year or two earlier and had the sort of infectious enthusiasm that I remember when I was a teenager and the training lenses had just come off my bins. Sometimes his enthusiasm got the better of him and he would muddle up the names of the birds he was looking at. For instance he might see a White-eared Honeyeater, a not uncommon bird in the heathy areas at Bunyip, but in his excitement to call it, something in his brain scrambled and came out as: 'White-cheeked Honeyeater!' White-cheeked Honeyeater is an absolute stonking crippler in Victoria, but Stu was not actually trying to string a rarity, he'd just got such a flood of new information swirling around his brain that sometimes it got jumbled up. I actually found this enviable as it brought back the excitement of those times when I would sit up all night dreaming of seeing the birds I was reading about, when the magic of something new was potentially there every time I raised my binoculars.

Stu hadn't seen a nightjar, nor had he seen any of the owls we might see there. Groobs, well he was just along for the ride, constantly reminding me all night that his year list was already bigger than mine. We arrived in the late afternoon and the forest was uncharacteristically slow. Even on Twitchathons when Murphy's law dictates that things will be quiet, we usually saw more birds than this. We did manage to see a few wet forest birds, including Scarlet and Rose Robins, Rufous Fantail, Crescent Honeyeater and, right on dusk, using the spotlight for confirmation, a male Australian King-Parrot. But it was dark that we had been waiting for. Tonight was the night…

Three hours later we admitted defeat and headed home. Whereas the day had been too hot for bush birds, with the coming of night the temperature in the mountain air had plummeted and with it our chances of seeing the nightjars, which many believe go into torpor if the night is too cold. As the large insects such as moths that they feed on are not very active on cold nights, it was more likely that they probably just couldn't be bothered getting out of bed.

The next day I heard some very interesting reports of waders at the top end of Westernport Bay, about an hour and a half south of Melbourne. They sounded too good to be true: Broad-billed Sandpiper, up to seventeen Terek Sandpipers and, most tantalisingly of all, a Little Stint. As small as a sparrow, the Little Stint is almost identical to the more numerous Red-necked Stint. To identify it correctly we would have to have exceptionally close views and, even then, without a photo some would be suspicious. Make no mistake, stint identification raises passions. The debate over the identity of the first Little Stints seen in Australia was a catalyst for one of the darkest and, to my mind, most hilarious episodes in Australian birdwatching history – 'Stint Wars!'

I arrived on the scene just a couple of years too late to witness it myself and most of the participants seem very reluctant to talk about it now but suffice to say the twitching community was soon divided into two camps: those who believed that these birds were Little Stints, a new record for Australia, and those who thought they weren't. As with any war there were other issues and subtexts at play, including generational and cultural change and, of course, a certain amount of ego, pride and obstinacy on both sides. It even came to blows. Apparently one day out at Werribee Sewage Farm the two opposing camps faced off and while punches may not have been thrown, physical contact was made. I can see it now, the two sides emerging from the mists that rise off the settling ponds, warriors clad in anoraks and beanies, their weapons – telescopes mounted on tripods. Fiery words are exchanged about tertials and attenuated rear ends. Someone snaps and the pushing and shoving begins. Oh the humanity.

Twenty-five years on it is now well established that Little Stints do in fact turn up in Australia from time to time, so it was essential I try and nail this baby as it was very unlikely I would get another chance. This was part of the reason I stayed down south for the beginning of the year: to ensure that I was around in case any vagrant waders turned up. I lined up a ride out to the private property on which the waders roosted with a couple of the staff from Birds Australia (the prime bird research and conservation organisation in the country), who shall remain nameless for professional reasons. I've always wondered what birders who work at BA do when a mega rarity turns up. For the rest of us we can just claim a sickie and head off to try and twitch the vagrant, but the BA worker is in a unique dilemma. If they skive off work then everyone else in the office will know damn well that they aren't sick at all. And as many of the staff at Birds Australia are keen twitchers themselves, if something as crippling as an Emperor Penguin were to turn up, I imagine that the entire office would be deserted. When Groober worked there he actually suggested staff should be allowed to substitute two sick days a year for 'twitching days'. I thought this was a great suggestion, one that acknowledged the reality of the workplace. Groober no longer works at BA. I wonder if that suggestion had anything to do with it?

Suffice to say, we didn't see any of the good birds we were hoping for and I found myself dipping out yet again. Not only was I starting to dip out on individual birds, I was dipping out on actual birding events. I was supposed to spend the previous weekend in Sydney on a boat trip but that had been cancelled due to lack of numbers. The following weekend the first Port Fairy pelagic trip for the year was also called off, this time due to a poor weather forecast. Because most of the participants drive the three hours from Melbourne the day before, the call on whether it is safe to go out to sea on the Sunday is made on the Friday night. All day Saturday I sat at home watching the brilliantly fine weather outside the window, finding it hard to believe that a ripping cold front could possibly have been on its way. By the time the cool change arrived it had run out of puff and we would have got out with very little drama. I was starting to feel like there was some sort of conspiracy developing to prevent me seeing crucial species. When I hear of someone suffering a mental illness that causes them to be riven with anxiety, socially isolated and prone to feelings of paranoia, I think, 'Yep, sounds like a twitcher to me.'

Deciding I needed to make my own luck I picked up the phone and asked, 'Stu, you want to have another crack at those nightjars?' Two hours later we were standing at the helicopter landing pad hewn out of the bush in Bunyip State Park, waiting for the last rays of daylight to fade and the night birds to come out. Cleared areas like this are supposed to be the best place to see the birds. I'm not sure whether they specifically like cleared areas or it is just easier to see them out in the open, but as far as I could tell it was our best shot. The night was much warmer than previous nights and even before it was completely dark I could see masses of moths beginning to rise from the trees, together with the sort of big-winged insects that make people freak out when they land anywhere near them. Things looked promising.

Ears straining, we listened across the valley for the first of the nightjar's cackles. As is often the case, the trailing end of the kookaburras' laugh as they settle in for the night confused the issue for a few minutes. But then out of the dark came a series of weird shrieks, wails and what sounded like a heavy door creaking open in an old horror film. This was not the call of a bird of the night, but rather, as the spotlight revealed, a flock of Yellow-tailed Black-Cockatoos bouncing above the canopy, calling into the growing darkness. Even in the dark they are mighty impressive birds, hauling themselves along on massive wings, in halting uneven wingbeats. They look like they've flown straight out of a Hollywood animatronics studio. It is a Yellow-tailed Black that plays the role of 'Polly' in Sydney Nolan's 1948 painting *Pretty Polly Mine*. In the picture it sits oddly, looking as if Nolan has stuck it in the corner at the last minute as a surreal afterthought. Apart from the fact that you would never find the bird in such an arid setting, he has captured the essence of the species, for it does look magnificently surreal even in its natural environment.

The cockatoos were immediately followed by a smaller hawk-like bird belting across the open canopy. Our spotlight picked up two plum-coloured orbs at the front of the bird. It was the amazing eye-shine of the White-throated Nightjar. At last, after almost twenty years, I finally got a decent view of this bird. Stu and I punched the air, whooping in delight. There may have even been hugging involved as the bird flew around and around our heads, giving us sensational views. Bird number 175 and my first lifer for the year. These are the birdwatching moments you treasure.

As soon as we'd had our fill of the nightjar we decided we'd move on and try to get Stu a couple of other lifers and me a few extra year ticks. We headed out to the gully where I had spent the first few hours of the New Year, hoping to find not only the Sooty Owl but also the Powerful Owl that had been calling. There were no hippies that night so I thought we'd have a chance. After an hour or so of nothing much stirring a four-wheel drive came rattling along the track. The only drawback with birding in this great forest is that it also attracts trail bike riders in plague proportions. I was fully expecting the typical interaction you get when encountering 'Aussie blokes' in the bush, like the one I'd had some time before with a couple of farm boys in a ute on the back blocks of northern Victoria:

Bloke 1: You need a hand, mate?

Me (holding up binoculars): Nah, I'm right, thanks. Just looking for birds.

Bloke 2: Need a gun?

I love that. So wonderfully Aussie: willing to lend a hand to a stranger, equally willing to blow something away with a 44.

Unfortunately the scenario is more often likely to unfold thus:

Bloke 1: What are you doin'?

Me: Just a bit of birdwatching.

Bloke 1: Fucking poofter.

Bloke 2: Yeah, get fucked poofter.

And then they drive off spinning the wheels in the dirt so I get covered in dust.

This has happened to me several times. On Flinders Island in Bass Strait I had a bloke approach me carrying a shotgun. My sin had been to walk along the road next to his property and, using my binoculars, peer into a tree in his paddock to see what bird was making that unfamiliar call. He suggested in no uncertain terms that if I persisted in such behaviour I was 'Likely to get yourself shot.' I protested that I was standing on a public road. He tapped the barrel of the gun and repeated his message.

The occupants of the car at Bunyip turned out not to be drunken bogans but, in fact, birdwatchers. Not that they were any friendlier. They didn't introduce themselves or get out of the vehicle's cabin at any stage but I'd heard about these guys before. Though I'd never met them till now, the Owl Brothers are quite legendary, having dedicated much of their life to the study of owls. Bunyip is one of their favourite study sites and rumour has it that they know each individual owl personally. It has also been said of them that, like many researchers, they are more territorial than the animals they study. We were on a public road and had every right to be there, but the grilling the Owl Brothers gave us distinctly indicated that they were pissed off that they didn't have the power to remove us from the premises. Perhaps they thought we might have been wildlife smugglers or egg collectors – whatever their reasons for the attitude, they kind of put a dampener on the evening. Half an hour after they drove off, not having heard another sound, Stu and I decided to call it quits. It was a pity really, as I was desperate to ask them about the whereabouts of Masked Owls in the forest. Though if I had, their heads might actually have exploded.

On the drive out I saw something very small flash across the beam of the headlights. Thinking it was probably a robin I almost didn't bother to spotlight it. When I did, I saw an Australian Owlet-nightjar, a tiny little night bird that, though common throughout Australia, you hardly ever see at night because it is so small and its eyes reflect absolutely no light whatsoever. They have a very cute little poppet face but when the big eyes staring back at you are absorbing light like two black holes, the effect can be a little disconcerting. Stu didn't mind. It was another lifer for him and we were still congratulating ourselves when five minutes later a massive shadow flew across the road in front of us.

Reversing the car I got the headlights on the bird sitting on the roadside fencepost to reveal a Powerful Owl imperiously staring back at us. This is some bird. Our largest owl, if you stood next to one it would come up to your knees. Not that you would dare get that close to it. It has enormous sharp talons, a vicious beak and a big 'What are you looking at?' stare. As if to prove how tough it is, you can often find one during the day perched on a branch with the carcass of half the previous night's prey clutched in its talons as if to say, 'Look what I did. And I'll do the same to you if you give me any lip.'

We had our fill of the owl and headed home, Stu almost bouncing off the roof with excitement and me feeling very, very content. Another tricky species out of the way, a bogey bird under the belt. Maybe my luck had turned the corner.

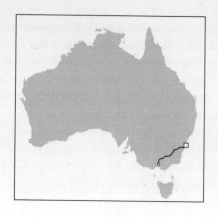

CHAPTER 8

26 January, Wollongong Pelagic, New South Wales: *193 species*

Dawn broke on Australia Day 2002, finding me standing on the edge of Wollongong harbour thinking that all seabirders must be mental. Pallid waves slapped petulantly against the breakwater suggesting that it was a pretty rough day out on the ocean, and yet the gathered throng of seabird enthusiasts who surrounded me seemed to relish the prospect. To spend a day out at sea, bobbing around throwing fish guts off the back of a boat in order to attract hungry seabirds is disturbing enough behaviour, but to actually pay for the privilege is surely a sign of abject mental deficiency. But if I was going to get anywhere near a total of seven hundred birds for the year I had to go out to sea. There was no avoiding it. There may be as many as seventy species that I would have no hope of seeing from land. These guys do it for fun. Every month. More if they get the chance. That is truly mental.

In case you haven't guessed I am not a big fan of pelagic boat trips. They're uncomfortable, they're wet, and the threat of seasickness is a constant Banquo's Ghost at the table of any enjoyment I might be having. Spending hours feeling queasy, bouncing around, getting covered in spray and watching other people throw up is not my idea of fun. Well, not since my Year 12 formal. Even though I've never actually vomited on a boat, I invest so much energy worrying about whether I will be sick that I can never relax enough to enjoy myself. None of the fifteen other birders waiting to board the 43-foot *Sandra K* seemed to have such reservations. Boat trips are one of the few social occasions for birders, normally solitary creatures who spend most of their time assiduously avoiding others of their kind, so the mood as we gathered on the dock was one of expectant bonhomie, like the first morning of school camp.

My vomit neurosis was compounded by the fact that I was utterly exhausted. I had driven up from Melbourne the day before, a nonstop trip of around eleven hours. Then to top it all off when I went to take my seasickness medication before going to sleep (apparently it works better that way) it was not where I thought I had packed it. A frantic search of my bags, motel room and entire car failed to reveal it. Faced with the torture of a day at sea without the crutch of my Dramamine, I spent hours driving around Wollongong in a futile quest for an all-night chemist. Eventually I settled for a pack of ginger tablets bought from the local supermarket. Ginger is supposed to have homeopathic anti-nausea properties but I wasn't convinced. I wanted hard-core, take-no-prisoner pharmaceuticals. I lay awake all night pondering the torture to come. At three I got out of bed and searched my bags again and, as if by magic, the tablets appeared in the pocket where they should have been in the first place. So by the time I boarded the *Sandra K* I'd had only three hours sleep and was definitely not looking forward to the next ten hours.

A pelagic trip generally follows the same pattern whether it is out of Wollongong, Port Fairy or Perth: departing early, a bunch of overexcited seabirders gather aboard a chartered fishing vessel that a generally bemused crew then takes out towards the continental shelf. Seabirds may be seen as soon as the boat leaves harbour but you can usually get these from land so unless something particularly special flies past, the boat continues punching into the waves. Beyond the initial activity of the coastal zone, bird numbers often drop off as you cruise over the mid depth waters of the continental plate. Wollongong birders have dubbed this the 'Abysmal Plain' because it can take hours to cross and the tedium can mount. On the way out everyone on board is keyed up, expecting that something really good would turn up. The first sighting of something vaguely interesting (say, a Flesh-footed Shearwater) will usually bring the boat to a stop even if the old salts know dozens of Fleshies are likely to be encountered out at the shelf break, which is where the continental plate drops – often dramatically – hundreds of metres to the true ocean floor. There is usually no change in water colour, no signage, no dotted line to tell you that you have arrived at the edge of the continental shelf but the experienced seabirder can tell when they've arrived even without the aid of a depth sounder or GPS, for this is when the truly pelagic species begin to reveal themselves. Some, such as the Great-winged Petrel, rarely come any closer to land.

This convergence zone where the nutrient laden colder water of the deep ocean wells up to mingle with the warmer continental stuff often brings to the surface a rich burst of marine life that can have the seabirds queuing up for a feed. At the first sign of any congregation of birds the boat will usually stop and the chumming begins. Ironically, the person doing the chumming has the least amount of chums around them, as the chum (or berley) used to throw over the side always comprises a foul-smelling substance. Sometimes rancid mutton fat infused with fish oil is used, sometimes part of last week's catch is chopped up and thrown out, but most prized of all is shark liver. Birds go nuts for this stuff and can smell it from miles off. I have been on a boat where not a bird was in sight. Within five minutes of the first of the shark liver being lobbed overboard, a lone albatross appeared. Five minutes later it had been joined by sixty mates gathered at the back of the boat in an orgy of feeding. They literally came from miles away. Birds that one would never see alive from land are now within touching distance, gorging themselves on the stinking bounty.

It's usually the first whiff of shark liver that finishes off the last of the green sailors on board, though few in this category usually last this long without losing their breakfast over the side. At least if they spew out at the shelf they can be comforted in the knowledge that it is adding to the general chum. Rod Gardner, one of the 'Gong regulars, later described there being 'not too much swell' on this particular trip. I'm not sure that the three people who were sick within the first hour would agree with his assessment.

I survived unscathed despite the lack of sleep. Over the years I have developed a few techniques to help quell my stomach. Once on board I try to synchronise myself with the rhythm of the rocking boat. I prefer to park myself near the rear of the boat where I can get as much fresh air and view of the horizon as possible, and just hope that we start seeing some interesting birds to take my mind off things. I also try to avoid conversation whenever possible. I find that the muscle effort required to get my voice heard above the churning throb of the diesel engines places too much stress on my already tense stomach, so I simply try not to talk. Letting out a series of enormous yawns seems to dissipate this tension. I also find singing songs under my breath to be quite soothing. For some reason The Beatles' 'In My Life' is the most calming of all. (However, due to the difficulty of getting permission to reproduce Beatles lyrics from the copyright holders, in the upcoming passage I have had to substitute the words to 'In My Life' with those of a song that is out of copyright – 'Botany Bay'.)

If I am just left alone this strategy works for me in even the roughest seas, but on a boat full of excited birders there is nowhere to flee, so I inevitably find myself wedged next to the biggest chatterbox on board who will take my Easter Island facade as an invitation for a chinwag. A typical conversation with me in the first hour of a pelagic boat trip would go along the lines of:

Chatty birder: So, Sean, how's the year list coming along? Good?
Me: Mmm.

Chatty birder: I suppose you've got all the easy ones out of the way, Willie Wagtails and the like.

Me: [Yawn]

Chatty birder: Yeah, we've got a pair that nest in our front garden.

Me: [Sung] *Farewell to Old England forever*

Chatty birder: Boy, if I had a dollar for every Willie Wagtail I've seen in my life.

Me: [Yawn]

Chatty birder: How many Willie Wagtails do you think you've seen in your lifetime?

Me: [Sung] *Singin' Too-ral-lie, oo-ra-lie attitty, Singin' too-ra-lie oo-ra-lie ay!*

Chatty birder: [Silence]

Me: [Silence – thank God, at last he's got the message]

Chatty birder: Of course, I've probably seen more magpies than I have Willie Wagtails.

The day was fairly typical for a summer trip off the 'Gong. We saw many species characteristic of the east coast in summer: once over the shelf the first of the Great-winged Petrels made an appearance. A little like a Fleshy-foot, the Great-winged has longer wings which it uses to cut through the air in graceful arcs, whereas the shearwaters seem to work a lot harder with their stiffer wingbeats. A little later they are joined by a greater number than usual of that pirate of the sea, the Pomarine Jaeger. The Pomarine looks very much like the Arctic Jaeger – jaeger being the Norwegian word for 'buggered if I can tell them apart' – which we had seen on the way out. Almost identical in plumage, the clinching detail is the shape of their tail streamers, small points on an Arctic, little twisted racquet shapes on the Pomarine. However, they tend to lose these within a few weeks of growing them so you have to rely on other more subtle features such as the bigger, barrel-chested appearance of the Pomarine, which flies belligerently amongst the other seabirds waiting to bully them into disgorging their catch.

Such identification differences fall into the realm of 'jizz'. Jizz is the indefinable quality of a particular species, the 'vibe' it gives off. Though dismissed by many as a kind of birding alchemy, there is some physical basis to the idea of jizz. Because every species is built differently, the way a bird holds itself physically can be just as important for identification purposes as the way its plumage looks. Feathers are the most variable part of a bird, so to rely purely on them can occasionally be misleading. A case in point is the Short-tailed and Sooty

Shearwaters, two species that look so superficially similar that laymen simply call them all 'muttonbirds' (supposedly they taste like mutton but to me they taste like chicken injected with a super-concentrated solution of cod liver oil – definitely one of the most revolting things ever to have passed my lips).

Most birders will look for the silvery underwing panels on the Sooty to clinch an ID but in bright sun the underwing of the Short-tailed can look just as pale. And while the Short-tailed does indeed have a shorter tail than the Sooty, which means its feet stick out slightly further from under the tail, we are only talking a centimetre or two at most and there is always the chance a Sooty's tail might be in moult or the ends of the tail feathers have been worn off, giving it a longer legged appearance. The same goes for their bills – the Sooty's is longer than a Short-tailed's by a whole 1.5 centimetres! If you can discern that difference at fifty metres as you lurch around on a rollicking boat you are doing very well indeed.

The wingspan on a Sooty, however, is about ten centimetres longer than on a Short-tailed. Again, this measurement can be difficult to detect at sea, but the longer wings do give the Sooty a different jizz as it flies. That's an extra ten centimetres (around ten per cent) of wing surface with which to fly so the Sooty doesn't have to work quite as hard to travel at the same speed as a Short-tailed. This means the Short-tailed Shearwater tends to flap its wings more often, whereas the Sooty has a more languid jizz in flight, something that you can pick up with practice almost every time. But jizz is a rather nebulous and subjective concept and gives rise to many a dispute. Everyone knows what you mean when you say a bird is black or white or grey, but how exactly do you define 'lazy' or 'loafing' or 'indolent' when referring to the flight of a bird? The concept of jizz relies on an innate sense of how a bird is rather than truly testable criteria, so it can lead to an awful lot of arguments.

And as seabirders are about as fanatical a bunch of birders as you are likely to get, (their motto is 'Sea Birders are Real Birders!') the arguments come thick and fast. Birding at sea is tough work, you're bouncing around and the birds are wheeling past at speed, disappearing behind waves. Just to get your bins to a bird is a feat in itself.

The absolute guns pride themselves on their ability not only to do this but be able to distinguish, in a split second, that some speck on the horizon is not just a Jaeger but a sub-adult, intermediate phase Arctic Jaeger. I've seen them do it time after time. They are almost never wrong. Almost. With such enormous powers comes the risk of hubris – a belief in one's own infallibility and distrust of anybody else's powers. Because glimpses are often only fleeting and the birds rarely hang around to settle disputes, there is a tendency to not back down once a call has been made. The resulting debates over the correct identity of an immature albatross or a distant storm-petrel make the Middle-East peace talks look like a love-in.

Luckily this day there were no contentious calls. There were also none of the target species I was hoping for – Tasman Sea and South West Pacific specialties such as Buller's Shearwater, White-necked and Gould's Petrels. We did see some more tropical species such as Brown Booby and Tahiti Petrel, the latter a new bird for me and one that I identified before anyone else. Usually I have to have a new seabird pointed out to me so I was quite chuffed to get this one myself. Both the booby and the Tahiti are birds I expected to see on the following month's Brisbane pelagic, so the excitement of adding them to the list was tempered somewhat by the knowledge that my opportunities for the Tasman birds were already running out.

Still, by the time we pulled into dock around five o'clock I was somewhat triumphant. I'd added fourteen species out at sea and, most importantly, I hadn't spewed! I just had to make sure I kept that record going on the fifteen or more pelagics I'd have to endure in order to get my quota of seabirds. One thing was for certain: Dramamine wouldn't be going out of business that year.

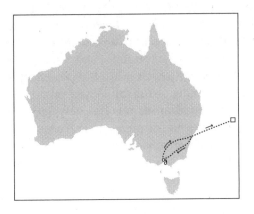

CHAPTER 9

3 February, Norfolk Island Botanic Gardens:
219 species

The plan was very simple: roll through Australia's first three convict settlements in order to rack up a swag of new species for the list. Straight after the Wollongong pelagic I was to head to Sydney (established January 1788) to catch a plane on Sunday 27 January to Norfolk Island (founded March 1788) then fly down to Hobart (convict settlement number three, 1803) for another pelagic. The first tourists to do this trip were clad in leg irons, crammed below decks in rotting hulks, suffering scurvy, malnutrition and body lice, and while modern airlines are trying their utmost to emulate such conditions, they were still going to deliver me to my destinations quickly and efficiently. I couldn't go wrong. Or could I?

By Wednesday 30 January I was still stuck in the long-term carpark at Sydney Airport, where my car had been parked since Sunday, when I should have been sipping cocktails from my Norfolk Island balcony as angelic White Terns fluttered past. The hitch? For the previous four days no-one had been able to get in or out of Norfolk Island. Anchored in the South Pacific more than a thousand kilometres from the mainland, Norfolk was fogged in and essentially the planes couldn't find it. I was left to cool my heels in Sydney, Australia's biggest and most exciting city. So naturally I turned my back on it and tried to make use of my time to pick a few extra species. This involved a quick dash down to Melbourne when I heard of a possible first for Australia, a Least Sandpiper being found. It turned out to not be a Least Sandpiper but its near relative, the Long-toed Stint, still a difficult species and no certainty for me to pick up that year, so I still decided to go for it. Of course I didn't see it and then found myself back in Sydney cooling my heels in the airport carpark with nothing to show for it other than a loss of 20,000 frequent flyer points.

Finally word came through that the fog had lifted and just before midnight the plane touched down on Norfolk Island. What was supposed to have been a leisurely week's birding now had to be three days of frenetic activity as I charged around making sure I saw everything I needed in time. Norfolk was the first place for the year where there were no second chances. There are birds there that live nowhere else in the world and if I missed them, I'd missed them for the entire year. For the first time the chill wind of a major dip was upon me, but as I headed out on my first morning, I was filled with an optimism fuelled by the excitement of birding in a new area.

Norfolk Island is simply beautiful. With its mix of lush green fields, stately Norfolk Island Pines, steep valleys and impenetrable bush set against the backdrop of a vivid blue ocean, Norfolk is far more reminiscent of New Zealand than anywhere in Australia. In fact some Kiwis claim it should be part of New Zealand, not least the members of the twitching community who include Norfolk for the purposes of their New Zealand bird lists. They say it's because Norfolk's birds have more of an affinity with New Zealand's avifauna but I suspect the real reason is that it gives them a couple of extra Australian species for their lists that they would otherwise not have.

Talk to many locals and you'll find they're adamant that the island belongs to no-one but the Norfolk Islanders. A curious mix of Aussies, Kiwis and Pitcairners – the descendants of the *Bounty* mutineers who moved here from Pitcairn Island in 1856 – Norfolkers possess a fiercely independent streak. The island has a slightly odd ambience to it, because although everyone is very friendly and laidback, there is the palpable 'us and them' sense found in all insular communities. Tourism is now the mainstay of the island but you get the sense that there is a lot more going on beneath the smiling welcome that greets the average tourist. My twitching quest was to bring me directly up against this more complex side of island interpersonal politics.

Overall, Norfolk is like a type of South Pacific Lite. It has all the beauty of an idyllic tropical island without any of the nasty, bitey stuff. The weather's not too humid, there is no malaria, and as most of the accommodation sits atop the main plateau one hundred metres above sea level, tsunamis shouldn't be much of a nuisance. There is a limit placed on how many tourists are allowed to visit at any one time, so there is little congestion.

Birds far outnumber the island's human inhabitants, including hundreds of White Terns flying about the island, while stunning Red-tailed Tropicbirds hang motionless on the breeze above the clifftops, red tail streamers protruding from their snowy bodies as though they have remote control antennas attached to them. The White Terns are remarkable not just for their beauty – they are elegant, long-winged birds that, apart from their black bill, feet and eyes, are so translucently white that with the sun behind them you can see the outline of the main bones of their wings – but because they have seemingly the most ridiculous nesting habits of any bird. Each year they lay a single egg on a horizontal branch of a tree usually more than ten metres above the ground. They make no attempt at a nest, merely depositing the egg on a notch in the bark that will supposedly stop it rolling off. It must be a successful strategy as there are plenty of terns on Norfolk, but I found one fluffy grey chick sitting on the ground, apparently having been blown out of its alleged nest. In the past this may not have been such a problem as there were no mammalian predators to knock off fallen chicks. I intervened in the cycle of nature and placed the bird in the care of a local wildlife handler, because I doubt the poor ball of fluff would have lasted the night amongst all the newly arrived cats and rats.

The mammals that settlers brought with them, particularly the rats that made it to the island when the first airstrip was built in the forties to help with the Pacific war effort, have wreaked a dreadful toll on Norfolk's wildlife. It may seem like a natural paradise today teeming as it is with fantastic seabirds such as Black-winged Petrel, Black Noddy and Masked Booby, but after a while you notice that most of them nest only on offshore stacks and islets where the rats can't reach them. The remaining forested areas still have a number of birds including Norfolk endemics such as the Norfolk Island Gerygone and Slender-billed White-eye, but it has also lost a clutch of unique species.

One such unfortunate bird is White-chested White-eye of which there has not been a confirmed sighting for over ten years. They keep being reported but every official search for the species since the 1980s has failed to detect any birds. The Norfolk community is now split into two camps: those who consider it extinct and those who believe it is still hanging on in some inaccessible slice of the island. On one side are the locals (though not all of them) who feel yet again their unique on-the-ground knowledge is being dismissed by arrogant, out-of-touch authorities, a classic case of (possibly justified) small town paranoia. Opposing them are some locals and some (though not all) off-island conservationists who believe that most recent reported sightings are misidentifications of the similar Silvereye. The self-introduced Silvereye, which is now the most common forest bird on the island, is a remarkably variable species so you'd have to be mighty careful to make sure what you thought was a White-chested wasn't in fact an odd looking Silvereye.

But merely calling into question somebody's claim can have dramatic reverberations on Norfolk Island. Resident bird enthusiasts constitute a doubly insular community – a narrowly focused interest group within a small local community – so that any difference of opinion is immediately known and can seriously affect the relationships between members of both groups. Luckily I didn't have to get involved in this particular debate, as despite scrutinising every bloody Silvereye I came across I saw nothing that remotely resembled a White-chested White-eye. My taste of the murky, internecine rivalries of Norfolk's natural history community would be served to me in my quest for two other species.

There are no full blood Norfolk Island Boobooks left. Rats may have had an impact on their population but the largest toll was most likely caused by land clearing and the loss of nesting hollows once all the largest trees were removed. By 1986 there was only one Norfolk Island Boobook left, a female. Essentially it was too late. In an attempt to save at least some of the genes, two male New Zealand Boobooks (the closest genetic relative to the Norfolk birds) were shipped in and the female mated with one. Though she died sometime around 1996, there are now thirty or so hybrid Boobooks still haunting the night with their calls.

Even though the Norfolk Island Boobook wouldn't count for my official Big Twitch list as it is currently considered by authorities to be a subspecies of the more widespread Southern Boobook, I was keen to see one. I dropped in to the national parks office to ask for advice on where I should look for the owls. Unfortunately most of the staff were on annual leave, including the person in charge of the boobook recovery program. The remaining staff members were strangely reluctant to give out any advice on where to look for the owls. I can understand them being reluctant to pass on information about where this critically endangered bird was nesting but they wouldn't even advise on a good place to just listen for them without getting the okay from the principal researcher.

The staff softened slightly when I returned the next day asking to borrow a spotlight to look for them myself. They didn't divulge any further information, but kindly provided me with a powerful torch for which I had to buy a battery at the island's one supermarket. I spent the next two nights clambering and sweating in the dark along the island's forest tracks, trying to save the juice in the torch battery for when I really needed it. Walking underneath the forest canopy at night was a slightly unnerving experience. All light from the stars was blocked out making it pitch black, aside from the glow of the luminescent fungi clusters on the ground. The ocean winds seemed to be magnified in the branches of the pines overhead creating an incessant sighing noise, pierced only by the demented cackling of nesting seabirds. Though I knew there had not been a violent death on Norfolk since the days of the convict settlement a hundred and fifty years ago, an irrational feeling of being in the presence of malevolent spirits began to take hold of me. Being in the bush at night by yourself, these sorts of feelings can creep up on you, but usually I am able to rationalise them away. That night it took all my strength to stop myself from wasting precious battery power by keeping the torch on the entire time, trying to ward off the ghost of a revenge-seeking convict.

I started to feel myself spiralling into my own 'Blair Witch' scenario, especially when I heard the distinctive real-life whoops and yelps of teenagers coming from somewhere deeper in the forest. Forget about the malevolent spirits that lurk within the dark recesses of the mind, the real terrors of the night I have found are more likely to spring from a bunch of young blokes in a small town who, having drunk their own body weight in beer and lucked out on scoring with the 'chicks', are looking to vent their frustration on something else. An out-of-towner wandering the bush at night with binoculars and a torch is a perfect target. As the banshee cries approached along the darkened track I braced myself for what was to come and shone the beam of the torch on them.

'Who are you?' one cried, startled.

'Who are you?' I fired back, trying to sound capable of handling myself in a stoush without seeming too aggressive.

'We're the Norfolk Island Christian Community Youth Group.'

'We're out on an evening ramble!' volunteered another chirpy kid.

Forget about broken-bottle-wielding delinquents braying for blood, those kids were straight out of 'The Famous Five'. They were fantastic. Bright eyed and well adjusted, they seemed too good to be true. They were fascinated to know why I was out in the forest and we spoke for about half an hour before they bounded off into the darkness hollering like Indians as they sought out their next rambling adventure, leaving me alone again with the owls. Or not. For two nights I hauled myself up and down the highest part of the island without so much as a 'boo' from the boobook. The Parks staff needn't have worried. The researcher's birds remained completely unscathed from a Dooley encounter.

It was in my attempt to see a White-necked Petrel that the intricacies of local politics were to fully confront me. The bird was as good as in the bag for me as one or two pairs breed on Phillip Island, six kilometres to the south of the main island. They nest in burrows that they only enter or leave at night, so finding them would normally be a problem. However, the researcher who had discovered the species on Phillip Island had placed a perspex tube over the burrow so that he could simply slide the cover open to check on the progress of the nesting bird without having to pull it out. A twitcher had recently reported that he had been out there and seen the bird through the window. All I had to do was get out to the island with a guide who could show me the burrow, and the White-necked Petrel was under my belt.

Getting to Phillip Island was proving problematic. For five days there was so little breeze that the fog had not cleared from around the island, but then the wind ripped through so fiercely that no charter boats dared go out to sea. By the third day I was desperate and luckily one operator, Mike Simpson of Land and Sea Charters, came to my aid. He has a reputation for being the only skipper to go out in rough weather so I was particularly lucky: as we approached Phillip Island, he said to me that if he'd known how rough the crossing would turn out to be he wouldn't have left the safety of the wharf. As I was the only tourist foolish enough to risk the conditions I had to pay the entire charter and guiding fee of $130.

To get to Phillip Island, which is a protected area, one needs to be accompanied by a registered guide, and mine was a direct descendant of *Bounty* mutineer Fletcher Christian. I would happily have paid double. Being guided by someone with such a historic surname added a touch more cachet and romance to the experience, a bit like being shown around Stratford-on-Avon by a Shakespeare, the battlefield of Marengo by a Napoleon, or the White House by a Lewinsky. There is no landing berth at Phillip Island and Mike had to negotiate his boat as close as he dared beneath the cliffs in the most sheltered part of the island. A dinghy transferred us to shore where, between waves, we had to jump over to the rock platform then haul ourselves up a series of ropes to the top of a rather daunting cliff.

Phillip Island is a simply awesome sight. In the early days of settlement someone stupidly let goats and rabbits loose on the uninhabited island. They went on a feeding rampage, reducing the vegetation cover to virtually zero, leaving an almost lunar landscape which forms a dramatic contrast to the swirling ocean below. In recent times the grazers have been removed and an active revegetation program is underway, but it will take decades to return the island to what it once was. Fortunately rats never made it here and the island is chockers with breeding seabirds which have retained a certain boldness about the presence of humans, so that you can walk quite easily amongst the colonies of noisy birds without causing too much consternation, provided you don't get too close. At times this is almost impossible, as birds will literally nest on the paths.

Having grown up on Norfolk and being absolutely passionate about the place, particularly its wildlife, my guide was superb. She knew the best route to take to get the best views of all the nesting species, including the raucous Sooty Terns, the clumsy looking Masked Boobies and what I consider to be possibly the cutest seabird of all, the Grey Ternlet. A relative of the larger White Tern, which tends to get all the press when it comes to the wow factor, the Grey Ternlet has a much subtler beauty. It too has the big black eyes and dark beak contrasting with a whitish head, giving it an innocent, baby-faced look, but rather than being dazzling white, its body is a soft powder grey. It is simply gorgeous when seen up close. We even detoured to the research hut to see the gecko endemic to Phillip Island hiding in the shade. She showed me everything, though whenever I asked about the White-necked Petrel she seemed cagey and evasive.

I still thought the White-necked was on the agenda and I asked again. She shifted uncomfortably and admitted that we'd passed their burrow and now didn't have enough time to go back for it. Exasperated, I began to plead with her. She explained that she was under orders not to show the Petrels to any more birders, mumbling something about the welfare of the birds. I was baffled. All the other seabirds on the island hardly glanced at us twice as we moved past their nests. All I wanted was a quick squiz – a few seconds would suffice.

I was convinced there was something else going on, and then I remembered my conversation the day before with the researcher and island resident who had discovered the White-necked Petrel. We had been getting on like a house on fire. He was interested to hear what I'd been seeing. He told me I'd just missed out on Long-tailed Cuckoo (a rare New Zealand visitor) by a fortnight. He filled me in on the politics of the White-chested White-eye sightings. And then I mentioned the White-necked Petrel. The laughter at the other end of the line immediately ceased and I was treated to a twenty-minute tirade on how a mainland twitcher had stolen all the glory over the discovery of the bird.

In fact I already knew the other side of the story. The two of them were on Phillip Island when the researcher told the twitcher of this strange petrel he had found in a nesting burrow. When shown the bird in question the twitcher immediately identified it as a White-necked Petrel. Back in Australia he wrote an article about Australia's first breeding record of White-necked Petrel. Because he had been the one to identify it, he didn't acknowledge the researcher which, though a bit rude, followed scientific protocol. If the researcher had correctly identified the bird, he would have been entitled to full recognition. Still, the snub rankled greatly and the next time the twitcher came to the island he was given a frosty reception indeed.

A reception that now seemed to be extended to me. I could see the boat setting out from Norfolk to pick us up. If I couldn't convince my guide to backtrack to the burrow I was screwed. She stood resolute. She said she would have loved to help me but when, a month earlier, she had shown another twitcher the bird and he reported it on the Internet, she incurred the wrath of the researcher. If word got out that she had shown me the bird, she feared strings would be pulled and she'd lose her guiding permit on the grounds that she'd placed the wildlife at risk of harm. By this time the boat was pulling in to pick us up and it was too late.

We boarded the boat in a rising swell and the ride back was extremely bumpy. I was spewing – not literally from the pounding of the waves, but because I'd dipped out all because of island politics. In such a small population you have to be very careful that you don't get on the wrong side of certain people. It is much less stressful to put up with the occasional angst-ridden rantings of a thwarted twitcher than to incur the wrath of those you have to deal with every day. I felt for my guide as she seemed genuinely upset that she couldn't show me the bird. Perhaps my evident agony at dipping out did have some effect, though, because on the next Wollongong boat trip a month later, I spoke to Jo Wieneke from Townsville and discovered that she had just come back from a trip to Norfolk where she had been shown the White-necked Petrel in the burrow by the same guide that I'd had. Maybe my desperate pleading had softened her resolve. Maybe it was just the fact that Jo is an exceptionally nice person and I come across as an annoying arsehole. Whatever the reason, it meant that I dipped on White-necked Petrel. I would not see one anywhere else for the entire year.

It looked like I was also about to dip on another Norfolk specialty, the Norfolk Island Red-crowned Parakeet. This endemic bird, recently split out as a separate species from its New Zealand relative, was so common at the time of settlement that its raids on the first crops almost sent the fledgling colony into famine. From then on it was heavily hunted. This, combined with competition for dwindling nesting hollows from the introduction to the island of the bigger and bolder Crimson Rosella, ensured the bird's inevitable decline. By the early 1980s there were only about thirty left. A rescue effort was undertaken, centred on a captive-breeding program at the Botanic Gardens, and now there are around two hundred birds roaming the island.

Not that I could bloody well find them. I'd been assured that the easiest method of getting onto the parakeets was to hang out at the Botanic Gardens next to the cage containing the captive birds. Apparently wild birds would come in and have a bit of a chat with their captive mates. Everyone I spoke to gave me different advice. 'You want to be there first thing in the morning.' 'Nah, they're more likely mid morning.' 'Rubbish! Late afternoon is when you want to go.' After three days of being there morning, noon and night I'd had no luck whatsoever – it wasn't until the end of the third day that I'd even managed to find one of the caged birds.

By the final morning I was pretty desperate. My plane was leaving at ten fifteen so I didn't have much time. One of the captive birds was calling at dawn but it didn't bring any wild birds in. I raced around to the other side of the island where I heard a bird calling from the depths of the forest, but it didn't show itself. Back to the Bot Gardens and still nothing. It was now after nine.

The airport is minutes away from the gardens so I nicked down there, checked in my luggage, went into town to refill the hire car – the bloke at the servo couldn't believe I'd done three hundred kilometres in three days on an island measuring only eight by five kilometres, reckoning it must be some kind of record. Speeding back to the parrot aviary I arrived at nine fifty-five for one last forlorn attempt.

At two minutes to ten I could see one of the aviary birds sitting mockingly on the edge of the cage. I scanned the surrounding bush. Nothing but a covey of introduced California Quail scampering for cover. I trained my binoculars back on the parrot in the cage and suddenly realised it was not actually in the cage, but sitting on the outside. It was a wild bird! At five past ten exactly I had Red-crowned Parakeet on my list.

Ten minutes later I was on the plane as it took off for the mainland.

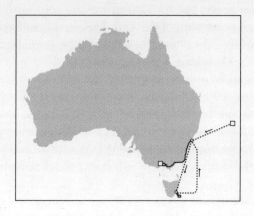

CHAPTER 10

10 February, Hospital Swamp, Victoria:
262 species

I arrived back on the mainland on 3 February. My next trip wasn't for another eight days, when I was to head to Brisbane. The intervening period gave me a foretaste of just what was involved in a year of twitching – a life on the road, last minute changes to schedules to accommodate rare birds turning up unexpectedly, and mad dashes across the country in order not to miss them.

First up was a quick detour down to Tasmania to join a boat trip of visiting Taiwanese birders that Groober had organised. Groober and I were having a sensational time as the little charter boat, *The Pauletta*, bobbed about in the steepling waves. There were albatrosses all around us. Dozens of White-chinned Petrels fought amongst themselves over the scraps we threw them. There were so many birds coming to the boat that I was supremely confident something brilliant was about to make an appearance. Pity the Taiwanese weren't seeing any of it. Despite assuring Groober that they'd taken their seasickness medication, seven of the nine were down for the count. They lay on the deck ashen faced, politely puking into plastic bags.

After two hours of this torture they finally mutinied. Rising from her prone, shivering misery, the one with the greatest command of English cried, 'No more. We go back now!' The others shakily but emphatically nodded in agreement.

The skipper turned to us and apologised, explaining that as it was their charter, he was obliged to head back to port. When *The Pauletta* went out the following weekend, there were five Gould's Petrels in the same vicinity. I'm sure if we had stayed out just half an hour longer, something as exceptional as this would have turned up. It was not be, though, and by nightfall I was touching down at Sydney Airport again.

A quick check of the Internet at the airport dictated my route for the drive back to Melbourne. A Ringed Plover had turned up at the mouth of the Snowy River in Victoria. This is possibly only the twelfth-ever sighting in Australia, and it is certainly a species I had not contemplated seeing in my original potential tally of 705. So I took the coastal route back to Melbourne picking up on the way not only the Ringed Plover but a swag of fantastic southeastern specialties such as Wonga Pigeon, Hooded Plover, Blue-winged Parrot, Red-browed Treecreeper, Glossy Black-Cockatoo, Southern Emu-wren and Pilotbird.

I saw the Blue-winged Parrots just before dark out on a bush block that I had looked at buying a little more than a year earlier. I was still in a relationship and we had walked the property and tried to imagine a future there together. I guess my imagination faltered and I looked over that block of forest in the fading light tinged with regret. If things had gone differently we might have been building a house there right then. Instead I was faced with a year and an entire continent unfurling before me, knowing that I would be alone most of the way. Well, not entirely alone. At times I'd be accompanied by other birdwatchers, like Groober. Gee, that really makes up for everything. As much as I like Groober, I know who I'd prefer to snuggle up with at night.

The day before I headed off to Brisbane I was out doing the February Seaford Swamp survey with Groober. The good wader areas had dried up and there wasn't much about, meaning we got through the survey earlier than anticipated. There were still a couple of hours of light left and Groober suggested we could try for the Red-necked Phalarope that had turned up down near Geelong. Of the 705 birds on my wish list, the Red-necked Phalarope is one I was least confident of seeing. Not sighted in Australia until 1962, since then one or two seem to turn up somewhere every year, but not always. They are almost annual on Rottnest Island near Perth and are virtually guaranteed at the Port Headland Saltworks but word was, it had become almost impossible to gain access there. I wouldn't be heading that way until much later in the year so it made sense to get it out of the way. We worked out sunset was a little over two hours away, almost the same time it would have taken to drive via Melbourne to get to Geelong, which lies on the almost exact opposite side of Port Phillip Bay to Seaford. We figured it might be quicker to head south and catch the ferry across the bay. We took the risk, not knowing what time the last ferry sailed.

We pulled in to Sorrento at five minutes to seven. The last ferry for the day left at seven and we were the final car aboard. Alighting at Queenscliff we raced up towards Hospital Swamp, which lies just south of Geelong, arriving with the sun dangling threateningly on the edge of the horizon. After getting permission from the bemused landholder we charged across to the swamp and desperately scanned the wader flocks. Nothing. It was getting too dark and I couldn't see how we'd have missed the phalarope if it had been there. I'd begun to pack up my scope, thinking at least it was a worthy effort, when Groober's sudden cry called me back. It had been hidden behind a tussock and had just swum out onto the open water.

Five minutes later it was too dark too see. We were the last observers ever to see the bird. It was gone by the time I got back from Brisbane. I didn't hear of another one anywhere in the country for the rest of the year.

CHAPTER 11

17 February, Slim Dusty billboard, Pacific Highway, New South Wales:
319 species

Brisbane is the capital of Queensland and Australia's third largest city. That's about as much as most other Australians know of Brisbane. When they visit southeast Queensland they usually head to the holiday resorts of the Gold and Sunshine Coasts, immediately to the south and north, ignoring the city itself. Over the last decade much has been done to shake off Brisbane's image as a sleepy country town with a bit of a seedy underbelly. In general it's failed. Not at building a vibrant cultural and business hub, but in convincing the rest of the country that Brisbane is a place that matters.

It most definitely matters for birders, though, for within Brisbane's hinterland is a richness of bird species surpassed only by the Wet Tropics of the Far North. The Brisbane area is essential for any birding tour of Australia. I was there for a week and hoped to add plenty to my list. After checking in to my bland inner city hotel room that looked like every other bland inner city hotel room in the rest of the world, I immediately felt compelled to get the hell out of there. I acclimatised myself by taking a stroll down to the Brisbane Botanic Gardens.

Brisbane's CBD is designed as if it is trying to deny the existence of the Brisbane River, which cuts a turbulent, mighty brown swathe around the city. About the only place you can get a river view is down by the Bot Gardens and this interface of river and park can make for some surprisingly good birdwatching. Even though I saw fewer species than on a similar stroll through Melbourne's Botanic Gardens, the birds seemed so much more exotic, with species such as Figbird, Australian Brush-Turkey, Spangled Drongo and the horn-bill-like Channel-billed Cuckoo. It had been Brisbane's hottest summer in years and by the time I got back to my hotel room I was soaking in sweat, a reminder that for much of the year I would be operating in areas with similar, if not higher, temperatures and humidity, but with no minibar full of drinks at the end of the day.

I was up at dawn the next morning which, thanks to Queensland's insistence on not adopting daylight savings time, meant I was on the road by 5 am. I was actually heading into New South Wales to try once again for the South Island Pied Oystercatcher. The SIPO, as it is known, looks very similar to the Pied Oystercatcher of Australia; in fact until recently they were considered the same species. In the late nineties somebody found that a couple of SIPOs had turned up on a beach near Ballina, about 200 kilometres south of Brisbane. It took me about two years to finally get up there to twitch them – more a slow stretch than a twitch – by which time the gen on where to find them had gone slightly cold as the twitching community had moved on to chasing other rarities. And to make matters worse I broke the crucial unspoken rule of twitching: I took my girlfriend along in a foolish attempt to combine a romantic getaway with a twitching trip. Promising her a stroll along a lovely ocean beach, I should have known I was in trouble when I first saw the smoke from the bushfire.

As the fire burned slowly through a paddock I made some disparaging comment to the effect of, 'These bloody cane farmers – they just can't help themselves.' Turned out it was not sugar cane farmers burning off but a serial firebug who had set things ablaze. Unaware and unconcerned we parked the car and headed off to the beach. I thought it would be a short stroll but three hours later, with nothing but the Aussie Pied Oystercatchers putting in an appearance and the plume of smoke coming from the direction of the car just getting bigger and bigger, I was beginning to worry just a little. My girlfriend was more than worried; she was bordering on distraught. Giving her the remaining water and assuring her I'd only be about twenty minutes, I set off further along the beach, leaving her to the mercy of the elements and the four-wheel drives rampaging up and down the sand. Two hours later I returned without having seen the birds. We had to trudge all the way back down the beach and then run through the flames of the bushfire to get back to the car. Suffice to say, we are no longer together.

I can't say that my twitching habit has ever actually broken up a relationship, but I think at times it hasn't helped. I've almost managed to convert a couple of girlfriends to birdwatching but even then, the amount of time they consider should be spent looking for birds versus nurturing the relationship is always vastly different to my estimation. No matter how open and understanding they are, they always end up feeling they come off second best, and I always feel like I have to hold in check my full effort in chasing after rarities. And it doesn't help matters when the romantic field trips you promise turn out to be long hard slogs through mosquito infested swamps. Try wooing a girl with a trip to a sewage farm.

And then there was the girlfriend who agreed to come with me on a trip to northern Victoria for a day's birding. She fell asleep in the car and woke to find herself alone in the middle of God-knows-where, with rising floodwaters lapping at the wheels of the car. I was nowhere to be seen but my shoes and – most disturbingly – pants were sitting on the roof of the car. In my mind the explanation was quite logical. The swamp was in flood and I couldn't risk getting the car bogged by going any further. The whole area looked great for Painted Snipe and Little Bitterns and as I didn't have any gumboots with me I had taken off my shoes and pants to stop them getting wet, not waking her because she looked so peaceful asleep. Simple. She didn't quite see it that way and no amount of explanation ever allayed her suspicions. As there are so few female twitchers and, as far as I know, absolutely none around my age, my choices are either to find a sympathetic and indulgent partner who can put up with my idiosyncratic hobby, or remain single.

Having remained single, I had no such encumbrances this time around and happily headed off along the beach at Ballina, extremely optimistic of finally adding SIPO to my list. It was the sort of day that, if I'd had a wife and had brought her along, divorce proceedings would have been initiated. Caught in the tail end of a tropical depression (just below a cyclone in terms of damage) I trudged for hours along the beach, soaked to the skin. I hadn't brought anything vaguely waterproof. The rain bucketed down and the wind howled, sending stinging salt spray in off the ocean horizontally, so that the microphone on my video camera totally packed it in, necessitating a thousand dollar replacement – the warranty covered everything except being stupid enough to expose the camera to salt. The squalls were so intense that whenever I did come across oystercatchers I lost them behind a grey curtain of rain if they moved more than ten metres from me. Eventually, after hours of hard slog, I came across a bird in a group of Aussie Pieds that seemed to have more white in the wing, and much shorter legs – when it ran it looked like a dinky little wind-up toy version of a real oystercatcher. Next day I showed the video of the bird to Andrew Stafford, a long-time buddy and Brisbane birder, and he confirmed it for me: South Island Pied Oystercatcher, on my list!

I first met Andrew on a Bird Observers' Club Young Members outing in the early eighties when I was about fourteen and Andrew around twelve. His mum was so terrified of letting her snowy-haired little boy out with these scruffy older kids that she had loaded him up with numerous packets of lollies. Whether the lollies were meant to be used as bribes or to provide the energy he'd need to outrun us when we started beating him up, I'm not sure, but it earned him the tag 'Sugarman' for years to come.

His family moved to BrisVegas a few years later and he embraced his adopted city with alacrity, particularly its music scene.

He had just started work on a definitive history of the Brisbane music scene, to be titled 'Pig City'. Andrew is one of the few people I know with whom I can discuss both the habitat preference of the Eastern Grass Owl and which Beatle plays which guitar solo on the final track of *Abbey Road*. Interestingly, he approaches both topics with the same methodical intensity and can rattle off which are the best months for seeing White-necked Petrel off Brisbane just as readily as he can give you a twenty-minute dissertation on his top three rock albums that contain seven tracks or less.

Given his propensity for the methodical approach, for the first time in the year, I left myself in the hands of the local expert – even though I'd done a bit of birding around Brisbane before I felt totally comfortable letting Andrew dictate the day's agenda. My initial confidence was dented slightly when, after picking him up for yet another 5 am start, he assured me our first stop would be at a 'dead cert' site for Comb-crested Jacana. Naturally we failed to find any whatsoever. My faith was restored dramatically when, after nursing my pathetic little hire car up to the top of the rainforest clad hills at Lacey's Creek, Andrew assured me that this was the best site around Brisbane for White-eared Monarch, a bird I had never seen. He finished this sentence with the caveat, 'Of course White-eared Monarchs can be very tricky.'

He immediately got out of the car and exclaimed, 'Good Lord, there's one now!'

That White-eared Monarch was a lifer for me. If only other birds were that easy to come by.

Later in the day we found ourselves in the vicinity of Lake Samsonvale. We weren't after waterbirds, but quail. Finding quail is hard work, requiring a hell of a lot of paddock bashing on foot through thick tropical grass. In these situations I am always apprehensive about snakes but Andrew laughed.

'You should be more worried about the paper wasps. When they attack it's like a million little hypodermics piercing your skin.'

He pointed out one of their paper bag like nests attached to a tall blade of grass and suggested I avoid banging into one. Then I noticed that there was a wasps' nest every metre or so, which put me on edge for the rest of the sweat-inducing hour we trudged through the grassland in the midday heat with no luck whatsoever.

We moved on to an area that Andrew assured me was reliable for King Quail, another species I had never seen before. With no success on the overgrown tracks we were forced to backtrack. Andrew was explaining to me that with King Quail it is a pretty hit and miss affair and I shouldn't be too disappointed, when suddenly a female King Quail literally flew up from under our feet. We tried to flush it again, to no avail. I expressed a little disappointment at the brevity of the view – we saw it for maybe three seconds at most. Andrew countered that he'd just had one of his most prolonged views ever of this elusive species; most of the time all you get is a blur of wings that flash past you in a millisecond.

En route back to Brisbane we stopped in at a few more sites. We had planned to do some spotlighting but after a solid day of birding, much of it flogging through impenetrable grasses under the blazing sun, we decided to call it quits. Though we'd dipped out on a couple of things, we'd seen ninety-six species for the day, twenty of which were new for the year.

The next day I did it all again. Heading south, I was trying to follow up reports of Painted Snipe on the Gold Coast. I'd looked for the alleged site two days earlier en route to the SIPO but all I'd found was a small wetland that seemed little better than a muddy ditch. It turned out this actually was the wetland where the Painted Snipe were. This is a nationally threatened species that is one of the most enigmatic of all Australian birds. They follow the ephemeral waters of inland floods but no-one can predict with any certainty where they will turn up, so as I arrived at the wetland I was not really that hopeful. To compound my doubts, bulldozers were operating nonstop a few hundred metres away as they gouged out the foundations for the next new 'Gold Coast lifestyle experience'. Bustling women in hot pink outfits power-walked by and older couples walked dogs on the adjacent fields. A council vehicle was slashing grass on the roadside verge. I just couldn't believe it was possible for a Painted Snipe to exist here at all. And then a lone male bird wandered into view. Bugger me. I take back all those flooded ditch comments. This place should be on the National Estate!

I made my way back along the coast, checking out the mangrove and mudflat habitats of Moreton Bay, not getting back to my stark hotel room till well after dark. I decided to dine at the hotel and realised, with all the cooing couples around me, that it was Valentine's Day, so I went back to my room to bring my loved one down to dine with me. I spent the meal staring lovingly across the table at my binoculars. We made a toast to having passed three hundred birds (Richard's Pipit at Hastings Point) but decorum prevents me from revealing whether the relationship was consummated that night. Let's just say that with my binoculars, I like to watch.

My alarm went off at four-thirty and yet again I was heading out before dawn. The birding had been great but the fatigue was really starting to kick in for the first time in the year.

The day turned out to be brilliant. I picked Andrew up and we headed out to the Conondale Ranges. The Conondales are one of the most underrated spots in the country, a superb area of rainforest, rivers and mountains only a couple of hours north of Brisbane. And they harbour some spectacular birdlife. We failed to find our target species, the Black-breasted Button-quail, despite finding some fresh platelets. When the button-quail feed they scratch at the forest floor in a circular motion that leaves telltale circular dishes of earth in the leaf litter, meaning that we knew they were in the area, but just not showing themselves.

This disappointment aside, the rest of the day was a nonstop natural wonder feast. Good birds like Cicadabird, Paradise Riflebird (a relative of New Guinea's birds of paradise) and Russet-tailed Thrush all showed well and we came eyeball to eyeball with a massive Diamond Python curled up in the hollow of a tree. A less fun encounter happened when my ankle brushed past a seedling of the Gympie Stinging Tree. Luckily it was just a juvenile plant and the sting was not as severe as it should have been, but my ankle itched madly for about three days. To cop a branch across the face would be sheer agony and I can't begin to imagine the pain felt by the tourist – as the legend goes – caught short in the rainforest who saw the nice big shiny green leaves and figured they would make a good substitute for toilet paper.

Andrew even managed to redeem on the jacana front as in nearby farmland he spied a pair on a dam. We arrived back in Brisbane satisfied but exhausted. The next day we were up just as early to get down to Southport on the Gold Coast for the pelagic trip. The boat we set out in was enormous, particularly when compared with the little tubs we use on the south coast. It had two levels and more than adequately catered for the thirty or so passengers setting sail. I couldn't believe either the luxury or the comfort, though the ample size of the boat was to have unforeseen consequences.

Proceedings started very well indeed, for just beyond the break-water was a massive feeding flock, mainly Wedge-tailed Shearwaters but something more exciting could have been lurking amongst them. Pretty soon my prayers seemed to be answered when the cry of 'Streaked Shearwater!' went up.

I definitely needed this, another bird I had never seen before. I was atop the upper section of the boat and could see the bird in question flying around amidst the general throng but every time I raised my binoculars the boat pitched violently and I got at best a shaky glimpse, certainly not enough to tick the bird off. If I'd been on the lower, more stable deck I would probably have been able to sat-isfactorily clinch the ID for myself. But I wasn't too worried as we were barely an hour into the trip and the birding had already been sensational. Streaked Shearwater was all but in the bag, not to men-tion what else was waiting out there at the shelf.

Oh how wrong I was. For the rest of the day we added just six other species, all in very low numbers, with a pair of Hutton's Shearwater the only new bird for the list. Early enthusiasm waned and as the swell died down and the sun heated up, we were soon adrift in our own version of the doldrums. While most moved down to the lower deck for some shade, I remained desperately vigilant with one or two other diehards, trying to squeeze out another Streaked Shearwater. The languid afternoon dragged on, sapping everybody's energy. Eventually it was time to head for shore…

About halfway back everyone had retreated to the lower deck save for a birder called Bill Moorhead and myself. Bill had driven all the way down from Bundaberg for this trip and was almost as disappointed as me in the day's outcome. Suddenly I saw two birds sitting on the water. They were a long way off and all we could pick up was that they were largish with pale heads – like nothing I'd ever seen before. I mentally rushed through the pages of the field guide in my head, trying to think what those birds could possibly have been. I was stumped. I yelled down through the hatch to alert the others that we had got something interesting. One or two people raised their heads disinterestedly and gestured that they couldn't hear me. I looked back out to sea and noted that the birds were still on the water but the boat was now starting to head away from them.

I raced up to the stern where the more expert seabirders had gathered. I approached Paul Wallbridge, the organiser of the trip and champion of Queensland pelagics, and started describing the birds to him. As I mentioned the pale heads he looked at me quizzically and it suddenly clicked. There was only one possibility of something that large with a pale head – Streaked Shearwater. We scanned the area where I'd seen the birds but we were too low to the water to get a good view. I was off, charging back to the upper deck. By the time I got there Bill was just putting down his binoculars.

'They've just flown off,' he said. 'You know what they are, they're – '

'Streaked Shearwaters.'

'Yeah. So you saw them then.' Bill seemed relieved for me.

'Nup.'

I tried to console myself that I'd pick up Streaked Shearwater in October on the Ashmore Reef trip, but nonetheless I disembarked at the end of the day extremely dejected. Two opportunities to tick this species had gone begging. There is no doubt about what I saw but because I wasn't satisfied within myself that I had got on to enough salient features, I couldn't in good conscience put the bird down on my list.

The drive back to Brissy was a rather subdued one. Andrew suggested we forget about birdwatching for a while and head out to catch a band, let him prove to me that the phrase 'Brisbane culture' is not an oxymoron. We headed to his mum's place for a shower and change of clothes. His mum greeted us with the news that he had to call Tony

Palliser in Sydney immediately as a – 'Hang on, I wrote the name down somewhere…Ah, there it is' – a Kentish Plover had been seen.

Andrew's mum is a very cool, open-minded woman who is obviously very proud of her son, but as Andrew raced to the phone and started going ballistic as he listened to Tony, I could see the same look of incomprehension on her face that my parents often wore: 'This person cannot possibly be related to me.'

While excited about the news of a Kentish Plover turning up on the New South Wales Central Coast, only the second Australian record ever, Andrew sensibly wasn't about to drop work and other responsibilities to go for it. I, on the other hand, who had only one more full day left in Brisbane, faced an agonising dilemma. I had organised with Paul Wallbridge to head out the next day to try for what I was assured were almost dead cert Bush-hen and Little Bittern, two elusive species that would be very handy to have nailed down. But a Kentish Plover. To miss out on that would be criminal. It's a 700-kilometre run from Brisbane to Old Bar where the Kentish had been found. It was Saturday evening. I was due to fly out Monday morning and as I was heading up to Wollongong from Melbourne the following weekend for another boat trip, I could easily go up a day or two earlier and go for the Kentish at a more leisurely pace. But by then it might have gone. Two guaranteed ticks if I stayed in Brisbane versus a highly risky 1400-kilometre dash for one. The choice was obvious.

I left Brisbane at five thirty the next morning, racing towards the target in constant contact with other twitchers who were also going for the bird. By the time I reached Murwillumbah a call from Mike Carter, who was heading up from Melbourne, confirmed that the bird had definitely been identified as a Kentish Plover. At Grafton Tony Palliser called from out at the site saying he couldn't find the bird. By the time I drove past the Big Banana at Coffs Harbour a devastated Tony had called again: he had to get back to Sydney to catch an international flight for work. On the outskirts of Port Macquarie a call from Andrew let me know the others had got both the bittern and the Bush-hen.

It took me nine hours of solid driving to reach my destination, stopping only for petrol and an enormous billboard of Slim Dusty that loomed incongruously on the highway just outside of Kempsey. After seven hours of driving my mind might have drifted off the main game for I felt compelled to pull the car over and take a photo. It also gave me the opportunity to have a sneaky leak beside the car; a much more preferable option than going in an empty bottle. It was, however, rather disconcerting to have a gigantic country and western icon peering down upon me as I went about my business.

I pulled into the carpark above the beach at Old Bar to see Mike Carter's long-suffering wife Trisha sitting in their car reading a magazine. Trisha is not a birder but has spent a lifetime accompanying Mike on his twitching expeditions, enduring along the way: being stranded in the desert for two weeks, almost being kidnapped by Rascals in Papua New Guinea and having their tent washed out to sea in North Queensland. This time she had only had to endure a mad last minute dash the thousand or so kilometres from Melbourne. She told me that they had arrived fifteen minutes earlier and Mike had just headed down to the beach. I assembled my gear and followed him to be met by a group of birders from Newcastle who had just spent the day searching for the bird. One of them offered to walk me to the beach to point out where they had seen it.

He was full of urgency as he said they discovered the Kentish Plover on a high tide roost and as the tide was rapidly turning he assumed the bird would soon move off to feed on the extensive mudflats where it would be almost impossible to find. Having given me the hurry-up, he then proceeded to go into lengthy detail about the bird: how they had found it; what other species it was associating with; plumage and behaviour details – everything I would ever want to know about this particular Kentish Plover – when all I really wanted was to get out there and see it. I stood on the sand waiting for him to finish his dissertation, hopping impatiently from one foot to the other. I could see Mike in the distance approaching the site where the bird was. He kept talking, Mike kept getting closer and the tide kept receding. I snapped and, without apology, left him mid sentence to charge up the beach towards Mike. Never get between a twitcher and a new bird. All social niceties go out the window.

When I arrived breathless about ten minutes later, Mike was in a state of extreme agitation. The bird was nowhere to be found. Damn, I knew I shouldn't have stopped for Slim Dusty. We scanned the surrounding beach, focusing our attention on a shingle bank. Nothing. Training our scopes on the bank revealed that there were birds there, resting amongst the pebbles, blending in remarkably well. Birds seemed to materialise in front of our eyes. First a Red-capped Plover, then another, then another three. Next a Double-banded Plover, and a Lesser Sand Plover – a new species for the year – but no Kentish.

Suddenly Mike cried, 'There's something with a collar!' referring not to some overly formal beach goer, but the white collar of a Kentish Plover that distinguishes it from the Red-capped. And sure enough, Australia's second Kentish Plover emerged magically from amongst the shingle. Not long after, a couple walking their dog put the little flock to flight and we couldn't relocate the Kentish. If I had been five minutes later I would have missed the bird entirely. Thank God I resisted the urge to stop at the Big Banana.

I made the flight back home from Brisbane the next morning with minutes to spare. As it happens, the Kentish hung around for another month, so I could have gone for it at my leisure. Trying to find another Bush-hen and Little Bittern would turn out to be quite another saga.

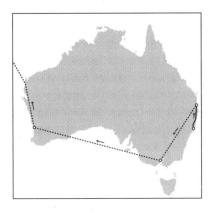

CHAPTER 12

15 March, Christmas Island Detention Centre:
353 species

If Christmas Island were to be invaded tomorrow I suspect that the only Australians who would bother trying to defend it would be the twitching community, who within minutes would be organising a strike force of angry nerds to protect their sacred soil. Lying less than four hundred kilometres from Indonesia and more than a thousand from mainland Australia, Christmas Island belongs to Australia only because of the quirks of international politics. Originally annexed as part of Britain's Strait's Settlements which also included such places as Singapore and Penang, the island was taken over by the Japanese in World War II. Once they got it back the British began looking to offload it and in 1958 the island was officially ceded to Australia. Because of its proximity to Asia, the addition of Christmas Island has seen the Australian bird list jump by more than twenty species and with more birders visiting every year it is not outrageous to imagine another twenty turning up in the next few decades. All it takes is a decent tropical storm to whip up and a bird that would normally be found on Java or Sumatra can suddenly find itself blown onto the Australian list – a case of 'I don't think we're in Yogyakarta anymore, Toto.'

The week before I left for Christmas Island just such an event occurred, with a bunch of Asian birds suddenly turning up on the island. Amongst them was a first for Australia, a Cinnamon Bittern. Sadly it had died, presumably of exhaustion soon after making landfall, and now resided in the freezer at the national parks office. I was due to land on Christmas Island on the Sunday. Glenn Holmes, one of the first generation of Aussie twitchers, now doing botanical fieldwork on the island with his wife, Jenny, had come across a Malayan Night Heron on the Friday and while looking for it the next morning, another birder-cum-researcher, David James, had also found a Watercock. Both these birds are incredible rarities on Australian soil and both would be new not just for me but also for Mike Carter, who has the greatest list of any Australian twitcher.

Mike was accompanying me on this trip. A civil engineer by profession, Mike was involved in the nascent twitching scene in England in the early sixties when he had the good fortune to marry a young Aussie girl named Trisha and moved here in 1964. His interest in twitching piqued by former record holder John McKean, by the early nineties Mike had seen just about every bird there was to see on the Australian mainland. Naturally his thoughts turned offshore. He virtually pioneered the twitching trip to Christmas Island but had never been there in the first half of a calender year. When I asked him if he was interested in joining me on this March trip, he immediately jumped at the chance.

With the tantalising prospect of two new birds in the offing Mike was almost in a state of apoplexy as we flew out over the Indian Ocean from Perth. The plane stopped en route at the Cocos Islands. A string of low-lying atolls almost closer to Sri Lanka than they are to Australia, the Cocos are Australian territory nonetheless. The islands contain no endemic species but they do have one species that occurs nowhere else in Australia: the Green Jungle Fowl. Introduced by plantation workers in the 1880s this is the Indonesian relative of the domestic chicken that originated in mainland South East Asia. The birds went feral on Cocos Island and can still be seen along the airstrip. We had our telescopes on board in case they were not easy to see from the terminal. On landing the dark forms of the jungle fowl could be seen scattering across the airfield, but we were moving too fast for me to get a tickable view. They herded us off the aircraft and we were told we had twenty minutes before reboarding. The terminal was filled with the local Malay population greeting relatives, farewelling others and the mood was quite festive. I was a little downcast as none of the green chooks had come back out onto the airstrip so we decided to wander across the runway to look for them in the scrub on the other side. We managed to get a good look at the birds, including a quite handsome male, and even had time to check out the idyllic tropical lagoon that lies next to the airfield.

Upon returning we were confronted by a horrified federal police officer. In the post–September 11 era, people are not supposed to be able to simply wander across the tarmac at international airports. We explained that we were just birdwatching but that seemed to exasperate him even more. He snapped that we were jeopardising our personal safety. I looked out along the runway to the waves crashing against the shore. There was probably not another plane within a thousand kilometres of us, ours being only one of two commercial flights a week. Smiling, I told him I didn't think any plane was likely to have sneaked up on us. This didn't help matters and he ushered us towards a small room in the terminal building. Suddenly I had visions of the week I was supposed to be ticking new birds on Christmas Island being spent in the Cocos lockup being interrogated about potential espionage activities.

Suddenly there was some sort of ruckus amongst the Malays and one of them raced over to our custodian demanding he urgently see to some crisis or other. Temporarily ignored, Mike and I joined the other passengers getting back on the plane and slunk back to our seats, keeping very quiet until it finally took off.

Rising dramatically out of the ocean like the island from *Jurassic Park*, Christmas Island's towering cliffs, an impediment to human settlement for centuries, provide a unique tropical environment that has developed with very little interference from the outside world. The island is a haven for birds and even in the main settlement, a town of around fifteen hundred people, ethereally beautiful seabirds, such as tropicbirds, wheel in the skies above. The golden hued White-tailed Tropicbird can even be found nesting right on the footpath. Pterodactyl-like frigatebirds, including the endemic Christmas Frigatebird, also patrol the skies. Swooping in to drink from any source of fresh water – including the swimming pool at the casino resort – only reinforcing the *Jurassic Park* feel.

But if Christmas Island was any movie it would be *Groundhog Day* for over the next seven days every day was identical in almost every respect. Same weather, same birds, same routine. The weather never changed – it was always stinking hot with a tropical downpour late in the morning alleviating the heat for about an hour before the humidity began to build up again to unbearable levels. The birds were almost always the same – we saw around twenty-two species every day. After the first full day we only added another eight more species during the entire trip. But we constantly kept trying for new species, especially the Malayan Night Heron, which eluded us seven mornings in a row despite us thoroughly searching the rainforest tracks every morning at dawn near where Glenn and David had seen it.

About the only place we spent more time than those tracks was the Christmas Island tip. As there is no sewage farm on the island I guess this is where all the rare birds feel compelled to go. If you look at the vagrant records from the island, you will notice that nearly all of them are of open country species. There may in fact be many rare forest dwellers that turn up on Christmas Island but they would tend to lurk in the actual rainforest itself which, though kept fairly open by the grazing of the island's famous red crabs (until the infestations of crazy ants started to take their toll), is made virtually impenetrable by the shards of limestone littered throughout. These shards are so sharp that they will slice the sturdiest of boots to shreds in a matter of days. So if you want to have a chance of finding rarities, you need to look in the more open, disturbed areas.

And places don't get much more disturbed than the tip. Every day there was a new pile of rubbish to attract new multitudes of flies. One day we arrived to find somebody had dumped the carcasses of around sixty chickens. As they festered in the equatorial sun the stench became unbearable and I found myself dry retching whenever we visited. The resulting bonanza of flies proved irresistible to insect feeding birds such as Barn Swallows, Christmas Island Glossy Swiftlets and at least two different White Wagtails, a very rare bird indeed for Australia. The flies were so abundant that while I was videoing one of the White Wagtails it yawned and a fly managed to buzz straight down its open throat. Now that's service.

To me, the place was paradise, with the rubbish tip at its epicentre. Which is, I suppose, why our benevolent and kind-hearted government decided to build the refugee detention centre immediately adjacent to the tip. Top blokes, our politicians – there's nothing they won't do to help make asylum seekers' lives just that little more unbearable. On the other side of the detention centre – a real prison with razor wire, real guards with real guns and accommodation that looks like it has been constructed out of shipping containers – is the island's sportsground, which is also a very good place for birds. We visited both the sportsground and the tip so frequently that the guards stopped bothering to check us out, leaving Mike and me alone. Far more unsettling than being searched by uniformed armed guards was the incongruity of how life pans out for different people. There was I, indulging in the ultimate freedom. I had the money and the means to visit this place in the pursuit of my own personal goals, for my own amusement. The people who stared forlornly (or is that resentfully?) at me through the wire had ended up there against their will, because they risked everything to try to reach a land where they could have the same opportunities I've had.

The reality of this contrast really hit home on the fifth morning when we discovered one of *the* birds of the trip. Having done the usual rounds of the forest tracks unsuccessfully looking for the Night Heron we decided we'd have a quick look around the overgrown go-cart track that lies between the sportsground and the detention centre. We had seen White-breasted Waterhens there and suspected they night have been breeding. As we searched the rank grasses, a plump, medium sized bird parachuted down in front of us. It was so short winged and short tailed that at first I thought it was a pigeon. I asked out loud, 'What was that?' and before Mike had a chance to answer I cried, 'It was a snipe! It was a snipe!'

I think Mike realised it was a snipe all along, but I was so surprised that I kept repeating the phrase like an idiot. We cautiously approached its landing place but as we did three more snipe flew past emitting a dull rasping call that seemed to spur the bird on the ground into action, and it rose up to join them. Snipe are notoriously difficult to identify in the field but on the basis of call, size, the small bill, short, rounded wings and short tail we were both happy to call this bird a Pin-tailed Snipe – that and the fact that Mike had also managed to see the definitive pin-like feathers on the tail. This is a very difficult bird to see in Australia. I was pretty excited. I was pumped. I looked across at the detention centre, my broad smile disappearing as I saw a little girl standing in the compound staring at me through the razor wire. Her mother came over, avoiding my gaze, and moved her away.

After almost a week on the island Mike's countenance started to seem almost as cloudy as the occupants of the detention centre, for although the birding had been pretty outstanding there was nothing Mike hadn't seen in Australia before. I added twenty species for the year, fourteen of which I couldn't hope to see anywhere else but Mike forked out a lot of money to come a long way with not a single addition to his life list to show for it. No wonder he was bummed.

Mike's contribution to the birding scene in Australia has been immense and not just because of the number of hours he's logged in the field, or the number of birds he's seen but, most importantly, because of his mentoring role. He basically discovered and nurtured some of Australia's most significant birdwatching talent – people such as Ian May, Chris Corben, Doug Robinson and Peter Lansley – and has provided guidance and support for countless others. Had it not been for Mike I know I would probably have lost interest in birdwatching once I hit my teenage years. It is because Mike invested the time, and even the money – he paid half my fare for boat trips because at the time my family couldn't afford to send me – that my interest in birdwatching was able to withstand the competing claims of mates, girls, sport and beer. The fact that I am still a birdwatcher has a lot to do with Mike's influence. And as I curl up at night with a copy of *The Atlas of Australian Birds* instead of the soft body of a loving partner, I like to think that Mike had something to do with it. It helps to blame other people for your loneliness.

The first time I met Mike was at Seaford Swamp. It was a lazy Saturday in March 1980 and I was riding my bike around the grounds of the primary school when I spied two men park their car and head out towards the swamp. Apart from my teacher, I'd never met any other birdwatchers before. Trying to be very cool I approached them and asked, 'You guys birdwatchers, are you?'

The older one (Mike) answered, 'Why yes we are. Are you?'

'Yep.'

'Seen anything interesting lately?' asked Doug Robinson, the younger man.

I brought myself up to my full eleven-year-old height and proudly told them of my latest amazing sighting: 'Yeah, I saw a Blue-winged Shoveler here last week.' Now known as the Australasian Shoveler, I was ever so pleased to have seen my first one the week before.

'Yes, it's been a very good year for them, there's been quite a few around,' responded Mike. He was not trying to belittle me, he was just stating a simple fact. The effect was to instantly deflate my cockiness.

'Oh. Have you seen anything interesting?'

'Well, there has been a Wood Sandpiper about.'

My eyes bulged out of their sockets. I'd read about the Wood Sandpiper in my *Gould League Rare Birds* book. And to think it could be living here on my swamp. Mike asked if I'd like to join them. I explained I didn't have my binoculars or gumboots on me but if they could wait ten minutes I would dash home and get them.

My mum later said that she'd never seen me move so fast in my entire life. Apparently I burst into the house, blurted, 'Mum, there's two men down at the swamp who said I could go birdwatching with them!' grabbed my binoculars and was gone, before she had time to ask who exactly these strange men were yet giving her plenty of time to ponder whether she would ever see her son alive again.

I saw the Wood Sandpiper as well as a couple of other new birds and, much to my Mum's relief, I was returned unharmed. Or so she thought, for Mike had planted in me the seeds of my doom as I became totally hooked on twitching. And now, twenty-two years on, that chance encounter at the swamp had led to me sitting in the middle of the Indian Ocean still looking for new birds. Oddly enough, after all those years this was the longest I had ever spent with Mike in one go. Even we couldn't rabbit on about birds for the entire time and I gained an insight into aspects of Mike's life outside birdwatching, such as the fact that his father was a World War I veteran who lost a hand at Gallipoli.

I also gained an insight into what makes Mike Australia's premier twitcher. It is impossible to say who is the best birdwatcher, it is such an esoteric concept, but by the one thing that can be measured – how many birds someone has seen – Mike is streets ahead of his nearest rivals. Some (mainly other twitchers who haven't seen as many birds as him) may say uncharitably it is due to his longevity (he started in 1964) or that he has been fortunate enough to be able to afford a lifestyle that allows him to travel at a moment's notice to chase after birds. But this is a churlish and superficial analysis. There are plenty of birders who have been around longer than Mike, many with access to greater funds, so why haven't they knocked Mike off his perch?

One answer is his passion. He simply loves birds and birdwatching. For him it is not simply a numbers game. I've seen him get almost as excited feeding a relatively common Grey Butcherbird in his backyard, pointing out the field marks that distinguish it as a female, as he is ticking off a new bird for his Australian list. In fact his passion for birding sees him out in the field so often that he has discovered more firsts for Australia than just about anybody. This is something you don't regularly achieve with mere dumb luck. Finding rarities is akin to goldmining. You may get the occasional dolt who strikes it big when they stub their toe on a huge nugget, but the miner with the greatest longevity is the one who can read the country, assess the lie of the land and search accordingly. He may not strike it rich every time but he won't ever be far off.

But this still doesn't fully explain Mike's birding success. Watching him on Christmas Island I think I finally figured it out. Mike has an innate curiosity for just about everything. He is always wanting to know how things work, or more precisely how they fit together, be it the feather structure on the wing of a White Wagtail or the plumbing system at the hotel. His nature is such that he isn't satisfied to simply accept what he sees, he wants to know the 'why' behind what he sees. This fascination for things can often mean he becomes oblivious to everything else aside from the object of his fascination. This is not to say he has no interest in things other than birds but when he is concentrating on them there is very little space left for anything else. It also means he can be quite a frustrating travelling companion as he is always stopping to look at or comment on something, often with much more intensity than seems warranted: 'Look at that crab!' 'Look at that butterfly!' 'Good Lord, look at that swiftlet, it's got two primaries missing from its left wing!'

Particularly when it extended to statements about what I'd ordered for breakfast – 'Baked beans *and* mushrooms. Good Lord!' – I couldn't help but wonder if he was being critical or taking the piss. Then it dawned on me that Mike is only stating the obvious because it seems fresh to him. I began to envy his capacity to see the wonder in almost anything. It is curiosity, it is engagement, it is, I am sure, the reason why, though approaching seventy, Mike can easily pass for someone twenty years younger – he has a refreshingly boundless enthusiasm for the world and all that it contains. This is why he is such a top birdwatcher; he is always on the lookout, always engaging directly with what he sees. It also explains why he is one of the most positive, refreshing and seemingly happy people I have ever met.

But after five days without a new bird I could see his enthusiasm was starting to flag. The night before he had declined to head out spotlighting around the airport in the hope of turning up an Asian nightjar or two. I was beginning to feel guilty that I'd dragged him all the way there for no reward. Then, on our second last morning, it looked as though we might have hit the jackpot.

We were again heading out before dawn to look for the Night Heron when the car headlights caught the unmistakable form of a bittern flying up from the gutter. There seemed to have been an influx of bitterns and herons on the island because, apart from the Night Heron and Cinnamon Bittern, we had seen six species, including the Asian form of Black Bittern. Slamming on the brakes we grabbed our spotlight and managed to flush it once again. Even though we'd had only two brief glimpses, we were pretty convinced it was a small bittern, most probably either a female Cinnamon or Von Schrenck's, both absolute cripplers. The second time we flushed the bird it landed on a grassy patch and ran toward the edge of the forest. In the pre-dawn gloom we could see its outline where it stopped to strike a typical cryptic bittern pose, its neck skyward, making itself as skinny as possible.

We debated our next move. Shining the spotlight might have disturbed it and as it was only a few metres away from the edge of the forest, we wouldn't get another shot at it if it bolted. As it was only twenty minutes till dawn we thought we'd keep vigil until the light got good enough to identify it. As long as it didn't move. There was an abandoned building nearby and we figured one of us could use it for camouflage to approach more closely. Mike moved off using the building as cover while I kept my stare fixated on the dark shape poking up from the grass. Hordes of mosquitoes swarmed in but to slap them away might have frightened the bird so I just had to let them have their way with my bare arms.

Eventually Mike signalled he was in position and I began the painfully slow crawl to join him. By the time I reached him the first morning songsters were starting up and it was almost light enough to see the bird. We focused our binoculars and the first light of dawn revealed the bird. It was a stick. The bittern had run behind the stick and straight into the forest. In the dark we hadn't seen the second part of its mad dash and had spent the last twenty minutes stalking a stick.

It looked like being a miserable flight home. I stared out the window for a last glimpse of Christmas Island. The sky was full of gathering storm clouds, the sort of sky you would expect in the tropics.

Mike leant over me to look out the window and burst forth in exclamation: 'Good Lord, look at all the clouds!'

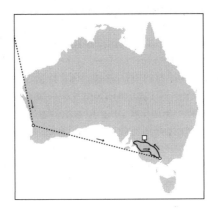

CHAPTER 13

23 March, Gluepot Reserve, South Australia:
373 species

I'm sure if I had something named after me I'd be quite chuffed. I imagine Louis Pasteur got a little tickle of satisfaction every time he bought a bottle of pasteurised milk, Dr Parkinson a small lump in his throat whenever he watched a Katharine Hepburn movie and Thomas Crapper must have really enjoyed his visits to the toilet. The only person I know that has had anything named after them is John Cox and interestingly he is rather embarrassed that the Cox's Sandpiper bears his name, but as it stands, it will forever be associated with one of the greatest controversies in Australian birdwatching history.

From the 1960s onwards the occasional odd looking sandpiper would turn up in wetlands around Melbourne and Adelaide. It seemed different to every other type of sandpiper then known. Nothing is more infuriating to birdwatchers than a bird that refuses to be categorised. Australia's leading birdwatcher of the time, Fred Smith, had a stab at it and though he wasn't completely happy, he declared these rogue birds to be Dunlin. It was a reasonable theory:

although Dunlin hadn't ever been seen in Australia before, these birds looked pretty close to what Dunlins were supposed to look like. Nobody had a better solution and so for quite a few years Dunlin was on the Australian list.

John Cox, having recently emigrated from England, had seen Dunlin before. They are one of the most common waders of his homeland. When he started seeing these Australian birds, he wasn't convinced. A correspondence began between John, Fred and other leading birders and over the years they all agreed that these probably weren't Dunlins, but what they were no-one was exactly sure. Throughout the seventies John found more of these mystery birds in the Penrice saltfields immediately north of Adelaide and he became the leading expert on them. John had his theories, as did others, and at this stage they were all cooperating with each other to solve the mystery. Then the late Shane Parker of the South Australian Museum jumped the gun and published a scientific paper proclaiming that these birds were not Dunlin but in fact an entirely new species which he named Cox's Sandpiper after the man who had contributed so much to solving the mystery.

People were not happy. Professional and personal relationships were soured, some felt their contributions had been ignored, and simmering rivalries burgeoned into vicious semi-public slanging matches. John Cox wasn't too happy either. He hadn't asked for his name to be used, and was more than a bit embarrassed that it was, particularly because he didn't think the bird deserved a species name at all. His suspicion, since confirmed by DNA testing, was that the Cox's Sandpiper was actually a hybrid of the Curlew and Pectoral Sandpipers. As John says, 'Waders are randy little buggers,' and will attempt to mate with practically anything they can mount. The breeding range of these two species has only a small area of overlap in the Siberian tundra and occasionally such interspecies trysts will produce a hybrid that, when it migrates to the saltfields and sewage farms of Australia, really sets the pulses and imaginations of bird-watchers racing.

John would have preferred not to have been so intricately involved in the entire sorry business; he is able to garner enough controversy on his own without the aid of a third party. He is very forthright in his opinions and calls a spade a spade. This may not endear him to some, but I find it refreshing that, on greeting me when Groober and I arrived at his place, his first words were, 'Christ, you've put on some weight!'

I hadn't seen John since I went to Adelaide to (unsuccessfully) twitch the '87 Northern Shoveler, when I was a skinny, eighteen-year-old kid. So, yes, I had put on weight. I countered his forthrightness by telling him that I may have gotten fat, but he'd lost a hell of a lot of hair. He was momentarily taken aback, but then a broad smile appeared across face and I knew we were going to get on just fine. The next thing he said to me was, 'What the bloody hell happened to your finger?' as he looked down at the bandage and sling on my left hand.

Basically the story was the latest in a long line of disasters that have befallen many a Groober-Dooley twitching expedition. We were on our way over to Adelaide to twitch the Hudsonian Godwit that had been found at Penrice saltfields via Gluepot Station in the Murray Mallee where we hoped to see the extremely rare Scarlet-chested Parrots that were coming in to drink at a dam near the homestead. I had been planning to head over to the Eyre Peninsula at Easter for this species and if I didn't see it there my only option was to mount an expedition into the Great Victoria Desert, so I jumped at the chance of looking for the bird relatively close to home. One measure of the Scarlet-chested Parrot's rarity is that it is one of the few Australian species that Groober hadn't seen, so it was easy to talk him into coming along for the ride.

I should have known something would go wrong as Groober and I have an atrocious record of disaster when twitching together. Outcomes of our previous expeditions include: writing off a car in Western Australia when we hit a kangaroo at over a hundred kilometres an hour; blowing up an engine on New Year's Eve in East Gippsland; and getting bogged in the Big Desert during a thunderstorm. We were crossing the Nepean Highway in Seaford once when Groober was run down by a horse. This is one of Melbourne's main thoroughfares, mind you, and as we crossed at the pedestrian lights to get to the beach to look for beachwashed Common Diving-Petrels, a rider appeared from nowhere, tried to jump the pedestrian safety barrier and managed to land the horse right on top of Groober.

At the beginning of that ill-fated Western Australian trip we had reached the South Australian border and the fruit fly inspection station. Rather than throw out the entire esky of fruit and veg we had bought the day before, Groober decided we should try to eat as much of it as possible there and then. It was 39 degrees and the fruit fly inspector stood dumbstruck as he attempted to demolish bags of apples, peaches and bananas. A queue was forming behind us so the attendant asked if we could move the car. While scoffing down an orange, Groober threw me the keys. I put the wrong key in the ignition and it snapped off, meaning we had to hotwire the car for the rest of the trip…until we hit the kangaroo. I know I'm pretty hopeless but when we get together we seem to dramatically ramp up the incompetency factor. Over the last ten years or so we hadn't had any major disasters and Groobs had travelled extensively throughout Asia without major incident, so I thought we must have been improving with age. Or perhaps our luck was due to run out.

Things began to unravel fairly quickly. We had hoped to arrive at Waikerie in South Australia around midnight. There we would sleep in the car then first thing next morning collect the key for Gluepot from the service station, catch the first ferry across the Murray and be lining up with the parrots at around 7.30 am. After stopping for dinner and supplies (no fresh fruit this time), and generally dawdling, we were running way behind schedule. Around 1 am I pulled in at the 24-hour servo in the Mallee town of Ouyen to grab a drink and have a stretch. I didn't really need a drink but as we still had around three hours to go to Waikerie, I wanted the chance to freshen up. I tell you, it does not pay to be safety conscious. If I had just driven straight through, none of the following would have happened.

In pulling off the road at Ouyen I managed to puncture one of the rear tyres. This was already my third flat for the year and the thought of changing it in the middle of the night did not put me in the best of moods. With my documentary in mind I brought out the video gear and asked Groober to film me changing the tyre – get some mileage out of wimpy bird boy trying to fix the wheel of the monstrous beast. After struggling for a good twenty minutes, as much from tiredness as from the physical exertion, I finally lugged the now expired tyre up onto the mount designed for it at the back of the car.

Groober had stopped filming by this stage and suggested that the sight of me trying to haul the tyre up would make hilarious footage. So I unhooked the tyre and set it back down on the ground. When he was ready I lifted the hulking tyre up again. This time as I tried to screw the first nut in, the tyre slipped and crushed my finger against the steel mounting, ripping a fingernail right out of my finger. It's all on video: me mugging to the camera, the crash of the falling tyre, my initial recoil, then the blood draining from my face as I look down and discover the fingernail gouged out of my flesh just dangling there cadaverously.

Instead of seeing in the dawn at Waikerie we found ourselves watching the sunrise from the emergency department of Mildura hospital. They bandaged me up and made me stick around for precautionary X-rays, so that by the time we finally made it to Gluepot we were around twelve hours behind schedule, and I had a throbbing, disfigured finger. It would take four months for the nail to grow back. Luckily for us the parrots did not come in to drink that morning. It would have been all the more excruciating if we had missed them.

Gluepot, which is now run as a conservation reserve by Birds Australia, has some of the best unburnt, mature mallee habitat in the country. We managed to see some much sought after dry country birds species – Pied Honeyeater, Striated Grasswren, Chestnut Quail-thrush, Gilbert's Whistler and Regent and Mulga Parrots – without any trouble at all, but it didn't make up for not seeing the Scarlet-chesteds. After we'd set up camp and rested, we made our way to the homestead dam for our evening vigil – the theory being that the parrots get very little moisture from their diet of seeds and need to drink every day. Scarlet-chested Parrots, being desert dwellers, have probably adapted to going without a drink for longer than other parrots but, particularly in hot weather, will partake of the water available in manmade dams. The five days the birds had been seen coming into this particular dam had been excessively hot, the day of our arrival relatively cool, perhaps explaining why they had failed to show that morning. Still, hope springs eternal and we positioned ourselves in the bird hide alongside the dam an hour and a half before dusk and waited.

And waited. Apart from a Common Bronzewing, a type of large brown pigeon, nothing came in to drink at all. We had another visitor in the form of a birdwatcher who had spent the past few weeks working as a volunteer on the reserve, a kind of birding busman's holiday. She had seen the parrots over the past week and we listened totally gripped off as she described a party of seven, including males with the stunning scarlet sash across their chest. She told us that as they hadn't come in that morning, she didn't like our chances in the evening. I thanked her for her honest assessment but said we'd stick around and try our luck. She seemed incredulous that we would even think about continuing our vigil and started chiding us for hanging around when we clearly had no chance of seeing the birds. What she didn't appreciate was that after travelling that far, disfiguring myself and ruining my potentially lucrative hand-modelling career, we weren't about to give up. Her incredulity turned to irritation and she countered with the news that a famous birder had come all the way from Canberra to see them and if such an expert had missed out on them, what chance did we have?

There again was that hierarchic deference that I had first encountered at the bird club meeting twenty years ago. Because this expert was known as someone who had seen over five thousand birds around the world, if he dipped out then we mere mortal birders had absolutely no hope of finding the parrots, did we? Frankly I didn't give a shit that the expert hadn't seen them. If he'd missed out that was his tough luck, it wasn't going to stop me. Luckily the painkillers had just kicked in so I didn't say anything like this to her face, just that we would take our chances. She walked off in quite a huff, muttering loudly under her breath, 'You're not going to see them!'

We didn't see them.

After a stunningly clear night serenaded by boobook owls and owlet-nightjars we were out the next morning before dawn, slightly less optimistic but unbowed nonetheless. I took up position in the bird hide and Groober went and secreted himself over at the next dam for our dawn vigil. Just after sunrise a Peregrine Falcon came flashing through, scattering all the birds coming in to drink. 'That's it,' I thought, 'show's over.' No parrot in its right mind would come in now with such a predator in the vicinity.

I wandered out of the hide and joined up with Groober. We stood on the open wall of the dam discussing our next move when suddenly a female Scarlet-chested Parrot flew in, circled around our heads giving us a superb view, wheeled around and flew off in the direction it had come from. No stunning male counterpart flew in, but there we were – one of the hardest birds to find in Australia had just made an exhibition flight around our heads. We were stoked. Oddly enough, when we bumped into the volunteer on our way out, rather than being pleased for us she seemed somewhat put out, as if a certainty in her view of the birdwatching world had been shaken – these punks succeeded where the expert dipped? Impossible. I wonder whether she even believed we'd really seen it.

'Well, you better come in and have a beer then, sounds like you've earned it,' John Cox responded to our tale. 'High tide's not for a couple of hours and you won't get the Hudwit coming in before then.'

John's house was a maelstrom of rambunctious chaos. David Harper, the birder who discovered the Hudsonian Godwit (Hudwit), and his family were visiting John and his wife Heather. Unlike most birding get-togethers, which are usually subdued affairs, when the Cox and Harper families gather the atmosphere is raucous and celebratory. David and his wife Sue's two daughters treat John and Heather like grandparents, and while John is somewhat of a father figure to Dave, it would probably be more accurate to say they are more like brothers, because although there is obviously a deep affection between the two, there is also a lot of rivalry and an endless stream of taunting and ribbing of each other.

Before I left Melbourne I'd rung John to ask if there were any other waders about that I needed. Aside from the Hudwit there were also Pectoral Sandpiper and Long-toed Stint literally, John assured me, over his back fence. When we arrived he had some bad news – he hadn't seen the Pec since the day I'd phoned, but not to worry, the Long-toed was still about, two of them that morning in fact. We grabbed our binoculars and went out to check the wetland that really does lie just beyond his back fence. Of all the birders I know, nobody looks more at home with a pair of binoculars than John Cox. He is the birdwatching equivalent of a great hunter, striding along the edge of the swamp with an almost leonine confidence, his large hands gripping his binoculars like a gunslinger wields a Colt 45. It didn't help that day, though. The Long-toed Stints had decided to up stumps and begin their migration back to the Northern Hemisphere – that morning's sighting turned out to be John's last for the year. I'd missed them by a couple of hours.

This dip did not bode well for the Hudwit. We made our way over to the saltworks and, when it had not come in after an hour it looked like it too might have begun the long journey north. For over an hour there was little to look at but the saltpans. Small flocks of waders kept arriving as the tide rose out on their feeding grounds on the mudflats of the Gulf of St Vincent, but there was no Hudwit amongst them. The flock of Grey Plovers that the Hudwit had been associating with arrived without it. Oddly enough, the Hudwit had been giving the flock of very similar Black-tailed Godwits a wide berth, so when they flew in, the last birds to do so because their longer legs and bill mean they can feed for longer on the rising tide, nobody particularly bothered to check them out. Then someone noticed the telltale black armpit of the Hudwit amongst the pale of the Black-taileds' underwings. Another bonus bird for me.

Back at John's place for victory celebrations, Dave Harper confessed to me that he'd become very stressed when the Hudwit didn't show. As the bird's discoverer, he somehow felt personally responsible for me seeing it. I assured him that I'd been birding long enough to know that there were no guarantees with birds and I wouldn't have held it against him if I'd dipped. Of course we both knew that if I had dipped, I'd see to it that his name was mud in the birding community, but as it did turn up, I can say without equivocation that he is a top bloke and a brilliant birder. Foolishly he said he could help me out with another bird, the Grey Falcon, as he knew a reliable site for this species in the South Australian desert and was planning a trip there later in the year coinciding roughly with the time I would be in that area. We made a plan to hook up.

My year was beginning to take shape quite nicely and on 24 March, with the total on 382, I headed back to Melbourne feeling very satisfied and optimistic.

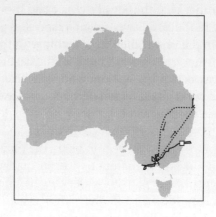

CHAPTER 14

30 April, Barren Grounds, New South Wales: *405 species*

The quietest time for Australian twitchers is probably late autumn–early winter. Most of the migrants have returned north, the locals have generally finished their breeding cycles and though the southern coast starts to be buffeted by cold fronts coming up from the Antarctic, they are generally not sufficiently strong or frequent enough to blow in most of the sought-after Southern Ocean species. My 350th bird – halfway to the target – was Java Sparrow on Christmas Island, yet it wasn't until 9 April that I reached four hundred, a Flame Robin, at ever reliable Seaford Swamp. By the start of June the total would only creep up to 416.

While I still continued birding, getting out into the field on twenty-six days, much of my time was spent on other matters. As I would be on the road for most of the second half of the year, staying in my comfortable but very expensive house by myself was financial madness, so I moved into a share house in North Fitzroy with an old friend. Moving in with her had several advantages. I had somewhere safe to store my stuff, my rent immediately dropped a thousand bucks a month and, most importantly, as I had lived with Indra in another share house twelve years earlier, I didn't have to break her in to the sick and twisted world of birdwatching. She'd been through the ordeal before and, while not exactly enthusiastic, could at least tolerate the vagaries of my behaviour with stoic acceptance.

I also attended the first match of the footy season where I witnessed my team, Collingwood, go down to a far less skilful side. Given such a shambolic performance on the part of the Magpies it looked like I'd picked the right year to be on the road.

In the midst of my preparations I even managed to pick up some real employment of sorts, two weeks working on a pilot for a new sketch comedy show for Channel Nine. As all the unemployed writers gathered for the first meeting, someone jadedly welcomed everyone to 'Generic Sketch Show Pilot Number 417'. We had all been through this roundabout so many times before that nobody had much enthusiasm for the task, taking the job for the pay rather than with any hope of the show getting the go-ahead and actually making it to air. I jokingly countered that with this attitude the show would actually get commissioned and turn out to be a huge hit.

Perversely, professional success was the last thing I wanted at that moment. If the pilot was to get up, the network might go into production immediately and there was a fair chance I'd be offered a good position. To turn it down would have been professional suicide. To take it would have meant saying goodbye to the record. It dawned on me that I was much more committed to breaking the record than I was to furthering the long-term prospects of my career. For the first couple of months I thought I could always call it off if things got too much. By this point, though, I was too steeped in blood to turn back. Even though I knew it was absurd, chasing that record meant too much to me.

As it seemed to mean to others. Thanks to the agency of the Internet my essentially personal quest had become rather public. I spent as much of this period dealing with birdwatchers as I did with birds: thanks to my postings to Birding-aus, people were following my progress with much interest. I was starting to receive emails of support and advice, both helpful and maybe not so helpful, and whenever there was a lull in my regular postings, speculation mounted as to my whereabouts. I even had a fan club, though from what I could gather it only comprised two members. My birding odyssey had become a spectator sport.

Essentially a loner when it comes to birdwatching, I found the attention a little surreal. While I had been birding for over twenty years I was not a huge part of the scene and I could go about my birding activities relatively anonymously. While I knew enough of the key players to be kept in the loop I was hardly the guy they went to to discuss tarsus length on Golden Plovers or the morphological differences in cranial structure of the Wandering Albatross complex. Now they were suddenly confronted with constant updates about my record attempt. My initial suspicion was that they might think I was a bit of an interloper who didn't deserve to have a crack at the record. What I found was quite the opposite, with birders from all over the country, both experienced and novice, showing me nothing but support. At times this was almost disquieting as some birders seemed almost obsessive in their efforts to help me out – the case of the Black-breasted Button-quail being a prime example.

It all began with a Laughing Gull turning up on Bribie Island, north of Brisbane, appropriately enough on April Fool's day. This was serious news as it was probably only the sixth record of this North American species in Australia. I waited by the phone for news.

At ten o'clock the next morning I got a call from Andrew Stafford on his mobile: 'Dools, I'm just looking at the bird now...'

You little beauty.

'...disappearing over the horizon on Moreton Bay. Sorry about that.'

Oh well, at least I'd saved myself an airfare.

A couple of hours later, Andrew called back with news that Paul Wallbridge had just seen the Laughing Gull come back in.

Game back on. I touched down at Brisbane Airport around five thirty the next afternoon and with the aid of Paul managed to see the Laughing Gull after a few hours' frustration. As a bonus he also got me a Broad-billed Sandpiper, an uncommon wader that was no dead cert. I had allowed two and a half days to try for the Laughing

Gull and with success on the first day I had to work out how best to spend my remaining time in Brisbane.

I retired to the house of a local birder who had kindly put me up and we indulged in a night of victory celebrations. Things were going very festively until the mood changed and I began to get an inkling of just how involved people wanted to be with the whole Big Twitch concept. The local birder had been incredibly generous in his hospitality but obviously felt he could do more. He had to work the next day but he assured me that he should be able to find me a species or two on Saturday morning before I flew out. I still needed Black-breasted Button-quail, having dipped out on it with Andrew in February, and I floated the idea with my host that I might try for it up the coast at a place called Inskip Point, where people had reported seeing them recently.

He didn't seem impressed with this plan. 'Have you been there before?' he asked with concern.

I told him I hadn't.

'Yeah, well if you haven't been there, you could be wasting your time.'

'Why, have you been there? Isn't any good?'

He hadn't, and that was troubling him. As he didn't know the site how could he could he give me any advice? He seemed pained at the prospect of me going up there when I could have been picking up some other species with his guidance. No, if I was to have a chance at the record it would be much easier if I accepted his help, so I'd probably 'want to give Inskip a miss'.

The topic of conversation moved on. A couple of drinks later he asked abruptly, 'So what are you doing tomorrow?' and before I could answer added, 'You're not still thinking about going to Inskip, are you?'

'Maybe. If I can get them there, it saves me having to look when I'm here again in September. There'll be no second chances then.'

'Nah, you don't want to go to Inskip,' my host declared. 'I don't know anyone who's been there. You'd be wasting your time going there at all. Why don't you wait until you're back this way and I'll take you out to my Black-breasted site? They're virtually guaranteed there.'

He became so insistent that I began to feel it would be taken as a personal betrayal if I did go. Eventually I decided to call it stumps and the last thing he said to me as I retired to his spare room was, 'So you're not going to Inskip are you?' I answered that no, he was right, I wouldn't go and he tottered off happy.

At 6 am I awoke to the first birdsong and opened my eyes to see my host standing in the doorway of my room. First thing he said after I had let out a startled expletive was, 'You're not going to Inskip, are you? That would be a stupid idea. You don't want to go to Inskip.'

'Nah, I don't think so. I think I might just have a bit of a sleep-in, actually.'

Placated, he readied himself for work. After he had gone I had a spot of breakfast, packed my things and headed for Inskip. After a few detours for other birds in and around Brisbane – such as the Bush Stone-curlews that stand like eerie, goggle-eyed sentinels over one of the carparks at the University of Queensland – I didn't roll into the campground at Inskip Point until just before dark.

I immediately realised I should have listened to my host. Even if there were button-quails here, it was the school holidays and the area was overrun with families camping. Man, was it going to be humiliating to have to tell him this. Then I noticed that in the middle of the camping ground, dodging kids on bikes and families playing cricket, was a covey of Brown Quail. I'd already seen this fairly common species on my previous Brisbane trip but if they could be amongst this seething mass of holidaying humanity, why couldn't a button-quail? I parked the car and wandered down the track to the point. There, right on the track in the fading light, was a male Black-breasted Button-quail having a dust bath. It was in exactly the same spot again the next morning. I kept in touch with my host but we never spoke of Inskip again.

At least my host was trying to be helpful. Though I had no evidence, I suspected that quite a few birding experts were sniggering behind my back at the audacity of my 700 target – they were all too polite to snigger directly to my face. All except for one. In April Stu Cooney and I headed out to Werribee in the hope that we might pick up an early arriving Orange-bellied Parrot. We did manage to get onto one, heard above the din of the engine as we drove along the coast. Jumping out of the car I could see the bird silhouetted against the sun giving its characteristic buzzing call which reminds me of the sound of marbles being rubbed together. Unfortunately we could get no better view and even though it was clearly an Orange-bellied, I didn't feel justified in ticking it. As it disappeared it flew over a carload of other birders. We drove down to ask whether they had seen it land. They'd missed it but we got talking. I knew one of them, and he asked me how the record attempt was going.

Another birder in the group, someone I'd never met before, hadn't heard of my record attempt. When I explained that I was hoping to top seven hundred, he burst into laughter. Not the kind of good-hearted, incredulous chuckle that I had come to expect; this was a vicious, scathing guffaw that lasted for minutes. I was reminded of a sitcom in which a bunch of characters see someone fall over. They all laugh for a minute until they realise the person is actually injured, but there is one Homer Simpson type who only laughs harder when he sees the blood spurting from the victim's head. Everyone else shifted uncomfortably as this guy continued his derisive laughter and proclaimed my quest the most idiotic thing he'd heard in his life. His contempt was totally unbridled, as though my goal was a personal affront to him and all humanity. Sure, secretly I might have agreed with him – it was a fairly idiotic venture – but to have someone spit that back in your face so venomously was quite confronting.

'Well even if I don't get to seven hundred,' I said with a smile, 'at the very least I'll keep cynical bastards like you amused.'

After we got back in the car Stu erupted: 'If that was me I would have punched that arsehole's lights out.' I laughed it off, saying it was probably what everyone thought and he'd been the only one honest enough to come out and say it. Stu couldn't believe I was so unfazed by the whole incident, though inwardly I resolved that I wouldn't let this bastard have the last laugh. Whenever things were getting on top of me over the year to come – the birds not showing, the distances too vast, the weather and the fatigue too overwhelming – I would think back to that anoraked figure quivering with derision and use the image of his smirking mug to keep going, determined that one day I would bump into him and quietly say, 'I did it.'

Most of my energy, however, was spent picking up as many species as possible during this relatively quiet period. This meant as many boat trips as I could muster. In March, the weather over Port Fairy cleared long enough for us to finally get out to sea. I saw my only Sooty Albatross for the year and managed to forget to bring along waterproof pants. The sea was quite lumpy, the spray constant; I got soaked through below the waist and remained that way until I finally arrived home in Melbourne fourteen hours later. While hanging on grimly as we bobbed about in the Southern Ocean, Mike Carter and I also saw a Grey-headed Albatross but it was so distant I declined to add it to my list because I wasn't happy with the views I'd got.

If I had been on board the April Port Fairy trip I would have seen not only another Grey-headed Albatross but also South Polar Skua and Great Shearwater. The shearwater would have been extra special as it was only the third record of this species in Australian waters, it normally being a denizen of the seas off southern Africa and the Atlantic. I missed a truly remarkable day at sea; a tragedy compounded by the fact that I actually should have been on board. Mike Carter thought I was still up in Brisbane with the Laughing Gull when a vacancy opened up for the trip, so he didn't ring me, although I'd specifically come back to Victoria in time for just such a contingency. Because of this mix-up I dipped on three species I would not see for the rest of the year.

I went on five more pelagics during this time and while I added at least one new species on each trip, none matched the excitement of the ones I'd missed. Not that there weren't highlights. Having both a Royal and a Wandering Albatross sitting side by side behind the boat for close comparison on one Port Fairy trip definitely qualified. As did the voyage back to Port Fairy in mid May when, in the soft afternoon light on a glassy green sea, we were surrounded not only by massive feeding flocks of gannets, shearwaters and Yellow-nosed Albatross but by a pod of around one hundred frolicking common dolphins. I didn't let on to anyone, but I was actually beginning to enjoy these pelagic trips.

With the lack of unusual birds and a growing sure-footedness at sea, I certainly had plenty of time to look around and observe the behaviour of that mental seabirding bunch, and how parochial they all seem to be. The boys from Wollongong think their patch of ocean rules; the Brisbane crew won't hear a bad word about their trips. Even on a local scale this rivalry can be intense. I've seen Portland aficionados pour scorn on trips out of Port Fairy even though they are only about seventy kilometres apart. A similar rivalry occurs between Sydney and Wollongong, which lie approximately the same distance from each other. This parochialism reached its ridiculous zenith when on one pelagic I commented to someone about the size of the shark liver being used as berley. Without a hint of irony, this person turned to me and boasted, 'Yeah, I bet you don't get shark liver that big down your way.' I couldn't believe it, he was actually using the 'my shark liver's bigger than your shark liver' line.

I wasn't buying into the argument. I didn't care what trip I was on as long as I was seeing new birds. Put simply I'd become a pelagic slut, would take a ride on whatever was on offer as long as it gave me every possible opportunity to see each species.

So it was that I headed up to Wollongong for the third time in the year in late April. Most probably the season was too far advanced for me to pick up any of those summer birds I'd already missed, but as there was a boat trip going it was still worth a try. My plans had me away from the eastern seaboard for the entire spring–summer season later in the year so, anything I got I would be grateful for.

Cruising up the Hume yet again the car started to swerve all over the highway. A blowout! After I got the two tonnes of car under control, I eased it over to the shoulder of the freeway and inspected the damage. The left rear tyre lay in a steaming, shredded mess – luckily the blowout hadn't occurred on one of the front tyres as that would have been far more difficult to control. Grumbling, in the fading light I changed my fourth tyre for the year. Then it came to putting the lacerated wheel up onto the mount that had only a month before claimed my fingernail. The finger throbbed every time I tried to lift the tyre and I could see the cadaver of the old nail staring up at me accusingly. Not being able to use my left hand efficiently I was having a hell of a time trying to hoick the tyre onto its mounting, and by the time it got dark I was so frustrated I ended up flinging the whole lot onto the side of the road. Not a great move, when I think about it, particularly when, a few days later, I replaced the tyre and also had to buy an entire new wheel.

On the previous Wollongong trip in February I didn't have a flat or misplace my seasickness medication, but a dodgy vegetable pastie bought at the Dog on the Tuckerbox Roadhouse at Gundagai ensured I spent most of the night sitting on the dunny, so again I got no sleep the night before we went out to sea. What is it about Wollongong pelagics and me? The Wollongong curse had struck again.

It wasn't just seabirds that occupied my time late autumn. I also tried to knock off as many tricky land birds as I could. I got Swift Parrot at Chiltern in May but dipped out on three attempts to pick up Regent Honeyeater there. I joined a National Parks Plains Wanderer census to pick up this most difficult to see quail-like species. An endangered bird of the inland grasslands, of which in Victoria there is only about one per cent left, the Plains Wanderer is not only rare but extremely cryptic. We managed to record twenty, including four chicks looking like little black balls of fluff on stilts, one rain-swept night out at the Terrick Terrick National Park about two hours north of Melbourne. It had not rained in the district for three months yet it bucketed down on us as we stood unprotected on the back of a ute scanning the grasslands with massive spotlights.

The things you'll do to see a rare bird. Like stand out in the literally freezing dawn in an exposed heathland waiting for a Ground Parrot. This extremely rare and shy heath dweller doesn't come out of the scrub for just anybody. Except David Attenborough. I'd heard from Brendan Neilly, the warden at the Barren Grounds Nature Reserve in the marvellous Illawarra district south of Wollongong, that an Attenborough film crew had recently shot footage of the birds coming in to drink at a roadside puddle at the same site. They didn't show for me. Bloody David Attenborough.

Even though the sun had started to rise it actually seemed to get colder so I went for a bracing walk up and down the road. Suddenly a ball of green feathers burst out of the heath beside me. For about five seconds the Ground Parrot remained in view before tumbling back down into the impenetrable scrub. I later mentioned the brevity of the sighting to Brendan, who responded that I'd seen it for about four seconds longer than most.

My trip to the Illawarra really produced the goods when it came to hard-to-see species. I managed to have the normally shy Eastern Bristlebird, one of the Barren Grounds specialties, hop along the track towards me as I was filming it. It got so close I couldn't focus the camera as it almost ran across my shoe. Following Brendan's advice I also got onto Chestnut-rumped Heathwren. He suggested I look for recently burnt areas in the heath. I found a suitable site and began bashing my way through it, the charcoal sticks of fried bushes turning my blue jeans black within minutes. After an hour of this I had no luck and returned to the car to find a pair of heathwrens foraging on the track in front of my car.

I owe Brendan big time. He really was incredibly helpful. When I was younger I harboured thoughts of becoming a park ranger – until I learned that rather than being glamorous, much of your time is spent as a glorified janitor. And you have to deal with the general public. During my stay I was constantly amazed at Brendan's cheerfulness and enthusiasm even when every single visiting birder asked the same questions – 'Where are the bristlebirds?' 'Where can I see a Ground Parrot?' and so on – often expressed as more of a demand than a question. He never seemed to tire of helping them. If it was me I'd soon have been screaming something like 'Do you have to be spoonfed everything? Go find them yourselves, you bloody slackers!' It's a pity that he was soon to lose his job as his employer, Birds Australia, which runs the observatory at Barren Grounds, decided the operation was economically unviable and it was to be closed down.

Before I left Brendan gave me one last tip: where to find Rock Warbler, New South Wales' only endemic species. A bird of the sandstone country that surrounds Sydney, Rock Warblers are not necessarily rare but as most of their habitat is inaccessible, they are not the easiest birds to see. Batting three from three, Brendan turned out to be spot on and along Bomaderry Creek on the outskirts of Nowra I spent half an hour watching a Rock Warbler feeding on the vertical cliff-face and boulders above the creek.

In the Sydney region, the more remote sandstone outcrops still harbour examples of Aboriginal art, recording the lives and spirituality of the original inhabitants of this land. Today a new generation of settlers is adding to the cultural record, reaching out across the ages in an act of spiritual solidarity and understanding. Where Rock Warblers would once have foraged amongst galleries resplendent with images of kangaroos and goannas these days at Bomaderry they feed amongst rocks emblazoned with: 'Mandy is a slut!' 'Bong on Australia' and 'F*** You'. I love culture.

CHAPTER 15

9 June, Pirates Bay, Eaglehawk Neck, Tasmania:
428 species

Eaglehawk Neck, a short distance from Hobart, is a small isthmus only a few metres wide connecting the Tasman Peninsula to the rest of Tasmania. In convict times the Neck was guarded by armed soldiers and vicious dogs to prevent convicts from escaping the hellhole that was Port Arthur prison. Standing at the jetty in Pirates Bay I felt similarly trapped as I watched the waves slapping against the hull of the fishing boat *Frustration* while it bobbed at its mooring. The name precisely summed up my mood at that moment, for I couldn't get off that piece of land either because of a huge weather cell the pelagic trip I had come specifically to Tasmania for had been cancelled.

I drove up to Tasman's Arch, one of the most dramatic examples of this area's spectacular cliff formations, and set up my telescope to gaze longingly out to sea. How times had changed – I was now aching to be out on the chop, being buffeted by the wind and waves. My frustration was compounded by the fact that between the coast and the Hippolyte Rocks dozens of albatrosses skimmed across the sea surface. If there were this many birds so close to shore it must have been an absolute ripper out at the shelf. To make matters even worse a couple of little tuna boats – half the size of the vessel we were to travel on – puttered out amongst the waves. The worst of the weather hadn't hit and I was convinced we could have had at least a couple of hours at sea. God knows what I was missing out there.

The rest of my Tassie jaunt had been going particularly well. Tasmania has twelve endemic species and I had them all within three days of setting sail on the ferry from Melbourne. This allowed me time to check out a part of the world I had never really visited before. I meandered across the north of the island to the famous Cradle Mountain, noting along the way how utterly beautiful the place is and how brazenly the timber industry struts its stuff here. On the mainland you very rarely come across logging on roadsides; in Tassie the foresters don't even attempt a nice facade, they just clear-fell their coupes right to the edges of the road. As I made my way up into the island's interior it seemed at nearly every turn a breathtaking vista bore the scar of clear-felled forest.

I had booked to stay for two nights in a cabin bordering Cradle Mountain National Park. As I was registering, the woman at the desk asked whether, having seen the area, I still wanted to stay two nights. Not the kind of ringing endorsement you'd normally expect from a tourist operator. It seemed bizarre because the area is quite stunning. Cradle Mountain is justifiably one of the country's most famous wilderness areas. Above the thousand-metre mark, the entire area has the stark beauty typical of alpine landscapes. But before I could even get to the national park I had already seen all my target species. There were Black Currawongs everywhere and, despite the freezing conditions, in the Myrtle Beech grove behind the cabins I managed to get onto Scrubtit, Tasmanian Thornbill and a gorgeous male Pink Robin. At night I spotlit wombats and wallabies, but not the Tasmanian Devils and quolls for which the area is famous. Overnight the temperature sank to below freezing, making me wonder how on earth any of these creatures survive there.

As I had seen everything I'd come for there was no point in hanging around, so I decided not to stay a second night, probably vindicating the woman at the desk. I decided I needed as much time as I could to find Tasmania's rarest endemic, the Forty-spotted Pardalote. Confined to just eight or nine small populations on islands and peninsulas around Hobart, this was the one bird I really didn't want to miss, so I decided an extra day's searching wouldn't go astray.

Turns out I made a good decision. In heading down to Hobart, I kept ahead of an oncoming blizzard that may well have snowed me in on the mountain and prevented me from making it to the boat trip, not that it went ahead anyway. Driving across the top of Tasmania through the alpine desolation of the Great Lakes area, every time I got out of the car to take in another breathtaking view I was almost swept away by the icy gale. Entering Hobart all was still and I made my way after dusk to the Waterworks Reserve just out of town for some spotlighting.

Andrew Stafford had told me he had seen Masked Owl there and while not an endemic species, the Tasmanian race is reputedly the easiest of the species to see. Because foxes never gained a foothold on the island, Tasmania is a sensational place for native mammals. Several species that have become extinct on the mainland survive here in good numbers and while looking for the owl I almost had to kick Eastern Barred Bandicoots, Southern Brown Bandicoots and Southern Bettongs, a very cute type of wallaby, out of the way. At one point I heard the distinctive shriek of a Masked Owl and thought I was going to catch up with this species at last. But precisely one minute later the cold front hit with a sonic boom and any chance of hearing anything above the roar of the gale became negligible so I yet again dipped out on the wretched thing.

The gale continued the next day; surely not a good sign for finding the pardalote, which usually dwells in the canopy of very tall eucalypts. I drove out to the Peter Murrell Reserve on the southern outskirts of Hobart, not particularly hopeful of finding my quarry, but perhaps the wind was actually working in my favour for down low in a sapling out of the gale was an adult Forty-spotted Pardalote. I'd always thought the attraction of these birds was solely their rarity for they always seem rather plain when illustrated, but up close in the flesh they are actually very dainty, decked out in subtle pastel shades of green and yellow.

The storm continued with sufficient ferocity to dump snow on Mount Wellington and cancel the boat trip the next day, and I was faced with a dilemma. Apart from Masked Owl and all those seabirds I was missing out on I had seen everything I'd come for, but still had two more days before I was due to catch the ferry back to Melbourne. What to do?

The solution was to swap one small island for an even smaller one. I got on the phone and booked a seat on a light plane to King Island, in the middle of windswept Bass Strait, to go for a trio of some of the more ridiculous birds I was seeking – peacock, pheasant and turkey. All three were introduced to fox-free King Island as game birds and all three have flourished so well they have made their way onto the Australian list. I hung around Hobart for one more unsuccessful bid to spotlight Masked Owl then drove across the state overnight hoping I might see one conveniently perched on a roadside marker. I didn't, but I did finally manage to spot a Tasmanian Devil as it attempted a kamikaze run at the wheels of my vehicle.

Early the next morning, in shocking conditions, I found myself taking off in a light plane from Devonport Airport. There was only one other passenger and I got the distinct impression the pilot would really have preferred to stay safely at home rather than risking his life for us. The conditions were atrocious. The little plane was tossed about the sky and visibility was near zero. After an hour of this buffeting a window appeared in the clouds and there was the green jewel of King Island sitting amidst an angry grey sea. As we made our approach to land, barely fifty metres above the runway the tiny plane was thrown almost at right angles by a gust of wind and all I could think was, 'Great, I'm going to die all for a bloody turkey.'

Miraculously we landed unscathed and I noticed the airport terminal was teeming with pheasant shooters and their dogs. There is one weekend per year where it is open season on pheasants and I happened to have flown right into the middle of it in a quest for… pheasants. As if to mock the shooters' very presence on the island, a male Common Pheasant flew onto the fringe of the airstrip and began to feed, blithely (or was that cockily?) unconcerned at the braying hunt dogs on the other side of the fence. Ticking off this bird so easily was a double bonus because it meant I wouldn't be running the risk of being mistaken for a pheasant by a myopic shooter as I searched the scrub for them. In fact the shooters didn't seem to have scared off anything much as within half an hour I came across parties of both Wild Turkey and Indian Peafowl grazing by the side of the road. It really was quite ridiculous counting these birds from India and southern America on my Australian list, but they are considered valid wild populations. I don't make the rules, I just follow them, so onto the list they went and my list moved onto 431.

It also meant I could get out of the driving winds (which surprisingly didn't seem to have blown any seabirds in) and sit in the warm pub talking to the locals. King Island is a fascinating place. Sitting at one end of one of the most treacherous stretches of water in the world, it has a miserable history of shipwrecks and hardship, yet it is now something of a haven from the stresses of the modern world. Although ninety per cent of the island has been cleared of vegetation it still retains a remarkably wild feel, but in this weather it is much nicer in the pub. I spent a very interesting and stimulating evening drinking with a couple of pheasant shooters. Despite a seemingly enormous gulf between us what emerged was how much we actually have in common – a love of the outdoors, an awareness of the environment and joy at being out amongst it. And we all love birds. It's just that they love them and then kill them. It got so chummy that by the end of the night we were almost indulging in the great Aussie blokes' ritual: 'I love you, mate.' 'No, I love you.' Almost.

The next day was much calmer for the flight back to Devonport, and the ferry crossing to Melbourne was similarly uneventful. As we steamed into Port Phillip Bay the next morning I took a stroll on deck to watch the sun rise. There were very few human passengers about but to my surprise we had picked up two hitchhikers in the form of prions, a delicate little dove-like seabird. There are six species of prion, three or four of which I'd hoped to see in Australian waters. They can be exceptionally difficult to identify from one another. Over the previous couple of months I felt like I'd been making real progress on my prion identification skills and had already ticked off the most common: Fairy and Slender-billed. I had seen the Antarctic but was holding off adding it to the list because I still felt I hadn't had a good enough look. Generally, however, I was pretty cocky that I now knew what I was on about when it came to identifying prions.

The two birds had come to rest on the deck because they were obviously exhausted. By the time we docked at Melbourne they still hadn't budged and I decided I'd better take them into care. I grabbed a couple of empty cardboard chocolate boxes from the kiosk and caught the exhausted birds fairly easily, assuring curious passengers that I was taking them in for their own welfare. I failed to mention that it would give me the opportunity to indulge in some prion identification at very close quarters.

My cockiness soon faded as I realised that, though I might have been able to identify them at sea, I was totally bamboozled as to which species I was holding in my hands. I was pretty certain one was a Fairy Prion; but the other bird was almost ten per cent lighter, which suggested a Slender-billed, but the plumage didn't seem quite right. I was sitting at the kitchen table weighing them on the kitchen scales when my housemate Indra came in sleepily for breakfast. Normally pretty tolerant of my eccentricities, the sight of a bedraggled seabird sitting on her kitchen scales set her off. Her reaction was nothing, however, compared to that of our new housemate, Nancy.

Nancy was a fast-talking Mancunian who seems preoccupied with that peculiarly English trait of washing pure white sheets and t-shirts several times a week in order to maintain their pristine whiteness. We hadn't spent much time together since she moved in and hadn't really made a connection. The sight of the prions didn't really help matters. Her shrieks sent one of the birds into a panic and it disappeared behind the dishwasher. While I was trying to retrieve it from its hiding place the other bird proceeded to shit on Nancy's fine white tablecloth, and I was ordered out of the house. 'Fine by me,' I thought, 'I need some help identifying these things anyway,' and I drove to Mike Carter's.

Mike immediately identified them as Fairy Prions, making me

realise I still had a long way to go before cracking this seabird thing. The reason one was lighter was because it was undernourished. I tried to release the birds down at the bay and the larger one immediately flew off. The other went nowhere and I was forced to take it to a wildlife carer. I never heard anything from them so I presume it didn't make it.

I drove back home and the girls never looked at me in quite the same way again.

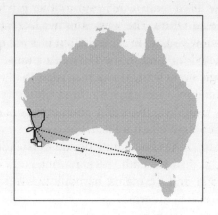

CHAPTER 16

24 June, Pemberton, Western Australia:
439 species

To someone from the east of the continent the southwest of Western Australia is familiar yet different. Perth has echoes of Sydney, being a harbour city lying on a similar latitude and possessing a hell of a lot of outrageously expensive waterfront property, but the sun in Perth sets over the ocean, rather than rising over it as it does in Sydney. In other ways Perth is reminiscent of Brisbane, without the humidity. The eighties white-shoe brigade casts a long shadow over the two cities, both of which have been substantially rebuilt in the last twenty years and still have a shininess and sense of possibility to them. Or maybe I just draw the comparison because I saw an Osprey circling next to Perth's main freeway – a bird that, though familiar to the two cities, always thrills a southern (or eastern) twitcher like myself.

Beyond Perth the landscape is distinctly Australian: the euca-lypts look the same, the pattern of settlement appears identical, even the birds are quite similar, yet something seems out of place. It's as if someone has taken a photograph of your family and altered every fifth detail. At first glance all seems normal but then you notice your father now has a moustache, your mother is a foot taller, your brother now has a tattoo. The west is rather like Tasmania in this respect – you know you are in Australia but it is not quite the same. Though connected by land to the rest of Australia, the southwest corner is, biologically at least, as much an island as Tasmania. Where Tassie is separated by a mere two hundred kilometres of ocean, the southwest has over two thousand kilometres of desert country, including the famous Nullarbor Plain, between it and the next patch of similar country. It has had a long period of isolation in which to develop along a distinct path. Perhaps not coincidentally, both Western Australia and Tasmania harbour twelve species of bird found nowhere else in the world.

The extreme southwest corner has the richest density of endemics, so on picking up my hire car at Perth Airport I immediately headed south. My plan was to spend around five days in the Albany area getting most of the area's specialties, including that trio of elusive skulkers – the Western Whipbird, Western Bristlebird and Noisy Scrub-bird – three of the most difficult birds on the continent to see. First stop was in the Busselton area where a Grey Heron had been seen in May. There has only ever been one previous record of Grey Heron in Australia and that was claimed by John Gould himself back in 1839. It goes to show the suspicious nature of the birdwatcher that Gould's record is now held to be quite dubious in spite of the fact that he was the seminal figure in Australian ornithology and would have known the bird well as it was a familiar sight in his English homeland.

Reading about the life of John Gould, he comes across as an archetypal twitcher totally obsessed with birds to the exclusion of everything and everyone else, including his wife, family, collectors and artists. Hand in hand with his passion for birds was an enormous ego and, like many a twitcher, you get the impression that he would not back down once he had made a declaration of a sighting. Such is his standing that it was almost a century before doubts began to be cast on his Grey Heron record.

No doubts are cast on the Busselton bird as it was photographed, even making the local paper. It disappeared before word had spread along the twitching grapevine, so nobody (myself included) had made the long flight across to Perth to twitch it. But seeing I had come all this way it seemed crazy not to check things out. Of course there was no sign of the heron but I did start seeing my first endemics – Western Thornbill, Western Rosella and Red-winged Fairy-wren, amongst others. Near the booming boutique town of Margaret River I stopped to watch a flock of Long-billed Black-Cockatoos using their deep bills to prise out gumnuts. Add to this a number of waterbirds on the lagoons around Busselton and the stunning vistas of windswept Capes Naturaliste and Leeuwin, and for the first time that year I actually had the feeling that I was on holiday rather than doing any kind of hard twitching yards.

This feeling was enhanced by the quality of the food I was eating. Not unexpectedly for such an upmarket tourist destination, the focaccia I had for lunch at Margaret River was as good as you find in the cafes of Bondi or South Yarra, but I wasn't prepared for the sensational Chinese dinner I had at Busselton. As a rule of thumb when travelling outside the big cities, I never eat at a restaurant that serves foreign cuisine of any sort. Even when it is run by genuine foreigners, to placate bland local palates they generally have to dilute the taste of their cuisine so much that the result is inevitably disappointing. My choice in Busselton was between the Chinese and the American style takeaways that line the highway so I opted for the Chinese. My expectations were fairly low, particularly when I saw they had a special 'Aussie' section on the menu – never a good sign when a Chinese restaurant also serves steak and chips. To my amazement, the meal I had was sensational, rivalling anything I'd eaten in Melbourne that cost less than fifty bucks.

I was similarly blown away the next night by the mixed seafood platter I ordered at the motel in Pemberton. Washed down with a couple of quality Margaret River reds, I was feeling most relaxed and comfortable on returning to my motel room. The next day I'd be off through the tall forest of the Karri country to the coast at Albany to have a crack at those three skulkers. I'd be coming through the region again in October, so I was feeling confident that by year's end I would have notched up all three species. I was feeling very peaceful about things.

Then my phone rang. It was Mike Carter in Melbourne. 'Where have you been?' Mike asked.

'At Busselton, looking for the Grey Heron.'

'You're looking in the wrong place, you know...'

Well derr. But why would Mike bother to ring me just for that? His next sentence explained all: 'It's just been seen at Geraldton.'

The Grey Heron must have been making its way back up the coast towards its Asian home as Geraldton is about six hundred kilometres north of Perth. My dilemma was that if I was to go for the heron I would need to head around eight hundred kilometres in the opposite direction and wouldn't have time to come back and try for the Albany rarities. No-one had been to look for the Grey Heron since it was reported three days ago, so did I risk three probable species for only one possible, no matter how much of a crippler it was? You bet I did. As if I'd want to dip out on a bird that might take another hundred and fifty years to reappear.

I left Pemberton at dawn, making a brief detour to check out the famous Gloucester Tree: you can climb a steel ladder that winds around it to the top of a mighty Karri for a canopy view of the forest. I took in the view of mist rising from the dew-soaked gullies and steeled myself for the ten-hour drive to Geraldton. The lush Karri forests give way to the coastal plain around Perth and then once out the other side of the metropolis the country starts to become noticeably drier. Sandy heaths start to thin out until the country around Geraldton has a distinctly desert-like feel; the roadhouse I stopped at for a dodgy curry dinner could just as easily have been a truck stopped in Arizona.

Driving in or out of Perth gives you a profound awareness that this is the most isolated capital city in the world. No wonder Perth people are often fiercely parochial, because when you drive just an hour out of town in almost any direction you start to get an unnerving feeling of being under siege and isolated, the desert and the ocean pressing in on you. It creates a sense of self-reliance and I guess a suspicion of the world beyond the seemingly endless horizon. Perhaps it was just the nerves of a big twitching effort like this that led to such thoughts. All this driving may turn out to be for naught.

If I was feeling the pressure, imagine how Mike Carter must have been feeling. I'd just come up from Pemberton, whereas Mike was flying over from Melbourne. I had a morning to see the bird before Mike and Frank O'Connor got there. Frank is the local Perth birder who told Mike about the initial sighting. A relative latecomer to birding, Frank has been bitten hard by the twitching bug, and is determinedly aiming to build the biggest Western Australian list of all time. The Grey Heron would be as much a coup for Frank as it would for Mike. Hopefully I'd have the bird lined up for them when they arrived – or at the very least I'd have ticked it off so I'd be able to grip them off and show them where the bird had been just minutes before them. There was not a single bird on my Australian list that Mike hadn't seen (and there were about a hundred and forty that Mike had ticked off that I hadn't). Maybe if I do see the Grey Heron, I should look around for a rock...

By the time Mike and Frank arrived the next morning, I'd spent hours scouring the banks of the Chapman River with no luck. We searched for the rest of the day, unsuccessfully. Like drowning men desperately clutching at straws, we kept looking for the Grey Heron the next day. Working on the theory that if the heron was the Busselton bird, it must have been heading slowly northward, back to Asia, we headed north to the next patch of likely habitat – the Murchison River at Kalbarri, one hundred and seventy kilometres away. No heron there but Kalbarri, with its swathes of heathland and surrounding dry country, provided many birding highlights, including Western Yellow Robin, Black-eared Cuckoo, Little Woodswallow and Tawny-crowned Honeyeater. The woodswallows were unexpected this far south and the cuckoo was most welcome as, although it has a wide distribution across Australia, nowhere is it easily twitchable. Not only was the robin a new bird but we were also privy to a pair of them mating. The female sat on a horizontal branch, quivering her wings seductively, and as the male approached she gave us a full view of all her bits before he hopped on and did the deed. Decorum prevents me from further description, but suffice to say the brevity of the proceedings gives hope to all us blokes – just compare yourself to a male Western Yellow Robin and you're looking pretty darn good in the bedroom stakes.

We agreed we couldn't keep following the coast northwards in the hope of catching up with the bird. Frank decided to head back to Perth, while I managed to con Mike into coming inland with me. I figured that I might as well make the most of being that far north and try to tick off a few desert species. We had a couple of great days' birding but we dipped on my two target birds. No Grey Honeyeater at Frank's site at Yalgoo, and no Chestnut-breasted Quail-thrush at the Mount Magnet 'golf course' which, aside from the pin flags, is indistinguishable from the surrounding gibber country. The greens would have been more aptly named reds for there was not a blade of grass to be seen and it appeared the greenkeeper must manicure them with a grader. I suppose it makes sense in such a dry, hot climate, as you would only need the one club – a sand wedge – in your bag, leaving more space for the ice-cold stubbies. I think even Tiger Woods would struggle on this course. We didn't do too well: few birdies, just the one distant eagle and not even a sniff of an albatross. I would have settled for a mere quail-thrush.

We made our way back towards Perth and once we hit the agricultural zone again I came across my first Western Corella for the year. Unfortunately it was fresh roadkill. As we were examining the corpse a few live birds flew over just as a couple of locals driving a ute pulled up and asked us what we were doing. We told them we were looking for corellas. Though threatened on a global scale, corellas can be locally abundant, a fact brought home to us by the women's response. After they had stopped laughing they offered to show us where a colony nested on one of the women's property, adding, 'You're welcome to take all those noisy buggers with you.'

At Northam on the Avon River I picked up one of the more ridiculous ticks of the year with the Mute Swan. There is hardly a more incongruous sight than these all-white English swans in the middle of rural Australia, but this one remaining population of this English species is regarded as self-sustaining and therefore tickable. And though rather laughable, I didn't mind as they are quite beautiful birds, really, and aren't doing anybody any harm, apart from the little girl who got a bit too close while trying to feed one. Sure, a crocodile attack may be messier, but I doubt she'll be approaching waterfowl with any enthusiasm in the near future.

A genuine highlight followed a couple of hours later in the form of a bird that, for the present, I couldn't even count on my official list. It is mooted that the western race of Crested Shrike-tit will be split out into full species status from the Crested Shrike-tit when the next official checklist is published, but back then I couldn't tick it. Despite this I was absolutely over the moon when we found a pair feeding quietly in a gully in the Darling Range on the outskirts of Perth. They are top-notch birds, striking in appearance and becoming scarcer by the year, having really suffered more than most species from habitat loss due to overlogging. I was astonished at how joyous seeing this bird made me feel when it didn't contribute to the immediate task at hand of adding ticks to the voracious list. A very un-mercenary attitude that could have me drummed out of the twitchers' union.

The next morning thirty eager sea-birders gathered at Hillary's boat harbour hoping the weather didn't turn any worse for the impending boat trip. Before the day's end a quarter of them would be chucking their guts out but I had under my belt not only the Soft-plumaged Petrel that I had come specifically to see, but also a couple of unexpected bonuses including Kerguelen Petrel and superb views of a pair of Humpback Whales. And to top it all off I felt totally relaxed. Even Mike confessed that on the long bumpy ride back in he was starting to feel a little queasy. This was a breakthrough moment for me, a sign that I was getting truly hardcore in my twitching if I could enjoy a boat trip that knocked about even a veteran of hundreds of such trips.

And to top the day off we saw a Salvin's Prion, a bird I hadn't even contemplated seeing at the beginning of the year. Prion identification is notoriously difficult and controversial with many top birders claiming they are impossible to tell apart at sea, but the bird that made a circuit around the boat showed enough distinctive features for us to be confident it was a Salvin's. If I'd been alone I wouldn't have been quite so confident but standing next to Mike who pointed out what features to look for made me feel a lot more comfortable. Who knows, this might be the most contentious bird in my entire year list, but being backed up by an expert kind of helps in rebutting the doubters. I remembered why I liked hanging out with the top rate twitchers – they might be freaks but they were awesomely brilliant freaks.

As we pounded back through the swell we came back into sight of land. I was feeling bloody tired but extremely satisfied. Smiling I turned to look at the Finnish biologist sitting hunched by the rail. She feebly smiled back, pieces of vomit plastering her hair to her cheek, turned away and began retching over the side.

Life was good.

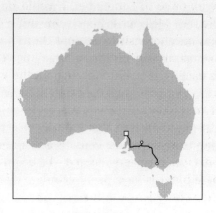

CHAPTER 17

14 July, Port Augusta, South Australia:
474 species

As I sat in the departure lounge of Perth Airport on 1 July making silly faces at the snotty toddler sitting opposite and hoping to God I wasn't allocated a seat anywhere near him or his frazzled parents, the clock ticked over to midday and I realised that the Big Twitch was now at the halfway point. Into the home stretch. Admittedly that stretch was tens of thousands of kilometres long, but for the first time a sense of the mortality of this venture kicked in. Six months might seem like a long time but suddenly it was beginning to feel claustrophobic. Although I had missed several species I was hoping for, it was only the summer east coast seabirds that I had most probably done my dash on. But even discounting them I was still on track for seven hundred, provided everything went to plan.

That plan involved a change of strategy. Back in Melbourne I loaded up the vehicle, steeling myself for months spent basically alone, and hit the road. For the first half of the year I was never away from home for more than ten days at a time; from this point on, apart from a week or so in September, I would be anywhere but home. But before I left Melbourne I had some unfinished business.

First up was another visit to Seaford Swamp where I finally caught up with Australasian Bittern, a large but very shy type of heron. They are usually at Seaford throughout the winter but their retiring habits mean you can walk right past them ensconced in the reeds and never know they are there. It was only now that the winter rains had filled Seaford Swamp that I finally managed to flush a bittern. As it disappeared over the reeds, its extraordinary green feet trailing behind it, I was very, very relieved – I'd be travelling through many areas where bitterns have been recorded, but they are not a bird that you often come across by luck.

Luck was something I'd been desperately short of while trying to find an Orange-bellied Parrot. Since seeing that untickable, silhouetted bird in April I'd lucked out on every follow up. These tiny parrots (known as OBPs) breed only in the isolated southwest of Tasmania and migrate across Bass Strait to spend the winter along the coastal saltmarsh of Victoria and the extreme southeast corner of South Australia. Until recently the bulk of the population wintered at only two sites: Point Wilson near Werribee and Swan Island near Queenscliff. Seeing them was a matter of turning up at either place at the right time of year. But something had happened to the OBP's age-old habits. While the breeding population stayed at roughly the same level, the birds stopped appearing at their regular mainland haunts and no-one can work out where they are going. Swan Island contains a secret service base, which means gaining access can be tricky, so I had focused my efforts on Point Wilson where, between the sewage farm and an armaments base, there is a narrow band of saltmarsh and grasslands perfect for OBPs. Well, it used to be.

I was supposed to go on one more Port Fairy pelagic but a massive low pressure cell with its accompanying gale force winds ensured yet another cancellation and I spent the weekend being blasted by Antarctic winds looking for OBPs with Groober in tow. On the Saturday the wind was so powerful we could barely hold our telescopes upright.

The birds were too sensible to show themselves in weather this bad so I delayed my departure for yet another day and headed out to Point Wilson once more early on Sunday morning. As it plays out in the best of twitching dreams, there was a flock of sixteen neophemas feeding by the side of the road as I arrived. I could hear both Blue-winged and OBPs calling but couldn't for the life of me pick out an OBP through my bins or scope. The birds started to move off and I was beginning to panic when up into the frame of my scope popped a juvenile Orange-bellied Parrot. It stayed still long enough for me to eliminate the possibility of juvenile Blue-winged Parrot (not an easy task) and I finally had the little mongrel under my belt. I was free to go.

I've never been fond of goodbyes. Many's the dud party I've stayed at till the bitter end because I haven't been able to work out a suitable departure strategy. And now, oddly enough, I was finding it very hard to say goodbye to Melbourne. I think I knew that once I was out the front door, it was crunch time – there'd be no going back. I found reasons to delay my departure. The day before I was due to leave I even found myself in a job interview for head writer of an as yet to be shot comedy series for Channel Seven. The first thing I said when I walked in was that I was leaving the next day for six months on the road birdwatching – a job application technique they had never come across before. The interview went brilliantly, mainly because we didn't talk about the job; they were so fascinated by the concept of the Big Twitch that they offered to screen updates of my journey over the credits of each week's show under the imaginative title of 'Sean's Crazy Birdwatching Adventures'. I turned them down. Who wants end credits? I insisted on nothing less than my own series. They said they loved the idea and would get back to me. I never heard from them again.

Monday 8 July was D-Day. The Land Cruiser was finally all packed and ready to go. One last supermarket run for fresh supplies and I'd be off. But then I managed to lock myself inside my house. When I came back from the supermarket, the front door slammed shut after I had entered. The whole house was deadlocked, and I couldn't get out. My keys were on the outside of the door, facing directly onto the street, with my open car, full of gear, parked invitingly across the street. I had

to ring my friend Anthony (one of the New Year's Eve owl imperson-
ators) to come over and free me from my house arrest. By seven that
night, a mere three days later than planned, I was finally ready to go.

What a night to head out: eighty-kilometre winds blasted
Melbourne, throwing my freshly loaded car all over the freeway. As is
often the case, the weather calmed down once I crossed the Great
Dividing Range and by the time I reached Bendigo the night was
perfectly clear and still with the great swathe of the Milky Way
splashed across the inky sky. Just north of Bendigo, at Kamarooka, I
flashed past what I thought was a Tawny Frogmouth sitting in a
roadside tree. I already had it on the year list but figured I may as
well check it out. It turned out to be a Barking Owl, a bird I had
dipped out on several on times around Chiltern. It was right on our
Twitchathon route but we'd never seen Barking Owl here before
despite driving this road dozens of times.

Staring at the owl staring back at me with its intense yellow
eyes, I couldn't help but feel this was a good omen for the trip. I
decided to sleep there the night, my first on the road, and as I settled
into the sleeping bag in the back seat of the car, I revelled in the glorious stillness of the country at night. The first night away from the
city you can feel the tension almost physically draining out of you as
you gaze at the achingly beautiful sky and greedily inhale the invigorating fresh scent of the country. My earlier trepidation gone, I now
felt like this thing was really happening. I felt alive.

I followed much of our Twitchathon route the next day picking
up Mallee species such as Purple-gaped Honeyeater and Shy
Heathwren until I eventually arrived at Hattah-Kulkyne National Park
with enough time to get out to my site for the star species of the day,
the Mallee Emu-wren. These tiny birds with long tails like Emu feathers are in quite a deal of strife. Being so small and such poor flyers they
don't do a great job of escaping bushfires and it might take decades for
them to recolonise an area they formerly occupied. In the past this
didn't matter so much as there were always refuge areas from which
the population could recover, but with the habitat so fragmented and
the frequency of massive high intensity fires increasing, the remaining
populations are becoming ever more isolated. South Australia was

their stronghold but over eighty-five per cent of the population there has disappeared as a result of fire in the past two decades. The area around Hattah is now crucial to these little birds' survival, so with a great deal of forethought and sensitivity, the state government has proposed building a toxic waste dump immediately next door on the site of some prime emu-wren habitat. Good one, fellas.

Right on dusk I finally heard one giving its tinny, barely audible squeak of a call. A sure sign of aging is when you can no longer hear an emu-wren. I have stood next to older birders while emu-wrens call their hearts out and they are totally oblivious. Hearing this bird saves me the price of a hearing test for another year. Unfortunately I'll still need an eye test, as the bird itself didn't show. Leading me a merry dance in what was probably my tensest birding so far that year, they always managed to stay ahead of me, darting from one clump of impenetrable porcupine grass to another.

Next morning I was out at the same spot at dawn. With the clear night skies, the temperature was literally freezing and though gloved my hands still kept getting stuck to the metal handle of my camera's tripod. Amazingly these birds, weighing only six grams, were already out and about. Six grams – it would take four Mallee Emu-wrens to equal the amount of fat in a single Big Mac – and there they were keeping ahead of me out in the scrub. Normally I would probably have given up looking after an hour but not that year. I couldn't afford for the birds to win these games of chasey. The adrenaline was pumping and each unsatisfactory half-glimpse only raised the stakes higher. It wasn't until the gold wash of the sun hit the red ridge of the sand dune that a Mallee Emu-wren finally poked its head up from a porcupine grass clump long enough for me to tick it off. The relief at seeing this little bird was physically palpable and I felt a surge of pure exhilaration. Unfortunately this triumphal rush only lasted a few minutes and it was on to the next bird for the next fix.

I'd brought a football along with me for company – a bit like the volleyball in that annoying Tom Hanks movie *Castaway*. Getting the footy out for a kick is actually a good ice-breaker when travelling – it's amazing who will join in with a game of kick to kick when you produce the pill at some remote Outback roadhouse. For some reason

I decided I'd kick the footy across the border every time I drove into a new state. The first opportunity for such an interstate kick came as I headed into South Australia along the Surt Highway, an occasion that met with near disaster. After I'd booted a nice looking drop punt across the border, it took a sharp leg-break and bounced precariously close to the wheels of an oncoming road train.

First stop in South Australia was a return to Gluepot where I could visit in a slightly more leisurely fashion than I had in March – and as an added bonus, this time I arrived with my finger unbandaged. Gluepot, so named because when it rains the dirt turns to a boggy, gluey consistency, is a superb wilderness experience, yet I suspect it will never attract the sort of eco-tourism numbers that will ensure its long-term economic future. Even though there are probably as many endangered species here as somewhere like Kruger National Park, you just aren't going to get the punters lining up en masse to look at Striated Grasswrens and Legless Lizards. The lack of dudes in safari trucks was a bonus for me, however, as I virtually had the entire reserve to myself and spent a glorious couple of days rambling through the place.

My prime target was the Black-eared Miner. A rather large, drab honeyeater, the Black-eared was damned by the invention of the stump jump plough. This icon of Aussie ingenuity was invented for the purpose of dealing with the large mallee roots that remained embedded in the soil long after the trees had been knocked down. It successfully opened up vast swathes of Black-eared Miner country, to their detriment. Gluepot is about the only place you get them these days.

For many the Mallee woodlands are unrelentingly drab and oppressive places – the worst the miserable Australian bush has to offer. 'Mallee' is the name given to a couple of dozen eucalypt species that grow in clumps on the poor sandy soils of the inland. Their thin, multi-stemmed trunks reach only to about three or four metres, too short to be terribly impressive, but just high enough to obscure the horizon. Particularly on a cloudy day, the Mallee is the easiest habitat in the world to get lost in. Despite having a compass I've become hopelessly disoriented in this habitat after walking just one hundred metres in from the road. The trees seem to close in on you and you barely have a sense of which way is up, let alone east or west. Even when you can scramble to a slight rise for a vista, for as far as you can see there is nothing but the uniform khaki of mallee-clad dunes. It is the sort of country that can infuriate, overwhelm and send people insane. Reassuringly I had a GPS unit with me this time, so as long as I remembered to log my starting point I shouldn't have any trouble.

I loved it. Not only are there great birds to be found in the Mallee but if you look closely enough the scene changes with every step you take. The Mallee operates on two dimensions of scale: the overwhelming enormity of the landscape and the intricacies of a lichen colony; a shred of peeling bark exposing the flesh-coloured limb of an ancient mallee tree; the parallel dapples of a set of lizard footprints in the soft sand; the hollowed-out centre of a ring of old growth porcupine grass.

Eventually I came across a party of twenty miners feeding loudly amongst one of the few flowering mallee trees on the reserve. Once the Black-eared Miner's territory was opened up it allowed the closely related open country species, the Yellow-throated Miner, to move in. They have genetically swamped the Black-eareds, hybridising with them to the point that now there are very few pure Black-eareds left. Most of this flock were 'mongrel' miners but there was one outstanding dark specimen that had enough distinctive features to allow me to distinguish it as a pure Black-eared Miner. Another of the really difficult birds out of the way.

So it was on to Adelaide where I dropped in on John Cox to see what was around and to pick up my toiletry bag that I had left there back in March. After three months it was nice to be able to brush my hair again. Also there was Dave Harper and we finalised our rendezvous point on the Strzelecki Track for three weeks' time. Dave was still way too confident about finding Grey Falcon for my liking. He maintained he had never dipped out on it at his special site but I couldn't share his confidence, especially as this time he'd have me tagging along to jinx him. With any luck I would pick up a Grey Falcon somewhere in the Centre, for in the next three weeks I'd be travelling some three and a half thousand kilometres through the core range of this elusive species.

The next morning in Port Augusta I took a quick detour down to the seashore. The next time I'd see the ocean would be in five weeks' time, on Cape York Peninsula on the opposite side of the country. Providing a farewell guard of honour, a small pod of Bottle-nosed Dolphins broke the surface right in front of me. I made my way to the Arid Lands Botanic Gardens where I picked up my first desert species, the Chirruping Wedgebill. Just beyond the gardens is the beginning of the Stuart Highway, the thread of bitumen that joins the north and south of this vast continent. Named after explorer John McDouall Stuart who set off from near here on a similar route one hundred and forty years ago, the trip north almost killed him. I stepped out of the car and looked at the entire continent stretching before me. Even this close to the coast the country is desolate. Not a tree protrudes into the sky. In the distance a couple of mesa-like hills break the horizon. When Stuart set off he had a few horses and camels. I was in an air-conditioned four-wheel drive and had the option of staying in a motel every night, yet still I was chilled with apprehension at the thought of what lay ahead.

After a seriously long pause in which I fought the irrational urge to turn around and go home, I got back in the car, cranked up the stereo and headed off into the vast interior.

CHAPTER 18

16 July, Stuart Highway, 19 kilometres south of the Northern Territory–South Australia border:
477 species

The minibus rolled at around a hundred kilometres an hour, killing the driver. Six passengers survived but due to the remoteness of the crash site it would be seven hours before they were finally airlifted by the Flying Doctor Service to Alice Springs. The greatest three weeks of my life were at an end.

It was August 1988 and we were on the homeward leg of a Monash University Biology Society field trip to Kakadu. I wasn't even a student at Monash but, through the agency of Puke, I had weaselled my way onto the trip. Puke and I had hijacked the itinerary somewhat in order to satiate our twitching needs. To that point it really had been the greatest three weeks of my life. Experiencing amazing country, hanging out with a bunch of like-minded souls. New birds every day, partying every night. And to top it all off I got together with a girl who actually had half an interest in birds.

The morning of the crash had started well enough. We had been at the campground at Uluru as the sun rose on that magnificent rock. Unfortunately, in our effort to distance ourselves from the rest of the group for a bit of privacy, my new friend and I had set our sleeping bags down by the path to the sunrise viewing spot and were caught *in flagrante delicto* by a party of middle-aged German tourists. Hours later, as we passed over the border from the Northern Territory into South Australia, we were lying together on the back seat of the minibus. For some reason I suggested that we shift positions and lie with our heads towards the centre of the road rather than, as we had been, with our heads facing the verge. A couple of minutes later the tyre on our trailer had a blowout causing it to jack-knife. Travelling at around a hundred kilometres per hour the violent swerving of the trailer brought the minibus over and we went off the road, rolling several times in the process.

The last thing I saw before I was blinded by the wave of red dust kicked up as we rolled off the road was my girlfriend falling backwards away from me. If we hadn't just changed positions we would have gone over on our necks. Goodbye Sean, goodbye sexy bird girl. As it was, things were pretty dire. The sensation was like being dumped by a giant wave – I couldn't see anything, I couldn't tell which way was up. The sound was extreme – tearing metal, screaming people, a deafening white noise. Suddenly everything stopped and I was lying on my back again, eyes closed. All was totally silent. I could feel pain in my ankles and wiggled my toes to check I hadn't broken anything. Expecting to still be on the back seat of the bus I opened my eyes to find I was staring at bright blue sky, and for a moment it actually did occur to me that I might be dead. Finally I sat up and looked around. The bus had come to rest about twenty metres away, upright in the scrub. Between it and me lay a couple of dust covered bodies, not moving.

Later there was an inquiry, legal action, compensation claims, all of which I turned my back on. No wonder I did so poorly as a law student – a pot of money to which I had a legitimate legal right and I walked away from it. Or more accurately hobbled. Though my injuries were comparatively slight, for years afterwards if I went to change direction as I was walking, my damaged ankles would lock and I would fall face forward onto the ground. This was but a minor and at times amusing after-effect of the accident. The real impact was psychological. Being one of the only victims not to be concussed meant I remembered it all: the crash, the bloody aftermath, the shattering of the invincibility of youth.

There is a component in compensation payments that provides for pain and suffering, including mental anguish. For many this legitimises what they have been through, recognises the trauma of their experience and helps with the healing process. Throughout the accident I had held it all together – bandaging the injured, flagging down help, keeping the flies out of gaping wounds, joking with the rescuers about their appalling musical taste. It was only after arriving back in Melbourne a week later that the impact really hit me. Lying in the darkness that first night in my own bed, I was overwhelmed by the enormity of the dark abyss that I had stared down on that lonely stretch of Outback highway. A matter of minutes, a matter of inches, and I would have ceased to exist out there under that piercing blue sky – a thought so powerful, so palpable, that it was overwhelming. I didn't know about post-traumatic stress syndrome at that time but I was self-aware enough to know I was very close to losing the plot.

The support of friends and family, a little bit of counselling, the supercilious sub-dean who refused my request to defer my studies, the fellow law student who risked expulsion by practically writing my overdue law assignment for me all pulled me back from a second abyss. The one thing I felt wouldn't have helped was money. Rather than compensate it would have felt like it was substituting for fully processing the experience of the accident. I didn't need to be placated, I needed to absorb what had happened in order to come to terms with it. After a few months life returned to normal. The fourth anniversary of the crash was the first to pass without me remembering it, but it was such a momentous event in my life that I always felt I wouldn't be fully healed until I returned to the site.

Now, on the sixteenth of July almost fourteen years later, I was finally there. I felt very strange. This was where I almost died. This was where we found the body of the driver, her neck snapped.

This was where the most violent moment of my life occurred. Yet it all felt so peaceful. This patch of highway is typical of much of the Outback. The soil is a vivid, almost blood red colour, contrasting with the stunningly blue sky that stretches overhead forever. At first glance the vegetation is a comparatively drab khaki and straw colour, but it actually works as a superb counterpoint to the vibrancy of the other elements in the landscape. There was much more vegetation now than there had been fourteen years earlier. The mulga was thicker and taller, the Centre having experienced a series of wetter than normal seasons. If the bus crashed today it would come to rest very close to the edge of the road, the robust mulga growth retarding its trajectory.

I walked twenty metres or so away from the verge and searched for evidence of the crash. It's amazing how quickly nature covers all signs of human activity, even in the desert. While the bus was towed away at the time and anything of value would have been quickly scavenged, I was expecting to find more debris. Eventually fragments of that long ago moment revealed themselves half buried in the red sand: the black snake of a rubber windscreen lining. A shattered side window. A plastic petrol cap. The hard black plastic casing of a rear view mirror. Not exactly Ozymandias but it was a reminder of the fragility of existence, and the hubris of youth. When these artifacts were so violently deposited there I had long, rock star hair, I was thin, my future was full of endless dreams and possibilities. Many of those dreams have disappeared under the desert sands of life – bird girl and I only lasted six months, for instance – but here I was, brought back to this place all these years later in the pursuit of the one dream I couldn't shake.

I had been hoping for some kind of momentous epiphany. But as I stood amongst the detritus of tragedy, with people burling past me on the Stuart Highway in their insulated bubbles of civilisation rushing to the next roadhouse for a refuelling and an ice cream, the only revelation I was aware of is that life moves on. And so must I. I was already running behind schedule.

This is a vast area and it had taken me the best part of two days to drive from Port Augusta to this point, in part because of a detour to Woomera. The settlement established to house the boffins and technicians working on the Woomera rocket range, the facility that helped develop the space race and enabled a foreign power to explode nuclear devices in our backyard, was now almost a ghost town. They don't fire rockets there much anymore though they did on the day that I decided to have a stickybeak. The multimillion-dollar satellite crashed to Earth within seconds of the launch. Sadly, I missed the explosion by a couple of hours although this probably saved me from being arrested.

As the site of yet another immigration detention centre Woomera was in the news at the time. The government and the private firm that ran the place had shown extreme reluctance to let people know what was going on behind the razor wire. As I drove up to the perimeter I expected to be approached by armed guards but it seemed most everyone had gone out to witness the aftermath of the failed rocket launch. Nobody challenged me as I parked and looked at the complex. On the drive in I had seen what was probably a Ground Cuckoo-shrike, a bird I still needed, flying in the distance. It occurred to me how thoughtful it was of the government to build a detention centre out there in the middle of a treeless desert where summer temperatures regularly climb above forty degrees Celsius and winter nights plummet to freezing. Because despite the extreme weather and the isolation and flies, these new arrivals to our country were at least being treated to sightings of rare desert birds. I was moved to think, 'Gee, I wish I was a refugee.'

I included this admittedly feeble gag in one of my reports to Birding-aus. The next time I got to a town to check my emails I received this message: 'Mate, stick to birds and lay off people who are locked up and less fortunate than you. You are not funny. Just pathetic.' My first ever hate mail! I was used to hearing 'You're not funny, Dooley, just pathetic,' from producers and former lovers, but from a total stranger? Ouch. Birdwatchers by their nature are generally a conservative lot so I was expecting to cop some flak for this little bit of Bolshie humour. I hadn't expected a barrage from someone who obviously shared a similar view to myself. Just goes to show satire is a weapon that, like a Woomera rocket, can easily backfire.

I decided to leave one hideous hellhole for another. A lot of people love Coober Pedy. I'm not one of them. I find it to be quite a hole. Well, thousands of holes, actually. The mullock heaps from the opal mines litter the countryside for miles around like giant ants' nests. The white clay that dots the surface has not oxidised like the surrounding red soil. It has a certain beauty, I suppose, but I found none at all in the town itself. Outback hype is always full of the characters that inhabit Coober Pedy, attracted by the lure of opal and the promise of riches, but all I ever saw were sad, desperate, generally drunk or borderline deranged wrecks of human beings lurking around dusty streets and tacky tourist stands. All the delightful characters must have been hanging around at the underground hotel.

Give me the surrounding countryside any day. There can be few landscapes in the world as desolate as the South Australian deserts. It is barrenness on such a mind-bogglingly enormous scale that it takes your breath away. At one point I pulled the car off the highway and scrambled onto the roof. There was not a stick of vegetation above ankle height to be seen for the entire 360-degree panorama. Nothing but red gibber plain all around me. I could have been on Mars.

Birds live here, though, and a couple of hundred kilometres north of Coober Pedy I was to stumble across one of these desert specialists and into another round of birdwatching politics. On the way I stopped at a site where Chestnut-breasted Whiteface had recently been seen. South Australia's only endemic species, this little brown and cream bird is regularly reported from only one site near Lyndhurst, about five hundred kilometres away. I was heading there in August but thought this place was worth a try.

At first glance it seemed like much of the rest of the country I'd been driving through. A large plain dotted with dry grass stretched to a small rise of barren, rocky hills a couple of kilometres away. Why the whitefaces would hang out here rather than the millions of hectares of similar country surrounding me is a mystery, but things looked promising as I pulled up and a pair of Southern Whitefaces flew from the side of the road. All three species of whiteface had been seen here recently. One down, two to go.

An hour later and no other whiteface of any description had put in an appearance. I was having a ball, though; the air was crisp, the landscape vivid and there were enough little dickie birds to keep me on my toes. A small flock of whiteface emerged from the bushes about eighty metres in front of me. They kept moving just far enough in front to stay out of identifiable range. Finally one popped up onto a small saltbush and I saw the flash of a reddish band across its chest – Chestnut-breasted Whiteface, one of Australia's least known birds. I was ecstatic. After I'd had my fill I was walking away, fists pumping in triumph like Lleyton Hewitt winning a match point, when I startled a flock of whitefaces. Over the next hour I saw at least twenty-two and possibly as many as forty Chestnut-breasted Whitefaces, an unprecedented number as the highest number ever reported to that point was only twelve. This was an exceptional birding moment, one of the highlights of the year.

Then, of course, came the repercussions. What I didn't realise at the time was that this location had been known for a number of years but people had kept schtoom about it. The primary reason given was to protect the birds from disturbance, though there was a rumour that at least one birding guide wanted to restrict knowledge of the place to a select few to give himself a competitive advantage when taking overseas clients around. The bloke who'd made a posting about the site on the Net had quickly been castigated and was soon backpedalling, contacting me to ask that I not publicise the site further. I was in a dilemma. In order to verify all my sightings I had to be open about where I had seen every species. I decided to describe the experience but be vague about specifics. But over the next few months other birders continually asked me to provide details so that they could have a look when they were in the area.

To a non-birder this may not seem like much of a dilemma, but as a twitcher I am torn between my desire to ensure the welfare of the birds and the unspoken obligation I have to enable others to experience them too. Why should I be privileged above others? In reality there is unlikely to be any serious threat to the whiteface from rabid twitchers swarming all over the place. The location is a long way from anywhere and even if it was well known, the amount of human traffic would increase from perhaps a couple of visits a year to a couple of dozen at most. Birders have been happily twitching the Lyndhurst whitefaces for almost twenty years now and they still seem to be going strong. The real danger comes from people whose interest in birds is far less benign than merely having a squiz at them through a pair of binoculars.

In Australia we are terribly naïve about the trade in wild birds and eggs. Because the country is so vast, much of the illicit activity of bird trappers and egg collectors goes unnoticed. Generally the black market aviarists aren't interested in little dickie birds like a whiteface, preferring to collect the colourful, iconic species such as parrots, but egg collectors would be very interested indeed in a bird like the Chestnut-breasted Whiteface, whose nest was not discovered until 1968. Not many collectors would have the eggs of this little one lying in their cotton wool filled drawers and the thought that I could be the one to tip them off about adding to their collection totally sickens me.

By the time I'd got back to the car after my whiteface encounter it was getting on. As I kicked the footy over the 'Welcome to the Northern Territory' sign, I realised that if I was to make it to my destination at King's Canyon I'd have to do a couple of hours of night driving. Forget your crocodiles and your venomous snakes and funnel-web spiders; about the most dangerous thing anyone can do in the Outback is drive at night. Nowhere are the roads fenced and there's a saying that hitting a kangaroo is the best thing that can happen to you when driving at night – it stops you from hitting something really dangerous, like a cow or a camel. Once the sun had set I slowed to around eighty kilometres an hour, adding at least half an hour to my trip but drastically reducing my chances of colliding with wandering wildlife. Well, that's the theory. I only managed to avoid smashing into a bullock by a matter of inches as its jet-black hide absorbed the beam of the headlights until I was almost upon it.

A little further down the track I came across one creature who hadn't been so lucky. A boobook owl was sitting stunned in the middle of the road having come off second best in an encounter with a road train. The temperature was beginning to plunge towards freezing and I didn't like its chances of surviving out there on the cold road, so I decided to take it into my care. Donning a thick pair of gardening gloves from my bag of tricks I approached, wary of that very sharp bill. The bird was too dazed to bother having a go but as soon as I picked it up it dug its talons into my hands in fear. I suddenly remembered the main weapon of this hunter is not its beak, which it only uses to tear its prey to pieces once it has been caught, but its talons. The more I tried to extricate myself the tighter its grip became and I had visions of me driving the rest of the way with the bird attached like some boobook-sized wristwatch. Eventually I disentangled myself and put the owl safely away in a box.

Driving along feeling smug for being such a good friend to the native creature I saw a car approaching from the opposite direction. Just as it was about to pass me a pair of Red Kangaroos bounded out onto the road. I hit them at about seventy kilometres an hour. The first merely bounced off the roo bar and hopped away. The second, however, copped the full impact and was thrown backwards into the path of the oncoming vehicle, which was travelling much faster and drove right over it without stopping. Guilty, I reversed back to assess the damage. Between the two cars we had broken both legs of this enormous big red male. It flailed hopelessly on the bitumen, unable to make a getaway. It would eventually bleed to death or more likely be crushed under a road train, but I couldn't bring myself to leave it lying there in agony like that. This was a beast of a roo and I realised I didn't have an implement big enough to finish it off with one blow, nor did I have the stomach for slitting its throat. There was only one thing left for me to do.

I got back in the car, turned the tape player right up so I couldn't hear anything and aimed the two tonnes of my four-wheel drive directly in line with its skull. Screaming at the top of my lungs to drown out any noise, I managed to hit the target first time and drove off into the night, shaking.

What a day. A reminder that in country like this there is both great beauty and great danger. When something stuffs up out here you really are on your own. And I was heading into the heart of it alone.

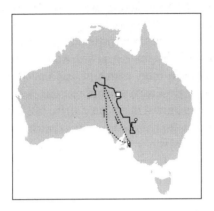

CHAPTER 19

30 July, Edge of the Simpson Desert, Northern Territory:
497 Species

The only other time my life has ever been in the slightest danger was on the night I attended my first ever rock concert. Forget a bus crash; you want truly life-threatening, try losing your footing as a skinny sixteen year old amongst the throng of burly blokes with t-shirts wrapped around their heads dancing in the mosh pit of a Midnight Oil concert. I had gone along with Groober and Puke but as I went down for the third time in that crush of sweaty bodies they were nowhere to be seen. Suddenly a hand grabbed hold of my collar and pulled me up from my impending doom. It was Jezz, a kid I knew from school. We have been firm friends ever since.

Jezz was working as head gardener for the King's Canyon Resort in the middle of Watarrka National Park. His girlfriend Karen worked there too so I decided to make their place my base for my Central Australian foray. King's Canyon is not a high priority for most birders but I managed to see some of the real Central Australian specialties here such as Rufous-crowned Emu-wren, Dusky Grasswren and Spinifex Pigeon which I first saw on a freezing dawn, curled up into a tight little ball, only its crest protruding so that it looked like a pigeon popsicle. And the scenery is second to none. There are magnificent ancient bluffs and canyons, hidden springs and rolling spinifex plains peppered with majestic Desert Oaks. Every day was a joy to be alive. Inspirational country, great birding by day, sitting around a campfire in Jezz and Karen's backyard by night, warding off the chill with a few beers and a whole lot of laughs. For the first time all year I felt I was home.

Too bad I almost got them both sacked.

Let this be a lesson to all: never invite a twitcher to stay. They cause havoc wherever they go. Not long after my disruptive presence on Norfolk Island they had their first murder in one hundred and fifty years. I turn up at Woomera and a multimillion-dollar rocket explodes. I was beginning to suspect I was some kind of chaos theory generator. It wasn't even what I did at King's Canyon that got them into trouble, but what I wrote about after the fact in my dispatch to Birding-aus. Using the inside dope I had from Jezz about the place, I merely mentioned a few management issues involved in running a resort in the middle of a national park in the middle of Australia. It didn't go down too well. Luckily for Jezz I had also included the Parks and Wildlife people in my assessment of the way things were run. There is always a certain tension between the Parks people and the resort management, so while Jezz's boss wasn't happy with what I'd said about his domain, at least he could have a good laugh at the expense of those uppity rangers. Not that I'd been particularly malicious but I did relay that they were nicknamed Sparks and Wildfires by locals because just before I arrived yet another of their prescriptive burns got out of control and set fire to half the park and neighbouring properties.

Still, I did make Jezz and Karen's social life a bit tricky for a while there, particularly with one of their mates from Parks and Wildlife. It all had to do with that injured boobook owl. To my surprise it had survived the night in its box but it looked in a bad way. I took it to the ranger's office hoping they might be able to look after it. The ranger on duty looked distinctly nonplussed and I wrote later that I got the impression that as soon as I left he most probably dashed its brains out against a tree. The ranger in question was a good friend of Jezz and Karen and he came to them almost in tears, protesting that he loved animals and how dare I think he would do that. They asked him what he had done with the boobook. He paused and then admitted he had dashed its brains out against a tree. He tried to explain that there was nothing that could be done for it, and he hadn't enjoyed doing it, but his protestations were drowned out by their laughter. I suspect it will be another decade before I can safely show my face around King's Canyon again.

Luckily I had left before everything hit the fan, heading into the MacDonnell Ranges. Welcome to superlative country. At nearly every turn was another staggering vista that would reduce me to the language of a second-rate sportscaster – the phrases 'magnificent', 'awesome' and 'absolutely f***ing brilliant' seemed to pass my lips with much regularity. The entire region is spectacular but I was particularly impressed with the road into Palm Valley along the Finke River, which apparently is the oldest river in the world. The landscape drips with sublime beauty both in the majesty of the big things, like huge rounded purple mountains and jagged red rock ridges, and on a micro scale: the subtle patterns of a spiky little Thorny Devil, a small lizard whose method of self-protection was to remain stock still even as I picked it up to move it from the middle of the road where it had defiantly taken up residence.

I felt more like a tourist than a twitcher. For days I happily moved through this area allowing myself to soak it all in rather than get too het up about my birding schedule. At Ormiston Gorge, somewhere that gives the Finke River Gorge a run for its money in terms of awesome beauty, I hooked up with a couple of nurses who were eighteen months into a round-Australia working holiday. Sharing my last bottle of beer as we laid back on the picnic table in the campground gazing at the enormous expanse of brilliant stars above us, I thought this must be how most people travelled. They were taking it easy, soaking it all in, mixing a bit of sightseeing with a bit of partying. They suggested I spend the next few days travelling with them. It was very tempting. But I was up before dawn, packing up the tent and heading out into the bush. It had been four days since I'd added a new bird for the year and sadly, the lure of a Spinifexbird was far greater than their feminine charms.

I had at least eight sites for Spinifexbird in the MacDonnell Ranges. I missed it every single time. Having no luck with what I thought would be a fairly straightforward bird I figured I may as well try for a really tough one – the Grey Honeyeater. So unassuming is this bird in both its dull plumage and preference for remote habitats that there are many very good twitchers who have never seen it. I had some recent gen that they had been seen quite recently at Kunoth Well, a little dot on the map on the edge of the Tanami Desert. I was heading out there early one morning hoping to beat the heat of the day when, just on the edge of mobile range, my phone rang. It was David Harper, his message brutally simple: Franklin's Gull, Adelaide, I better get down there pronto.

I swung the car around and headed straight for Alice Springs Airport. This American gull very rarely turns up in Australia and when it does it seldom stays very long in the one place. I simply couldn't miss it. The first plane to Adelaide wasn't until that evening so I booked my spot and headed out to Kunoth Well again.

I didn't like my chances now that the day had heated up but when I arrived at the site I had one of those rare, golden birding moments for as soon as I got out of the car a pair of Grey Honeyeaters flew into the nearest tree. This was a bird I had been expecting to spend days trying to find, one that has eluded some of the best birders in the land. And yet I still couldn't see a bloody Spinifexbird.

Next morning I was in Adelaide standing at a suburban football oval amongst a throng of thirty or forty excited twitchers lapping up the antics of a Franklin's Gull in full breeding plumage. It even accepted breadcrumbs from a happy fan – what a performance. It was quite a surreal scene. This is how twitching in England must be. Here such gatherings are still a novelty. Just as surreal was my arrival in Adelaide. As I came through the arrivals lounge I was descended on by a massive media horde. I didn't know my Big Twitch had become such big news. But it turned out the passenger next to me was the former leader of the Australian Democrats, Meg Lees. She was just about to announce her resignation and the establishment of a new political party, and I got caught in the middle of the impromptu press conference. Even more surreal was that by the next day I was back in the Alice, hauling my sorry carcass up yet another escarpment in another unsuccessful Spinifexbird hunt, not a hundred per cent sure I hadn't dreamt the whole Adelaide thing.

I needed to move on so I decided I would have to look for Spinifexbird in Western Australia later in the year. It wasn't until I was driving past the Santa Teresa Mission heading toward the Simpson Desert that I suddenly realised I had also missed out on Chiming Wedgebill a bird I had figured I would pick up somewhere along the way and hadn't made any particular effort to search for. Oops. Just outside Santa Teresa (aptly named as the village sits on the side of a mesa looking for all the world like it is waiting for Sergio Leone to start filming one of his spaghetti westerns) I stopped in what seemed like the last suitable habitat for both of these species and failed to find either, yet I had great views of Rufous-crowned Emu-wren, a species that most birders struggle with.

Heading south along the Old Andado Track the country becomes drier and drier as it skirts the western fringe of the Simpson Desert. After clearing the last of the mulga woodland the vegetation becomes stunted and sparse, perfect habitat for desert species such as Cinnamon Quail-thrush, Gibberbird and Banded Whiteface. All three species are regarded as hard to see but I got them whilst driving along the track, indicative, I suspect, of the fact that birders hardly ever get out into this remote country.

By nightfall I was well and truly alone. I found a bore to stake out hoping that the elusive Flock Bronzewing would come in to drink. Apart from a few curious cattle, nothing came in and as night fell I moved back to my camp and lit a fire to cook my dinner. The utter silence was amazing. Unlike many who feel compelled to build enormous bonfires every time they camp, I use just a few pieces of wood, enough to build up some good cooking coals and provide a modicum of warmth and light. As the fire died down the peaceful-ness of the chilly desert air took over. I suddenly felt very insignificant. The thought occurred that if a psychopathic killer were to pull up just then, no one would ever find my body. I could so easily have disappeared into that vastness forever.

I found that strangely comforting and slept well, wrapped up in my sleeping bag under the incandescence of the Outback sky, awoken only briefly by the distant creaking of the bore's windmill which, in the inky night, sounded suspiciously like a serial killer sharpening his implements.

I survived the night unscathed and next morning travelled along the edge of the Simpson Desert. Fingers of red sand dunes ran parallel to the track, clumps of cane grass on their sides. This is the habitat of the Eyrean Grasswren. So remote is the habitat of this bird that after its initial discovery in 1874 it wasn't conclusively seen again until 1961. I stopped several times with no luck; it felt like it would take me eighty-seven years to find it too. I pulled up yet again, this time armed with a shovel and toilet paper as I had to make a pit stop. Though I hadn't seen a vehicle all day, as soon as I went to drop my pants one rumbled into view, forcing me to move further away from the track. As usual, I dug a little hole and was squatting over it when I heard a barely audible squeak. It hadn't come from me (my campfire cooking is not that dire), but from a party of small birds moving about in the cane grass a few metres away. My binoculars were laid out just beyond my reach so, like a scene from *Carry On Birdwatching*, I struggled, pants around ankles, to reach for the bins without scaring the birds. Finally, bouncing out in front of me was a pair of Eyrean Grasswrens. I think I may have stumbled across a sure-fire method to see these elusive birds.

And so it was back into South Australia to meet up with Dave, birding all the way of course. I passed the five hundred mark with a group of four stately Australian Bustards. It was nice to have these big turkey-like birds as the milestone bird. At the time of European settlement I could have got them on the outskirts of Melbourne but these slow-moving creatures apparently taste delicious and were quickly shot out. Even in these remote areas where their habitat hasn't gone under the plough, they make a nice meal for the locals, who can easily pick them off from the back of a four-wheel drive. They are now only commonly found in conservation zones and in fact the birds I saw were within the borders of a national park.

From there it was in for a welcome dip at the thermal pools of Dalhousie Springs and then down the Oodnadatta Track, camping along the Aglebuckina Waterhole, which rang with the croaking calls of cormorants, Darters and other waterbirds attracted by the permanent waters, and then on down past Lake Eyre. Both the largest lake and lowest elevation point in Australia, almost a third of the continent drains into Lake Eyre. Not that you could tell when I visited as it was totally dry, one enormous shimmering expanse of salt, a stunning sight nonetheless. At this point it occurred to me that I was knocking off more places I'd always wanted to visit than I was target species. The Flinders Ranges were another such place. This impressive chain of mountains features in plenty of tourism ads for Australia because they are so spectacular, but I had never made the effort because until recently there were no birds in the Flinders that didn't occur elsewhere. But word was that in the new checklist the Flinders Ranges form of Striated Grasswren was to be promoted to full species status. Now I had a reason to go. And after spending one of the coldest mornings of my life stuck out on the all too exposed slopes of Stokes Hill, I finally tracked one down. I was now free to move on to the rendezvous point at Lyndhurst on the Strzelecki Track where after a long morning's search I added another grasswren, the Thick-billed, to the list.

Lyndhurst is the traditional site for Chestnut-breasted Whiteface, a bird I no longer needed, which was looking kind of lucky as for a while there I saw no sign of them. It wasn't until Dave and his travelling companion Marco arrived that their vehicle disturbed a group of four whitefaces which were conveniently herded towards me for my second up-close encounter with this bird in a month. As Dave pulled up I asked him what his secret to conjuring the whitefaces was. He loudly exclaimed, 'Because I'm a South Australian mate!'

Bloody South Australians. It's as if they are fearful that they're going to be forgotten by the rest of the country (too far from the action on the east coast but not as far west as Perth to claim a distinct identity) so they try to make up for it by crowing about every minor triumph. Now normally I love to see such Croweater cockiness shot down in flames, especially on the football field, but not out there. There were too many important target birds to get, most importantly, the Grey Falcon. All year Dave had assured me we would see it on the Strzelecki. The moment of truth had arrived.

CHAPTER 20

5 August, Yaningurie Waterhole, South Australia: *501 species*

Sitting atop the dune above Yaningurie Waterhole at dawn was a lesson in contrasts. The temperature was just on freezing yet I was in the middle of a dry, sun-scorched desert. The dune itself is a mighty blood red serpent commanding a view over the dull grey of the Strzelecki Creek floodplain. The surrounding countryside, having missed out on rain of any description for over a year, was dry and desolate, but water from previous years' thunderstorms had percolated through the big red bulk of the dune to seep out in tiny pools at its base attracting masses of wildlife. Supposedly, it also attracts the rare Grey Falcon, a predator that swoops in to feed on the throngs of parched birds that gather of a morning to slake their desert-created thirsts.

The Grey Falcon is an almost mythical bird. In fact, I am of the firm opinion that it doesn't actually exist. I have a theory that a cabal of evil twitchers got together to play a prank on unsuspecting birders and came up with a new species of raptor they called 'Grey Falcon'. Sure, there are photographs of alleged Grey Falcons in existence, but if you look closely you can see that they have obviously just taken a regular (and much more common) Brown Falcon and spray-painted it grey. As you can probably tell, I have never seen a Grey Falcon. Once I do I will happily join in the conspiracy but for now I hold firm that the Grey Falcon is about as real as Donald Trump's hair.

As a matter of fact in 1981 I did see a Grey Falcon. Well, I think I saw one. But Dad wouldn't stop the car. It was a family holiday in northeast Victoria and I was twelve. Like all summers of youth it seemed so much hotter than the summers of today. The family was cramped and miserable in our tiny Valiant Gallant, lost in the back-blocks of Benalla, the same countryside that the Kelly Gang had roamed eluding police a century before. Dad was particularly irritable that day as he was the one who had got us lost and was copping it from all quarters. My brother and I were playing up in the back seat and my mother had banned Dad from smoking in the car. These factors combined with the first stirrings of an undiagnosed duodenal ulcer and bowel cancer led to, as Bart Simpson would put it, 'one unhappy pappy'.

Dad's mood was further dragged down by my incessant demands to reverse the car to check out every bird we saw. Rather than uttering that ubiquitous paternal catch-cry, 'Why didn't you go before we left?', he found himself repeatedly asking, 'Why do you want to stop here? It's just another bird.' What he could never understand was that it was never 'just another bird'. It always could have been something new, something rare. Sure, every bird we had stopped for inevitably turned out to be quite mundane (or chooks, as they are known in birding parlance), the pale bird hawking over that parched field was surely the jackpot. But Dad would simply not stop.

That was a pivotal moment in our relationship; that adolescent catharsis when you realise your parents cannot sustain you as they once did – the moment you leave the nest. I began to drift apart from my father. I sought out other birdwatchers and they took me under their wing. He was one of those real Aussie blokes who loved his footy, his beer and his races, and he had a total mistrust of other men who were not interested in the same. And things only got worse when he actually started to meet my new, adult birdwatching friends. I guess, looking back now, I can see why he might have had some grounds for concern. Here was his twelve-year-old son going off to all sorts of out of the way places with strange, pasty, unshaven men wearing thick coats with binoculars draped around their necks, who always seemed to be talking about things like boobies, tits and shags. God knows what he made of 'We had a Fairy Tern down the Mud Islands.'

I was never so embarrassed as on Christmas Eve 1982 when my two worlds collided rather catastrophically. That day my father had arrived home from the annual work Christmas bash with considerably more than a skinful, just as university professor and birdwatcher Aidan Sudbury was focusing his binoculars on a male Black Honeyeater in the flowering gum trees of Seaford North Primary School. My local patch. Aidan immediately raced off to ring Mike Carter who, before he frantically dashed off to see the Black Honeyeater for himself, thoughtfully rang to tell me there was a mega rarity just around the corner. I was the second person to see this amazing bird, normally a denizen of the dry country north of Victoria, driven to the coast by one of the worst droughts in recorded history. Mike was the third. He was ecstatic. This was a new bird for his Victorian list. For me it was new bird full stop.

This was in the days before mobile phones, and rather than use a phone box to contact the birdwatching grapevine, as Aidan had done, Mike asked to use my home phone. My elation was immediately wiped as I remembered the state Dad was in. For an agonising hour I had to endure the naked clash of the two most influential adult men in my life. There was Mike going absolutely nuts over the phone, telling various birdwatchers about the exceptional plumage of this rare visitor, totally oblivious to my Dad's seething drunken animosity. And to top it off, Mike had broken a cardinal rule of the Aussie male etiquette by having the temerity to ask for a light beer when offered a drink.

From then on I assiduously kept these disparate elements of my life well apart – until one fateful day, a couple of days after Christmas 1998, when it was all brought horrifyingly close to home.

I was staying with Dad. By this time my parents had moved from humble Seaford to the affluent canal development of nearby Patterson Lakes. Two kilometres and three tax brackets away from where we lived in Seaford, Patterson Lakes lay atop the corpse of the former bird haven, Carrum Swamp. My parents had built their dream home by the water but, cruelly, Mum was robbed of much time to enjoy it, having passed away the year before after a long struggle with cancer. Dad had been amazing in caring for her and that experience, as well as his own successful battle against bowel cancer, had certainly mellowed him. But this mellowness was to be fully tested the moment I laid eyes on the bird sheltering from the storm on our jetty.

I commented, 'It must be pretty windy out in the bay, Dad, that Crested Tern's come in to rest on the jetty.' I casually grabbed my spare set of binoculars fully expecting to see the pearl grey back, black cap and yellow bill of the Crested Tern, but instead the bird was a dark, chocolate brown tern, the kind you just don't get in Victoria. In fact it was the first Bridled Tern ever seen in Victoria. A dinky-di Christmas miracle right in my own backyard, this was my shot at twitching immortality.

Then the fear took hold. The only thing worse than dipping in the birdwatching world is if you actually see something and no-one believes you, so I raced to the phone and frantically dialled all the other twitchers I knew. But being the Christmas break they were all out twitching, hoping to find a rarity. Well suckers, the rare bird was right here! Finally I managed to rouse Mike Carter from out of the bath, of all places, and he was already on his way, still half naked and dripping I imagine.

In the meantime a thought even more horrible than a dripping, naked twitcher occurred to me: what if the Bridled Tern flew away before Mike arrived? I grabbed my bemused father and made him look at the poor bird while I directed him to its diagnostic features. Luckily Mike arrived with a couple of local birders, the indomitable Peggy Mitchell and her daughter-in-law and partner in crime, Bette, so I never had to rely on my father's dodgy birding credentials as a back-up. When Dad realised twitchers were pulling up in the drive, he exclaimed, 'Not those bloody freaks – I'm off to the pub,' and scarpered out the side door as they came in through the front. My sighting was duly confirmed, photographed and copiously noted. Then for no discernible reason, the Bridled Tern decided to brave the storm and flapped off towards Port Phillip Bay, never to be seen again.

Until my quest for twitching glory with the Big Twitch the Patterson Lakes Bridled Tern had been my greatest birding triumph. But this wayward bird is even more important to me for another reason. Within two years of this momentous sighting, my father would be dead. He had beaten bowel cancer outright, but at the time of the Bridled Tern he did not know that he was already harbouring a fatal case of lung cancer, the product of a thirty-five year, pack-a-day smoking habit. His decline was rapid – a matter of six months from diagnosis to death. In those months, as he suffered the combined ravages of the disease and the chemotherapy designed to cure it, one of his greatest sources of solace was to sit by the window and look out at the birds going about their business on the lake.

About a week before the end as he sat there, breathing with the aid of an oxygen tank, my father turned to me and said,

'You know what, Sean? I've seen a Bridled Tern in Victoria. How many people can say that?' And he smiled a very satisfied smile.

At that moment I knew that finally, after all these years, he had an understanding of my birdwatching addiction. And also at that moment I knew that I would trade all the Grey Falcons and Bridled Terns in the world to have my father back.

And so, a little over two years later, I sat shivering in the Outback dawn, waiting for the Grey Falcon. The bastard never showed.

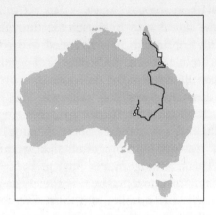

CHAPTER 21

14 August, Cairns, Queensland:
528 species

We not only missed out on the Grey Falcon, but also other important birds such as Rufous Fieldwren, Inland Dotterel and Flock Bronzewing. By the time we set up camp alongside the permanent waters of Cullyamurra Waterhole on the banks of Cooper's Creek Dave was uncharacteristically quiet. I told him, 'It's a good thing you got me that Hudwit in March or else I'd be seriously calling your creditability into question.' His only response was, 'You see, Marco, this is why you should never travel with a Victorian. They're a bloody jinx.' Marco, who is Swiss, wasn't buying into the argument and merely replied, 'I think you are both crazy.'

What Marco's earnest Swiss sensibility failed to pick up was that despite our baiting of each other, Dave and I get on exceptionally well. Actually born a Pom (with links, he claims, back to Gilbert White, one of the first naturalists in print with his delightful *The Natural History of Selborne* published in 1789), Dave comes across like an ocker Australian. He's one of the few birders my father would have hit it off with. And as much as I stir him, the fact is the reason we weren't seeing the birds he normally sees on this part of the Strzelecki is that it was such an extraordinarily dry season that away from the permanent waters of the Cooper there was not much for birds to survive on.

The Cooper is as wide as the Murray at this point and so deep here that the waterhole has never been known to dry out. Sitting by its banks is an incredibly peaceful experience. This is where the ill-fated Burke and Wills saw out the last days of their disastrous 1861 expedition. Having made it back from some of the most desolate land in the country, they slowly perished here surrounded by plenty of game, fish and water due to Burke's pig-headed refusal to accept the help of the local Aboriginal people. I could think of worse places to see out your days. Suddenly I felt tired and could easily have stayed here for a week or longer but time was moving on.

My original plan had been to accompany Marco and Dave onto the Birdsville Track, picking up Flock Bronzewing and Grey Grasswren, amongst others, before heading up into western Queensland, but I realised that would take me too far west to see Hall's Babbler so I only accompanied them for half a day or so into the parched country north of Innamincka, where again we had no luck. I parted company with them near Leap Year Bore and as they drove off in a plume of red dust I realised I was alone again. Just me and the enormity of the Outback. For about half an hour I had to focus all my mental energy on not chasing after them.

Yet again I spent another night alone in the Outback but for the first time I found the isolation disquieting. Maybe the camaraderie of the past few days triggered a desire not to be alone anymore. Maybe having knocked off one sizeable chunk of the country my body felt like the trip should be coming to an end when in reality it was only beginning. In the past month I had driven almost eight thousand kilometres; in the coming month I expected to be driving just as far. I should have been excited: I had just passed the five hundred mark and had the whole of Queensland, the most bird-rich state in the country, stretching before me, yet part of me just wanted to go home.

That feeling grew stronger over the next few days. I camped by a dry little watercourse called Candradecka Creek that hardly rates a mention on any of the maps, and all night I was unable to shake an unsettling feeling of being surrounded by malevolence. Normally as the darkness of the night closes in I can reason away such irrational thoughts; that night I couldn't.

After a fitful sleep I rose before dawn for another stakeout for Flock Bronzewing. They failed to show, as did the Grey Falcon, which had been reported from this area. To make matters worse, I later heard from Dave and Marco that the next night whilst camped by a waterhole near Birdsville they had a phenomenal forty thousand Flock Bronzewings come in to drink. I would have settled for just one.

Back at Innamincka the waterhole on the Cooper was still several metres deep. Even though it had hardly rained here for years, the creek was still teeming with life courtesy of monsoonal rains that had fallen several months earlier in the Gulf Country many hundreds of kilometres away. The wildlife follows the water. Big flocks of Cockatiels and budgies and corellas came in to drink before heading out onto the parched plains to pick through the deserted seeds of the previous boom times. Pelicans and cormorants and herons fed on the fish that had gathered in these residual pools waiting for the next big flush of water from the north.

And like the wildlife, the water attracts all sorts of people. This was my second visit to Innamincka, having headed up this way the previous year in a sort of dry run for the Big Twitch. I had come from the Queensland side, travelling for fourteen hours from Cunnamulla over six hundred kilometres of bone-shattering corrugations. By the time I rolled into Innamincka it had been dark for two hours. I was completely knackered to the point of delirium and all I wanted was a bed to fall into. If it did occur to me that there were an awful lot of cars in the carpark for a remote Outback pub, I was too tired to dwell on it. I opened the door of the hotel to be greeted by the beaming face of Dick Smith, adventurer, entrepreneur and Australia's most famous nerd. Before I could process any of this information properly he thrust his manic dial right up to mine and enthused, 'Are you one of us?!'

'One of us?' I thought, startled. 'Oh my God, it's true. Dick Smith really is a pod person.'

What he actually meant was whether I was with the charity car rally he was involved in. The inn was full as was the dining room and

I had to eat my dinner in the midst of the celebrity auction. Dick Smith was running about like an excited toddler cajoling all the middle-aged businessmen to put in a bid for the items. I left when Dick started getting way too excited about a life-sized Elle Macpherson poster.

I was chatting to a guy outside near my car when I noticed all the rally participants spilling from the pub. Just then a four-wheel drive decked out in flashing coloured lights started doing burnouts in the carpark with a guy in a harness performing gymnastic tricks off the back of the car. This was all getting far too surreal for me so I decided to leave. At that precise moment the first of the fireworks started. The guy I had been talking to was the pyrotechnician. Right where I was standing he had laid out his incendiary devices and they were going off in a series of exceptionally loud explosions. Through the flashing lights, smell of gunpowder and overwhelming cacophony, there was Dick Smith in an apoplexy of excitement. Fourteen hours of absolute solitude then this. I was in hell. But even then I knew I would have revenge on Dick, for I knew that if one day I could break the Australian birdwatching record and then write a book about it, I could knock Dick Smith off his perch as Australia's number one nerd. Oh God, shoot me now.

Happily Innamincka was far quieter on my second visit, though it was busy compared to the road to Tibooburra. On three hundred-plus kilometres of track I passed just four vehicles. The countryside was even drier than it had been the previous year and there were far fewer birds. I only stopped a couple of times, including once atop a large sand dune where I managed to find another pair of Eyrean Grasswrens, this time without having to drop my trousers.

At Cameron's Corner, the point where the states of Queensland, New South Wales and South Australia meet, I brought out the footy. Physics has never been my strong point so it took me several attempts to work out how to kick the ball from South Australia into New South Wales then curl it around into Queensland until it eventually landed back in South Australia. But I finally did it – perhaps the first tri-state kick in history?

Tibooburra, in the extreme northwestern corner of New South Wales, is one of those great little Outback towns that still retain a frontier feel. Remnants of its old mining past lay strewn on the outskirts of town. Rugged hills of red boulders surround the town and further out the even redder gibber plains are interrupted by the flat topped mesas of the 'jump-up country'. The motel room was most welcome, though dipping out yet again on Flock Bronzewing and Grey Falcon was not. Sadly, I had no time for a sleep-in as I needed to get to Wompah Gate on the Queensland border by dawn to have a crack at Grey Grasswren.

This was the point at which my Big Twitch trial run had come horribly unstuck the year before. At that stage I didn't have a four-wheel drive and managed to completely trash the underside of the Toyota Cressida I had inherited from my father. There are some serious boulders and potholes on the road to Wompah Gate and even with the high clearance of the Cruiser I was worried about doing my loved one some damage. For, yes, I have to admit it, and I never thought it would happen to me, but I had become one of those guys who is in love with his car. I still didn't know my sparks from my elbow, but God I love driving the thing. Sometimes as I drove along I was overcome with a sense of wellbeing and just had to give the dashboard an affectionate pat. There would be plenty of opportunities to wear the dash down to nothing in the coming weeks as I drove across the entire length of Queensland – roughly equivalent to travelling from Paris to Moscow or from New York to Texas without ever leaving the same state.

But first there was the small matter of the Grey Grasswren. This time I was determined not to dip out but when I crossed the dingo-proof fence at Wompah Gate and entered Queensland, I was in for a major disappointment. Grey Grasswrens live only in the remote lignum swamps of the Outback. There are very few easily accessible points into this sort of habitat, the road through Pyampa Station on the Queensland–New South Wales border being one. In recent years birders reported good numbers here, but as I pulled up at the site the full impact of the drought in this part of the world fully hit me. I was expecting to be greeted with a picturesque vista – a lovely old windmill by a full dam in a vast sea of green lignum, but what had once been a vast overflow was now a desolate, dry, dusty plain. The dam was almost dry and on it the stinking carcass of a cow lay rotting in the drying mud. There was not a blade of vegetation within cooee of the dam, a result of the lack of rain and the voracious appetites of the cattle and kangaroos that had been coming in to drink the last of the dam's waters.

The first stands of lignum were several hundred metres away. Lignum grows in thick tangled clumps on inland wetlands, the foliage more like spindly twigs than leaves. In poor seasons it dies off, only to bloom into life come the next flood. The pathetic clumps of lignum that clung to drainage lines here looked like they were well beyond resuscitating and I had to walk several kilometres into the sepulchral swamp before I came across any half-decent habitat. Every step I took across this desolate plain raised a puff of grey dust which the morning breeze started to blow around in eddies.

This was the most dispiriting day of the year so far. After today I wouldn't be in the Grey Grasswrens' range for the rest of the year, so if I missed it, that was it. I was convinced I wasn't going to get it and the thought of staying overnight only blackened my mood. To fail at this first hurdle meant I would have to find one extra species somewhere further down the track and if I couldn't get this first difficult one, and there would be plenty more just as hard, then why even bother?

Despairing but pressing on grimly, eventually I heard a hopeful tinkle. ('Hopeful Tinkle' – a good biography title for a man recovering from prostate surgery). Hearing is one thing; seeing is an altogether more difficult prospect. Over the next hour the slowest chase in history ensued with me on my hands and knees, down amongst the grey powdery dust and cattle dung and roo pellets, peering into the impenetrable lignum bushes hoping for a glimpse. A movement caught my eye and I got an almost subliminal view of something darting to another bush. Somehow the birds got around behind me and ten minutes later a pair made a quick flight across twenty metres of open terrain to the next cover. Streaky backs, chunky trailing tails and a distinctive black moustachial stripe, there was no doubt they were Grey Grasswrens.

I stooged around for another half an hour with no further sign of the grasswrens. The wind had picked up, the sun was beating down and I had had enough of the shitty place. I'd had a view that allowed me to see enough of their salient features to identify these birds as Grey Grasswrens, although I never really got a sense of the birds' essence. Bugger it, I'd had it. The bird went down in the list as number 503 and it was onward to the next tick.

My sense of despair refused to lift, perhaps a reflection of the landscape I was driving through. To get to the lush northeast of the state I had to pass through its dry heart that had been devastated by drought. Leaving the desolate gibber rises I entered the broad sweep of the Bulloo River flats which were equally desolate, every blade of grass gone. Great drifts of sand had formed along fence-lines, blown in from the bare paddocks.

After all these years of trying to farm the land with European techniques you'd think we would have cottoned by now – when there is no rain the first thing that goes is the grass. Even if the drought is so dire that it kills the deeper rooted trees and shrubs, they will still stand for many years, their roots holding the soil in place. Take out the trees and shrubs and, come the first big dry, you'll have nothing but bare earth, which will very quickly blow away. A pretty simple demonstration of cause and effect, one would have thought, yet in this most drought prone of lands we are still taking out the trees and shrubs at an alarming rate. Driving through the ripped-out guts of Queensland it was astonishing to see kilometre after kilometre of bare paddocks with nothing on them – a legacy of the panic clearing of the late nineties, when the government mooted putting a moratorium on broadscale destruction of native vegetation.

It made for depressing driving, exacerbated by the amount of dead wildlife rotting by the side of the road. I gave up trying to count roo carcasses per kilometre after my first three counts tallied seventeen, twenty-three and twenty-seven. Instead I tried to remember the name of every kid in my year at school, but that eventually depressed me even more so I started to count dead Emus. That took more skill as I could travel for as many as twenty kilometres between piles of feathers. The Emu is either less common or much smarter than the kangaroo. Perhaps it is just quicker at dodging road trains. It was like this for the best part of a week as I made my way through towns that sound like they were named out of Outback central casting – Thargomindah, Cunnamulla, Augathella (Home of the Meat Ant, according to the town sign) and Muttaburra (home to the Muttaburrasaurus, complete with a life-sized model).

Throughout all this death, gloom and carnage there were a few highlights, though. A patch of flowering Coolabah trees near Thargomindah that yielded hundreds of woodswallows and a few Painted Honeyeaters, a rare bird that I had missed down south over the summer and one that I really needed.

I finally picked up Hall's Babbler on 'Bowra', a working sheep and cattle property just outside Cunnamulla run by Ian and Julie McLaren, though I managed to dip out on Chestnut-breasted Quail-thrush and yet another Grey Falcon as well as picking up another puncture out on the backblocks.

And so, just shy of forty days in the desert, I drove up to the lookout on Mount Stuart on the outskirts of Townsville and gazed longingly at the ocean. To steal a line from David Andrew, former editor of *Australian Birding*, I felt like I was a birding Moses, looking out over the Land of Milk and Honeyeaters. For birders, the north-east of Queensland is indeed the Promised Land. More birds squeeze into its rainforests, reefs, swamps and woodlands than in any other part of the country.

I was especially pleased to have hit the coast at Townsville as it holds a very important place in my personal story. My mother was an only child but she bonded so closely with her cousin Kay that they were more like sisters. For the first seven years of my life Kay and her family lived next door to us. My cousin Michael, though five years older, was my closest friend and I was devastated when Kay's husband Frank moved them up to Townsville for work and to be closer to their eldest son. Over the years I visited often, to go birding as well as to catch up with family, and Townsville became a second home.

I hadn't actually been there since 1991 when I drove up from Melbourne with my Mum. Not exactly Kerouac, but a road trip nonetheless. Frank had died a couple of years earlier and Kay was in the final stages of breast cancer. In the eleven years since, Townsville had kicked on – in places it was almost unrecognisable. It was like seeing a family member for the first time in years: they might look different but there is a familiar resonance to their presence. The huge mango tree in the backyard of Kay and Frank's Housing Commission place had been cut down to make way for a subdivision. It had obviously been sold to a private developer and I noticed the washhouse that had been home to a family of Green Tree Frogs was also gone. Like the frogs, any traces of the people who once lived there had been obliterated, covered up with a fresh coat of paint and some aluminium cladding.

I could happily have rested up in Townsville, but I was due in the Torres Strait in a week's time so after a day of replacing tyres, doing washing and sending emails, I was off moving ever further north, picking up as many ticks in a couple of days as I had over the previous month. By the time I reached Cairns I'd had but a taste of the delights of the tropics. There were Spotted Catbirds, Macleay's Honeyeaters and Grey-headed Robins in the rainforests. A dazzling male Victoria's Riflebird gave a bravura performance, flashing his iridescent velvet blues and blacks as he celebrated stealing a scone from my plate at the Ivy Cottage Tea Rooms in the little village of Paluma. There were Crimson Finches on the edge of the canefields and Green Pygmygeese in the wetlands. A pair of Beach Stone-curlew circled noisily around my budget motel room in Cairns at night.

I should have been flying high but in reality I was exhausted in both mind and body. Perhaps it was the sudden humidity of the coast, or maybe sheer exhaustion after driving an average of two thousand kilometres a week for the past six weeks, but I was starting to feel fluey and one of my glands had swollen into a rock-hard lump in my throat. I dropped in at the doctor's to see what shots I'd need for the Torres Strait. This was predominantly a clinic for travellers so the doctor usually only treated ear infections, coral cuts and various backpackers' social diseases. He'd never had a patient heading to Torres Strait before so was a bit flummoxed as to what I would need to take. Looking up the books, he told me that while there had been recent cases of Japanese encephalitis they generally occurred only in the wet season. As I was leaving too soon for any precautionary shots to be effective, he suggested I simply avoid being bitten by mosquitoes. Easy for him to say; he wasn't going to be spending his time trudging through mangrove swamps trying to find new birds for Australia.

He gave me a shot for Hepatitis A and asked amid the general conversation if I had any other health problems. I told him about my travels and how tired I was and mentioned the swollen gland. He felt it, looking very serious, and inquired whether I'd ever had mumps. Mumps? That can make you sterile. I figured that with all the DEET-based insect repellant I'd been slapping on my body over the year (not to mention lack of a partner) my chances of becoming a daddy were pretty shaky anyway, but mumps? This was serious.

Unfortunately the doctor didn't finish his sentence. Sidetracked by my story about catching the plane with Senator Meg Lees, he proceeded to launch into an impassioned tirade on the leadership of the Democrats and barely drew breath for ten minutes. I never found out what he thought the lump might be and I left for Cape York Peninsula wondering whether I should have got my sperm frozen before I embarked on this adventure.

One of my longest held dreams (apart from the one in which I am transformed into a cartoon character and get to hang around with the Scooby Doo gang – that Daphne, she's a fox!) had been to make it to Cape York. And as I left the bitumen north of Lakeland, after yet another blowout, I was finally there in one of the great frontiers. Pity I was feeling so crappy. The swelling had hardened into a golf ball in my throat and I winced in pain every time I turned my head to take in another stunning vista.

Many imagine that Cape York is all jungle and are rather disappointed when they first get there to realise that ninety per cent of it is woodland. To me this is what makes this place so special. Cape York is roughly the size of Victoria yet only a fraction of it has been cleared. The woodland seems to stretch on forever, an absolutely thrilling sight for someone who has grown up amongst fragmented remnant blocks of habitat. The bird life was incredible. Some, like the White-throated Gerygone, will spend the summer down south at places like Chiltern while others – the Yellow Honeyeater and Black-backed

Butcherbird, for example – don't get much further south. And then there is the Golden-shouldered Parrot.

Hammered by trapping for the aviary trade, and the introduction of cattle grazing and the resultant change in fire regimes, this exquisitely beautiful parrot is now found in only a fraction of its former range. The only site I knew of was adjacent to the main road. When I arrived several hundred of the smelliest cattle I have ever come across were crowded around the dam where I had been told the parrots also liked to loaf during the heat of the day. I usually don't mind the smell of cattle – quite invigorating, really – but these beasts reeked so badly I couldn't get near the dam without gagging. Instead I wandered through the woodland, scanning the ground ahead for feeding parrots. I should have been looking above me for when I did there was a group of about eight Golden-shouldered Parrots sitting quietly in the trees, occasionally calling softly to each other, a kind of laidback chuckle. All the birds I could see were females or immatures, lovely birds in themselves but without the wow factor of the adult males. I would have stayed longer but the golf ball in my throat throbbed with every pulse of blood. Reluctantly I headed off and reached the mining town of Weipa just before dark.

Weipa is the Cape's largest settlement. Built on the back of an enormous bauxite deposit, the town has a shopping centre, motel and sports clubs to cater for the miners and their families. I had been planning to camp out in the rainforest for a couple of days but decided my body needed some dude comforts. I ate in the hotel's restaurant, slept a lot and did the odd bit of birding. Such is the abundance of birdlife in the tropics that over a couple of days I managed to see around eighty species without having to work too hard, though I dipped out on the Spotted Whistling-Duck, a New Guinea species that has snuck into the northern tip of Australia and can usually be found near one or more of the three wastewater ponds around Weipa. It's typical of my quest that, while most people drive to the top of Australia to visit the spectacular waterfalls and gorges, I spend my time hanging around the shit pits.

Miraculously, a couple of days' rest was enough to clear my symptoms and, come 21 August, I was at the airport waiting for my flight to Cairns and then Horn Island, where I'd begin a nine-day cruise through the Torres Strait. For most people a tropical cruise would involve snorkelling, sunbaking and fishing. Me, I'm looking forward to mangroves and mudflats with a bunch of other freaks who are into the same things. I was raring to go, because I'm a twitcher, that's what I do. Or maybe my enthusiasm was due to the golf ball moving from my throat into my brain.

CHAPTER 22

26 August, Saibai Island, Torres Strait:
561 species

With the stroke of a colonial pen in 1879, it was decided that the
islands of the Torres Strait belonged to Queensland despite the fact
that some of them were less than a decent drop kick away from the
New Guinea mainland. One hundred and twenty-three years later a
group of ten twitchers gathered aboard the yacht *Jodie Ann II* at
Horn Island hoping to exploit this historic anomaly in order to add
some New Guinea species to their Australian lists. When I originally
compiled my list of 705 species I hadn't included any birds from this
part of the world so anything that wandered over from New Guinea
would be a bonus.

I had already added two new birds to my list before we set sail,
having come in to Horn on the morning flight. I managed to bump
into Bill Watson, who had already been on the island a couple of
days, and he showed me a good spot in the mangroves where I
picked up Red-headed Honeyeater, Shining Flycatcher and my first
mozzie bite. Most of the other participants were arriving in the afternoon which is when I thought I'd be arriving too. I'd been planning

a big night out in the fleshpots of Cairns, thinking I could sleep in the next morning. I'd even confirmed with Mike Carter that I'd see him on that flight. Just as I was heading out the door I checked my ticket and realised I was actually on the early flight, too late to get in touch with Mike and inform him of my error. Mike almost got himself thrown off the plane as, thinking I was running late, he tried to hold it up to allow me to board.

When Mike finally arrived with the others in the afternoon he had some very bad news. We were meant to be going to Ashmore Reef in October in this same boat. I knew that they were one short, and so desperate was I to get out there that, if worse came to worst, I was going to offer to pay for the other berth myself – my chances of getting to seven hundred were negligible without the minimum of five species I could get out at Ashmore and nowhere else. But Mike's news was that the skipper had accepted another charter. No other skipper was mad enough to ferry a bunch of tick-hungry twitchers out on the ocean for a week at a time, so it was goodbye seven hundred. It was a rather inauspicious start to what should have been one of the highlights of the year. There was nothing to be done so I had to surmount my disappointment and make the most of what I had – nine days cruising in the tropics. Perhaps I'd pick up an unexpected five species and wouldn't need Ashmore anyway.

By the afternoon all ten of us had gathered on the dock at Horn Island ready for our assault on the Torres Strait Islands. Perhaps assault is too strong a word as I doubt that a posse of middle-aged teachers, accountants, engineers and public servants would strike fear into anyone's heart, though the residents of Dauan Island, our first destination, looked quite shocked as we stormed their beach at first light the next morning. We were all loaded up in camouflage gear, wielding an awful lot of hardware and raring to go. The entire village turned out to bemusedly watch us come ashore on the *Jodi Anne*'s dinghy.

Dauan Island is a picturesque, continental island with a white sand beach and a dominant central mountain. The tides only allowed us to spend a couple of hours there, so we hustled our way over to the uninhabited side of the island to check out what was around. Though quite close to New Guinea, the birds still had a distinctly Australian flavour but I managed a few newies, including Mangrove Golden Whistler and Eclectus Parrot, calling loudly as it flew over the island as if in some sort of traditional island greeting.

It was quite an esteemed party that the Eclectus greeted. All ten of us had seen well over six hundred and fifty Australian birds (hence the need to visit the extremities of the country in order to find new ones), and there were some serious birdwatching heavyweights on board, including the two people with the biggest lists in the country, Mike Carter and Fred Smith, who between them have almost a century of Australian birding experience. In comparison the rest of us were relative newcomers, although Bill Watson had been on the scene for a while, having been part of the first generation of twitchers, in the seventies, who regarded birding as a sport as much as a deadly earnest study and Bill still birds with that same spirit of fun. A school principal used to getting his own way, even on this first morning he was starting to get a bit antsy over the drawn-out debates as to the identity of a particular kingfisher or whether the Little Bronze-Cuckoo that one person claimed to have heard was actually a Broad-billed Flycatcher.

It was a long time since I'd been birdwatching in a group and I'd forgotten just how charged the dynamics could become. Especially amongst really good birders, a sense of competition inevitably develops. Sometimes it can be a fine line between healthy competition and a sniping battle of personalities and egos. Within minutes the race to be the first to call every bird was on, some coming the occasional cropper with a rash early call. It had happened to me before and it can be very embarrassing, especially if you mistake something very common for a rarity. The fear of this embarrassment has probably made me too conservative and often I'll sit on a sighting until I am absolutely certain, by which time somebody else has usually seen the bird and is incredulous that I hadn't been able to identify it.

Others hold what they have seen close to their chests for other, more competitive reasons: waiting for the moment they can trump somebody else's sighting. 'Well, Mangrove Golden Whistler is nice, but didn't you see the Flame-crested Ooomidoodle Bird? It was just back there in that tree. It was so obvious I thought everyone must have seen it.' On more than one occasion a statement such as this forces the rest of the group to substantially backtrack for a bird they have missed. It is a risky strategy, however, for if the bird has flown off, which birds tend to do, the deprived twitchers start to question whether it was ever there in the first place. Especially if they twig that there is no such thing as an Ooomidoodle Bird.

All this, just in the first couple of hours. The next few days were set to be very interesting.

Whereas Dauan had that tropical paradise feel, Boigu Island, our next port of call, is a big flat swampy blob of land surrounded by shallow, muddy seas. The only village clings to the one substantial beach on the whole island. The rest of the coast is forbidding mangrove swamp filled with crocs and in the wet season the interior of the island becomes a massive lake that is also filled with crocs. Just across from Boigu is the New Guinea mainland but, try as I did, I was unable to see any birds flying above its intimidating land mass to get my New Guinea list kick-started.

We arrived with enough time to check out the lay of the land before sunset. The little tin dinghy (tinnie) was the only way for us to get ashore but it only held half of us at most so usually we were ferried in two or three groups. The first party landed and almost immediately saw a Singing Starling, a highly sought-after New Guinea species. By the time the rest of us arrived it had flown. Those of us who didn't see it rushed around the village desperately searching every tree, much to the amusement of the locals who rarely have white people visit, aside from white bureaucrats and doctors – and now these crazy birdwatchers. I'm surprised they haven't tried to secede. Everyone eventually got to see the Singing Starling and the irony is, every other time we visited the village it was about the most common bird. All that angst for nothing, aside from providing some free entertainment for the villagers.

I was about to provide a whole lot more. On our final day at Boigu we were all coming back from a day birding the interior of the island. I had finally landed Pectoral Sandpiper, but aside from that the afternoon's birding has been hard work for little reward. As we headed back to the dock, Mike, Bill and I straggling at the rear, two large pigeons flew in from the general direction of New Guinea. As they passed overhead the rosy glow of the setting sun really showed up their plum-coloured bodies. They were Collared Imperial-Pigeons, one of the species we were specifically hoping to see. By this stage the others were strung out along the length of the village, too far away to be able to see what we were looking at. For all my selfish sins, I must have a certain dash of altruism because I immediately worried that they'd miss out on these cripplers. It is one of the paradoxes of twitching that it is those who don't get a crippler that wind up in agony.

So, barely having time to look at the birds as they flew over, I began sprinting after the others, yelling for them to turn back. But as I reached each person with the news, they simply charged off in the direction of the birds rather than passing it on to the next person down the line, which meant I had to run the entire length of the village screaming, 'Collared Imperial-Pigeon! Collared Imperial-Pigeon!' The others might have had difficulty hearing me but the villagers certainly didn't and they all came out to see what this crazy whitefella was up to. To make matters worse, as I ran along the zip on my backpack came undone and its contents began to spill out. By the time I got to the last member of our group I could barely speak. They'd bolt off after it and I was left panting on my hands and knees, my gear strewn along the length of the village and the entire population of Boigu collapsing with laughter.

Of the others, only Fred was able to get a tickable view of the pigeons, which made for a rather subdued evening aboard. And this was not the only little storm cloud brewing over us. There was also the pratincole protocol. The Australian Pratincole is a graceful wader that spends most of its time marching along the ground but when it takes flight it does so on elegant swallow-like wings. At the end of each day we did what is referred to as a bird-call, in which someone goes through the list of birds and whoever has seen that species yells out. I find it can be a rather tedious process at times. For Bill Watson it was like pulling teeth. Mike, who organised the trip, automatically assumed the role of recorder and led the bird-call, a situation that I'm not sure everybody was completely happy with.

When Mike got to pratincoles everybody agreed on Australian, but then somebody chimed in that they'd seen an Oriental Pratincole as well. Another couple of people concurred. Oriental Pratincole was quite unusual for the time of year and so far east – there are very few records for coastal Queensland. Mike and I had been through the flock of pratincoles with the telescope and hadn't seen anything but Aussie Prats. Mike grills the Orientalists, who'd looked at it through binoculars and noticed a much darker bird, which would suggest Oriental. I volunteered that we had scoped those birds for a better view and while there was a darker one it lacked the distinctive throat pattern of an Oriental. One of the others immediately and without any problem backed down saying they must have made a mistake. The others remained adamant that the bird was too dark to have been anything but an Oriental.

Looking for a way around the impasse and not wanting to antagonise anyone by directly challenging them, I offered the old two-bird theory: 'Maybe there was another darker bird and it had flown away before we could scope it?'

'Yes there must have been,' came the grim-faced reply.

Who knows if there was a second bird? There may well have been but I think Mike put Oriental Pratincole down with a question mark, a move that I suspect wasn't too warmly received as after that night two bird-calls were held. Officially it was done because people worked to different time frames. Mike liked to have a shower and freshen up before he settled down to write up his notes for the day; others liked to get it done straight away. But a schism was definitely developing and as a result we had the phenomenon of the double bird-call. This drove Bill absolutely bonkers as now he had two lots of tedium to rail against.

Things could have got worse. The next day, with half of us in the *Jodi Anne*'s tinnie and the rest of us in a local's boat, we explored the Boigu River, a mangrove lined channel that splits the island in two. Our deckie managed to spot what ten pairs of birders' eyes had missed: a juvenile Spotted Whistling-Duck hiding on the bank amongst the mangrove roots, desperately trying not to wind up in the dinner pot of our guide. This was the bird I had gone specifically to Weipa to see so I was particularly relieved. The trouble was that the other boat was further up the creek and it was a tense wait indeed before they got back to see the bird.

After this incident and another, in which one group got onto an unusual bird of prey that could well have turned out to be a new bird for Australia, it was decided that whenever the party split in two we would use the yacht's walkie-talkies to keep in touch in case one group found something interesting. The first test of the technology came when we headed to the other main island in the northern straits, Saibai Island.

After a couple of days' hard slog on Boigu and a fairly rough overnight crossing, the group was a little low on energy on our first morning there, at least until we got onto some more Collared Imperial-Pigeons down past the village cemetery and everybody finally saw them. Saibai had as many species as Boigu, but it didn't seem alluring. Perhaps it was just the tiredness. I did manage to add two new species, Little and Shining Bronze-Cuckoos. I expected to see both further south later in the year, particularly the quite common Shining Bronze. I'd actually heard one in January near Port Fairy and hadn't bothered chasing it up, figuring I'd see it at some stage during the year. I didn't. When I told the others this they couldn't believe I'd missed it. To shatter my credibility even further I admitted that I hadn't seen either species of triller. Again, I'd heard White-winged Triller in January, this time at Chiltern, and again I'd been too lazy to chase it. The others were astonished at this, particularly Chris Lester, who claimed he'd seen both species on this trip and hadn't bothered telling me because he assumed I'd have knocked them off ages ago. To rub it in, a few minutes later he pointed to a female Varied Triller in the bush in front of us. Ross and Jan Mullholland saw it immediately but I couldn't. Eventually the whole party was onto it and I still couldn't see it and this bush was only ten metres away. Either they were all in on an elaborate joke or I have a blind spot when it comes to trillers. I looked stupid either way.

For a few years after my twenty-first birthday when I turned my back on a typical party and went searching for Black-eared Miners instead, I always tried to see a new bird on my birthday. That lasted until I was twenty-six and failed in my attempt to see King Quail on French Island. Since then I'd never bothered and celebrated my birthday in the usual way: work colleagues singing a half-arsed version of 'Happy Birthday' and a few drinks at the pub. But in 2002 I hoped it would be different. Unfortunately I'd accidentally let slip that it was my birthday to the others. The boat's chef immediately said that he could make me a birthday pav and with the promise of another half-arsed rendition of 'Happy Birthday', I prayed that at least I might get a new species.

My prayers were answered. Waiting for the tinnie to take us ashore on the morning of my birthday a pod of Irrawaddy Dolphins breached the surface right next to the boat. I had never seen this tropical species before so it was a birthday tick, even if it was only a mammal. Once ashore, the schism in the group finally cracked into open rebellion. Mike had suggested we return to the cemetery area as that was where the Red-capped Flowerpecker, the main bird we were after, had been seen in the past. Some of the others decided they'd had enough of Mike calling the shots and announced they were going to the opposite end of the village. I preferred Mike's option, as did Bill Watson and Neil McCumber. As we started to walk away, Warwick Pickwell, who had more mates in the other group, changed his mind and joined us, saying to me, 'I'm going to stick with Mike like glue. Wherever he goes, that's where the rare birds turn up.'

For the first hour or two we saw nothing new and then a heavy downpour forced us to retreat to the newly built shelter in the middle of the cemetery. Before the rain had fully eased, Bill's ants got the better of his pants and he was up and out birding while the rest of us stayed in the shelter chatting. Suddenly Bill yelled, 'What's this flowerpecker with a red breast and red cap?' There is only one thing it possibly could be: a Red-capped Flowerpecker. This is another New Guinea species known previously from only two records, both at this exact location. Sensational. We tried contacting the others on the radio but there was no response, and as the village on Saibai stretched out for a couple of kilometres, there was no way I was going to run that far to tell them this time. They didn't find out until a couple of hours later and I must say they took the news with great magnanimity. They spent the entire afternoon at the cemetery but the bird failed to show. We had to leave for Darnley Island that night, and the tragedy is that on the follow-up trip a week later another party saw the flowerpecker on the same branch at exactly the same time of day. I felt terrible for those who had dipped out, especially Fred. It had taken Fred almost eighty years to get here, and it was probably his only chance for a Red-capped Flowerpecker. All that night as we ploughed through the heavy seas to Darnley which sits on the edge of the Coral Sea I noticed that Fred was poring through the New Guinea bird book, returning time after time to the flowerpecker page.

Dawn finally arrived to reveal a real Robinson Crusoe–style island. The village was on the opposite side of the island to our mooring, and looking up at its hills and untouched beaches it was easy to fool ourselves into thinking we were the first people ever to lay eyes on it. This illusion was shattered once we were on the island. A big funeral for a community leader was taking place and the airstrip, perched on the tip of the island, was in constant use as light planes dropped off dignitaries from all the other islands.

There were far fewer birds than on Boigu or Saibai, but there was still plenty of interest. Doves were everywhere, hundreds of Bar-shouldered Doves, a common bird on the mainland, and dozens of Rose-crowned Fruit-Doves, much more scarce back in Australia. There were also familiar birds such as orioles and white-eyes that seemed to show so much variation, some of us felt we might be looking at different species. Maybe days and days in the tropical sun were playing tricks on our eyes.

It had certainly taken a toll on the bulk of the group. After our first foray into this steeply inclined island, many decided to take it easy and spend the day on the beach or on the boat. Neil McCumber and I even took some time out from birding to go snorkelling on the coral reef around the island. It was such a sensational experience – the amount of life in these waters was simply astonishing – that I found it hard to drag myself away, but Neil and I finally headed off in a half-hearted attempt to track down Bill, who had not returned from the morning's sojourn. I think the constriction of being with the group had finally got to him and he needed to do a geographic away from everyone. We found him, late in the day, red-faced but otherwise fine. He had walked most of the island, finding a wild paw-paw tree that provided his lunch, and was as happy as Larry is often reputed to be.

Still, Neil and I had a great day of it. As lovely as the rest of the group were, they were all much older than me and although Neil was well into his forties, he and I share a similar juvenile humour and many cultural reference points. While I appreciate the dry humour of Chris Lester and have much in common with Mike, in some ways Neil was my release valve on this trip – I even found myself enjoying his improbable, bawdy stories. Not only is Neil a great storyteller, he is also the jammiest twitcher I've ever known. On more than one occasion he has been the last person to see a rare bird. Someone coming along even minutes later would dip out as the bird would have flown off just after Neil had seen it. I'm not saying he'd throw rocks at these birds to scare them off before anyone else could see them, rather that he had the amazing knack of turning up at the last possible moment.

But the cosmic forces that rule twitching have a way of evening things out and we were just about to miss out on what could have been the bird of the trip. The three of us were heading back when we bumped into Fred and Mike. We stopped to ponder the identity of a raptor, eventually deciding it was only an immature Pacific Baza, the common bird of prey on the islands. During our deliberations Fred had wandered away and when we came across him on the track a few minutes later he asked us if we had seen the strange dove. For two minutes he had been watching a bird the likes of which he said he'd never seen before. He hadn't called us over because he didn't want to scare it. It had flown off anyway, apparently in our direction, but the rest of us had missed it. Back on the boat Fred picked up the New Guinea book he had forlornly been flicking through the previous night and very quickly found the bird he was after – Black-billed Cuckoo-Dove, a new species for Australia.

We tried for it again the next day, with no luck. Fred later submitted his record to the rarities committee, who narrowly voted against accepting the record, not necessarily because they didn't believe Fred but because it is very difficult for an individual observer to get a sighting through without corroborating evidence, no matter what their reputation. If only he had been able to alert us to the bird's presence we all could have ended up with quite a coup.

The rest of the trip felt a little anticlimactic after this despite visiting two more islands: Dove Islet, a small, uninhabited cay where we found breeding terns, including my old friend the Bridled Tern, and Warraber Island, which had good numbers of waders for us to sort through. Our final night celebrations were curtailed somewhat by the rough conditions. At one stage the wind registered thirty-seven knots and the waves rose to three metres. Most retreated to their cabins for the bumpy overnight ride home, leaving a rather flat ending to what had been some extraordinary birding. Despite a couple of disappointments everyone had seen at least two lifers and got to experience an amazing part of the world that very few get to see, and we'd done it in relative comfort and style. I added eight lifers and twenty-two new birds for the year, four of which I couldn't possibly have seen elsewhere.

The *Jodi Ann* was a delight to sail on – a beautiful yacht of almost seventy feet, it looked just like a tropical cruise boat should, though cabin size was a bit of a shock. I was sharing with Mike and despite ours being slightly larger than some of the other cabins, the only way I could stand up was to leave the entrance hatch open, so that my head poked out, gopher-like, onto the deck. But after spending weeks alone in the Outback, I'd been grateful to spend rare time in the company of people I liked who all shared the same passion I did. For nine days it was nothing but looking at birds, talking about birds and thinking about birds. It was all so pure, so intense. And now, I couldn't wait to be alone again.

CHAPTER 23

9 September, Mission Beach, Queensland:
599 species

After nine days of glorious drifting about the Torres Strait I was thrown back into the depressing reality of the modern world at Cairns Airport, where I had only minutes to spare before my flight to Weipa was due to take off. The ever so helpful guy at the check-in informed me that the Weipa flight was closed and that even though I had a ticket I was too late. I'd have to wait for the next day's flight. When I forced the issue he admitted that he could get me on the plane but not my luggage. I informed him through gritted teeth that I had to drive to Hobart, the absolute opposite end of the country, in exactly twenty-two days, and I had a hell of a lot of birdwatching to squeeze in between now and then, so I couldn't afford any delays. He seemed shocked into action, and maybe just a little bit frightened, and checked my luggage in.

It turned out the plane was delayed by more than half an hour. I actually had time to eat a leisurely breakfast, read the paper and go for a Tosca. At the terminal I bumped into Tony Palliser, who was about to board the flight to Horn Island to join the second of the

Torres Strait birding trips. He was simultaneously relieved to hear we'd seen some good stuff and also panic-stricken because now the pressure would be on to emulate our success. Tony was third on the twitchers' tally and to dip on things like Red-capped Flowerpecker would see Fred and Mike move even further ahead of him. Sitting that high up in the twitching order is enough to give you an ulcer. Everyone below you has more options for new birds than you and when one does turn up that you haven't seen, if you blow it you may never have the chance to catch up with that bird ever again. The flowerpecker may turn out to be a resident on Saibai and may be a relatively easy get. Or it may never be seen again. For me the Blue Rock Thrush is just such a bird. I was in one of my non-twitching phases (probably due to poverty as much as anything else) and failed to go for it when it turned up at Noosa in Queensland in 1997 – the first Australian record of a bird that normally winters only as far south as Indonesia and the Philippines. There was conjecture that it had overshot its migration due to the massive fires in Indonesia that year, a set of conditions that may never happen again. At the time I wasn't so concerned that I'd missed it, but now, as my list started to rocket past many twitchers, I know that it is a bird I will never get back. When I think of Blue Rock Thrush now I feel the anguish of regret.

Before I left Weipa I quickly checked out the sewage ponds and sure enough, now that I didn't need them for the list, there was a flock of eighteen Spotted Whistling-Ducks as well as my first Sarus Cranes of the year, and I also found my first Eastern Grass Owl, though unfortunately this one was dead, squashed flat by one of the mining juggernauts making its way down to the port. Now for the main course, somewhere I had really been looking forward to all year – the rainforests of Iron Range. One of the few areas of the country I had never visited, this place has at least sixteen species I had never seen before. The road to Iron Range is only about a hundred kilometres, but it took three bone-jarring hours to drive. Such was my enthusiasm to get there, I probably went faster than was prudent over such a dodgy road, but by the time I arrived the only damage was that the glove compartment had rattled loose. An exceptional reprieve considering I was already down to only the one spare tyre.

Iron Range was every bit as magical as I'd imagined. The largest area of lowland rainforest in the country, Iron Range was teeming with wildlife. Within just three days I added twenty species, half of which were lifers: Palm Cockatoo, White-faced Robin, Magnificent Riflebird, Yellow-billed Kingfisher, Trumpet Manucode – until this moment they had only existed for me in the bird books I would read before going to bed. Now they were before me in all their vibrancy. For once reality matched fantasy. I even caught up with that bloody Varied Triller, but of course nobody from the Torres Strait trip was around to witness that I was not completely hopeless and could actually find these birds.

What really distinguishes Iron Range from much of the rest of Australia is the amount of activity at night. The forest is literally crawling with creatures all night, including some really good birds such as Rufous Owl and Marbled and Papuan Frogmouth. On my second night I was planning to head out again for some more spot-lighting. I sought permission to search the grasslands around the Lockhart River airstrip, hoping to flush the exceedingly little known Buff-breasted Button-quail. It had just gone dark and I was finishing up the last of my dinner when I heard three blasts from a shotgun echo through the forest. In the rainforest the thick canopy overhead cuts out all starlight and it is pitch black. The cicadas had yet to crank up and in the humidity of the still tropical night it was impossible to tell how close the shots were.

Never is the vulnerability of travelling in the bush alone brought home more viscerally than when someone starts shooting firearms around you. Trying to be rational about the situation I figured that it was either (a) rangers shooting feral pigs or (b) some of the traditional owners out hunting some bush tucker. Either scenario made it too dangerous to go wandering off into the rainforest in the dark where I might be mistaken for said pigs. What kept irrationally playing on my mind, however, was option (c): that the lone gunman who had recently held a German tourist and her mother hostage in the Northern Territory had somehow made his way two and a half thousand kilometres to end up directly at my campsite looking for a new victim.

After half an hour there had not been another human sound. The cicadas had started up and the night animals were on the move. Still wary, I decided to go and check on the couple I'd seen camping about a kilometre up the road at the next campsite. It turned out that Fran and Bob, from the Whitsundays, were birders themselves and we ended up talking about all the fantastic birds we'd been seeing. There were no more gunshots so, after an hour or so spent chewing the fat, I bid them farewell and jumped back in the car to head out to the airstrip for my spotlighting session.

As I was passing the turnoff to my camp a glint in the forest caught my eye. Thinking it was the eyeshine of an animal, I turned the spotlight on it. Rather than a startled cuscus staring back at me, it was the blade of a knife thrust into the trunk of a tree. My knife. Or at least the same type of knife that I had just been preparing my dinner with. Same size, same coloured handle. I went back to my camp. No-one was around but my knife was missing from the rest of the cooking implements. As was my lantern.

It didn't make sense. Why would someone plunge my knife in a tree? Was it some kind of warning? Had I disturbed them and they wedged it into a convenient spot where they could come back for it later to finish the job? Why would they steal my lantern? Did they want to put me at a disadvantage, groping around in the dark? Thoughts of Marbled Frogmouths now furthest from my mind, I was totally wired, waiting for the onslaught, occasionally scanning the surrounding jungle for anyone lurking about. After about an hour with no attack forthcoming, I became aware that I was incredibly tired and with a resigned, fatalistic shrug I decided I might as well retire to bed – if anyone out there had malicious intent there was very little I could do about it.

I opened the tent and sitting there were both my knife and my lantern. In all the excitement I'd forgotten that I'd put them and some other valuables out of sight in the tent when I'd headed off to visit the neighbouring camp. On closer inspection I realised that the blade on the other knife was quite rusty. It had probably been stuck in that tree for years.

I had to content myself with searching for the button-quail during the day – unsuccessfully. I continued to see more new birds, though, including Frilled Monarch, White-streaked Honeyeater (found only in this part of the world) and, thanks to a tip-off from Steve Murphy, a PhD student who was up there studying Palm Cockatoos, Fawn-breasted Bowerbird. Steve had said that the bowerbird could be very tricky but as I pulled up at the site there it was sitting atop a bushy tree, belting out its rasping call. I love it when a plan comes together. It happens so rarely.

One bird I hadn't been able to get onto was the Red-cheeked Parrot. Several times I'd heard them above the canopy making their incredibly frantic songflights but I hadn't been able to get a decent, sustained view. Even so, their flights were hilarious events. They manically burst forth from the canopy screeching as if petrified that their rapid, shallow wingbeats will send them crashing into the forest below. Their flight has the same quality as the movements of someone who's fallen into the water but can't swim. As I was packing up my camp on the last morning I heard that now familiar cry but this time it got closer and, as if offering himself as a parting gift, a male Red-cheeked Parrot landed in the fig tree above me.

As I was gawping at the parrot in gratitude the campsite's resident male Australian Brush-turkey swung into action. He had come to learn that the pesky humans that kept turning up in his territory were a free meal ticket. Curse the camper who first fed this eating machine, as they have created a voracious, tenacious monster. All foodstuffs had to be safely stored away because it would quickly raid whatever was lying around. As soon as I got anything out of the car to prepare a meal it would be in like a shot. When it realised I was not forthcoming with a handout it would target my rubbish bag, tearing through it and scattering rubbish across the campground. I put a bag around the first bag and hung it in a tree. That went too. So eventually I had to store my rubbish in the car – triple bagged, but still not the greatest vehicle deodorant in the world. As I was glassing the parrot (through my binoculars, not with a broken bottle) the brush-turkey jumped into the open car and ripped into the triple bag, strewing crap all through the car and leaving a smelly deposit of his own on the front seat.

All rubbish has to be taken out of the national park so the drive out was extremely bumpy, slow and whiffy. Halfway along the track out I thought the rotting fumes must have been causing hallucinations as I came across the most surreal scene of the entire Big Twitch. In the middle of the tropical woodland, hundreds of miles from anywhere on this heavily rutted track, was a classic old-time carnival troupe. One of the trailers carrying a carnival ride had broken an axle and the convoy had halted while repairs were made. They must have been heading to the Lockhart River Community where I suspect the carnies would outnumber the locals. I didn't see any bearded ladies or dwarves but I fully expected David Lynch to walk out on set at any minute.

Normally coming back from a place such as Iron Range is akin to coming down. But the next few days promised almost as much action, though I didn't know whether it would involve a carnival. First on the agenda was Red Goshawk, on a par with Grey Falcon as Australia's most elusive bird of prey – they had eluded me for years and defeated many a better birder than I. From two different sources I had been given directions to a nest in the vicinity of Lakefield National Park. This is really a dude approach to twitching: just follow the map and the bird should be sitting there. Well it was. A magnificent imperious female on her massive stick nest in a tree overhanging the road. I felt like I was in the presence of a rock star. I was so overawed with this creature that I dared not move any closer to the nest lest I disturbed it. It looked unfazed by my presence but I remained about a hundred metres away, thereby losing a superb photographic opportunity. I had put virtually no effort into finding this rarity yet I was totally overjoyed. Absolutely elated. This was a bird I'd had no confidence of seeing and now, having got it so easily, I felt anything was possible. For the first time in the whole year reaching seven hundred seemed a tangible prospect.

That elation was dented somewhat when, half an hour later, I took a pothole a bit too exuberantly and the vehicle was thrown across the road. The oil gauge suddenly lurched to empty, and a quick check under the vehicle revealed a reddish liquid leaking out from somewhere near the rear. This was not good. Rather than head through the national park I backtracked the forty kilometres or so to the main road and the Musgrave Station Roadhouse. Once there

I launched myself under the car for the grim assessment. It turned out the leakage was coming not from the fuel tank or oil sump but was actually water leaking from the punctured tyre stored under the car. At every creek crossing it had filled with muddy water which was now harmlessly dripping out. The oil indicator had resumed its normal position too. Suitably chastened I decided not to risk the rough track through the national park and headed down the comparatively benign and quicker main track. Even so by the time I rolled into my next destination it was right on dusk and I had been on the road for an exhausting twelve hours.

Julatten is a tiny village in the hinterland behind the coastal tourist mecca of Port Douglas. It has none of the glamour, none of the luxury hotels or eighty-foot pleasure cruisers. No white shoes, white sands or fake tans. Stretched out over a couple of kilometres are a school, a couple of houses, a tavern and that's about it, but to birdwatchers there is probably no more revered place in the entire country. The one thing Julatten does have is a caravan park, now known as Kingfisher Park Birdwatchers Lodge and the one thing the caravan park has is birds. Plenty of them. In the grounds of Kingfisher Park itself is a small patch of rainforest alive with birds. You can spend the day stooging around and easily see seventy plus birds without leaving the boundaries of the park. Foremost amongst these is the highly sought after Lesser Sooty Owl.

My previous attempts to see this bird here had all been failures. The best I ever did was to find a freshly dead bird, still warm, its skull crushed by a truck taking sugar cane to the refinery. Thanks to Carol and Andrew Iles, the guides at Kingfisher Park, I managed to see it. They were so intimate with the routines of all the local wildlife that they could pinpoint the precise moment when a fledgling young bird poked its head out of the hollow and sat on the edge for a couple of minutes before flying off. I would have spent night after night wandering around forlornly in the hope that a Lesser Sooty would fly into the beam of my spotlight.

The other great advantage of Julatten is its proximity to Mount Lewis, an area of upland rainforest that is a one-stop shop for all the North Queensland endemics. Over a couple of days I completed the set with some really great birds such as Golden and Tooth-billed Bowerbird. The male Golden Bowerbird is a beautiful bird that builds one of the greatest structures in the natural world, a maypole up to three metres tall constructed of sticks and festooned with decorative clusters of flowers and lichens. Or so they tell me. You'd reckon something that big would be pretty easy to find. Even when I've had directions I've always managed to overlook them. On Mount Lewis I managed to find a female on the nest. The female was just a plain brown bird and the nest was a small cup hidden behind a vine in the darkness of a crevice of a road culvert. I could find that all right, but a bloody great three-metre structure? No chance.

I found the bower of the Tooth-billed Bowerbird after a great struggle up a steep, vine-clad rainforest slope. There's actually not much to see. Tooth-billeds don't build elaborate structures, merely scratching out a space on the rainforest floor that they decorate fussily with soft green leaves. I sat quietly by one of these platforms and waited for its owner to return. After a few minutes he did, carrying a freshly plucked leaf of the wild ginger plant. Initially startled by my presence, he darted behind the buttress of a rainforest giant. Then he cheekily poked his head around one side of the trunk and began to act rather like a child in a game of peek-a-boo. It craned its thick neck around one side of the trunk, waited until we made eye contact, then pulled back away out of sight, only to emerge on the other side to peer at me again. This went on for several minutes, an incredible cross-species interaction that brought a delighted smile to even this hardened, callous twitcher.

Though not a huge tourist destination, Kingfisher Park had a steady stream of visitors coming through. It has a deserved international reputation as a great place for birds and during the four nights I stayed I bumped into people not just from Australia, but from the UK, Europe and the States. The only other person camping there was a German woman. She and her husband had planned to migrate to Australia to set up a new business. He had sent her on ahead while he sorted out a few things at home. Weeks turned into months with no sign of him arriving. Then one day she got a call saying he would not be coming to Australia, wanted a divorce, and was marrying someone else. She was up here trying to clear her head and take stock of this bombshell.

On hearing her story I reacted the way a decent, caring Aussie bloke should: I offered her a beer. She accepted, saying it was her first alcohol in years, as she and her husband were part of the raw food movement. They would not eat any food that had been cooked or processed in any way. There must be something to it as she looked at least ten years younger than she actually was, but she did seem rather fragile, an impression furthered when, after half a glass of beer, she staggered off saying she was a bit dizzy and needed to lie down. She accompanied me on a trek up to Mount Lewis but after an hour or two suddenly became listless and I thought she must have been bored. She replied that no, she was having a good time, but if she didn't munch on her handfuls of raw vegies every couple of hours she started to pass out.

John Young didn't strike me as a raw vegetables kind of guy – perhaps he did chomp down on a few raw vegies but they would probably have been accompanied by a chunk of crocodile that he'd killed with his own hands. Dressed in khaki shorts, shirt and bush hat with an enormous Merv Hughes–style handlebar moustache, John makes Crocodile Hunter Steve Irwin seem like a pale impostor. One of the most remarkable naturalists going, John is also one of the biggest personalities. A wildlife tour guide, environmental consult- ant and natural history filmmaker, he turned up with gear and assistant in tow to do a bit of filming around Kingfisher Park, giving me the chance to finally meet this legendary character. When he found out about my quest his interest was piqued and within min- utes he had provided me with loads of information on species I still needed to get, including about five sites for Grey Falcon along the route through the Outback I had just travelled.

It is rather appropriate that John has such intimate knowledge of such a mythical bird, as he has a mythic quality himself. There are more rumours and stories floating around this guy than anyone else in the entire birding scene. Talk of a dodgy past and run-ins with the authorities abound. Whether these stem from actual incidents or from the fact that people wonder what he must be up to out there in the bush all that time, I don't know. What I do know is that if you ever need to find a bird, any bird, particularly at its nest, John Young is your man. He has an uncanny knack for reading the country and finding birds and animals in it. You'd expect someone who spends so much time in the bush to be something of an introverted hermit. You'd be wrong. John is a total extrovert. After telling him of my encounter with the Tooth-billed Bowerbird, he just happened to have a leaf of the wild ginger in his truck and he brought it out, taking enormous delight in regaling the women present with a demonstration of the sensual delights of the soft leaf. His laugh is so infectiously raucous I am surprised he gets within cooee of any wildlife.

The night we went out spotlighting he had set up his camera gear at a feeding station hoping to get some good footage of mammals. His battery ran out ten minutes before the Greater White-tailed Rat, one of the species he had come specifically to film, turned up. Comparing this dip with some of mine over the past few months, we resolved to make a nature documentary entitled 'You Should Have Been Here Yesterday', which would feature shots of the perches that rare species had just vacated only moments before.

By now it was time to head south. The total when I left Julatten was 597 so the big question was what the milestone six hundredth bird would be. In the drier country around Big Mitchell Creek I fairly easily picked up White-browed Robin, an uncommon and much underrated bird, but I dipped out on Black-throated Finch, meaning that the special bird I had lined up as the six hundredth would actually only be 599. That's if I managed to see it.

For such an enormous bird (third only in size to its relatives the Ostrich and Emu) the Southern Cassowary is notoriously difficult to see, being remarkably adept at disappearing into its rainforest habitat. And to compound matters, most of its rainforest habitat has been lost to sugar cane fields. There is something romantic about the sugar industry. The fields of green cane glistening in the morning dew are a terribly pretty sight and the image of the cane cutter is right up there with the Man from Snowy River in terms of Australian bush iconography, but man they're bad news for cassowaries.

The one area of remnant lowland rainforest that is large enough to support a population of cassowaries lies between the towns of Tully and Mission Beach. Once in the forest zone there are roadside signs everywhere warning motorists to slow down. Not many drivers take heed and an average of four cassowaries a year get wiped out, not a great figure when it is thought only forty adults survive in this part of the world. I tried the walk along Lacey's Creek hoping to pick up a Pied Monarch as bird number 599 and then a cassowary as 600. I saw neither and moved on to the Licuala Forest where I had never missed on cassowary before. This time I did.

Looking for cassowary is just that bit more exciting than looking for other birds, not only because of their scarcity and magnificence, but because they are so bloody big. If you come across one unexpectedly in the rainforest, one kick to the guts from those enormously powerful legs with their razor sharp claws and it's bye-bye bowels. So every rustle in the undergrowth creates an extra frisson of tension. The first time I saw one was back in 1987. I was so intent on watching it wandering along the track toward me as it picked at the ground for fallen fruit that I wasn't aware how close the bird was getting until it filled the lenses of my binoculars. When I looked up it was only a couple of metres away. I began to back off slowly. The bird followed. The quicker I moved, the quicker the bird, almost as tall as me, would move. In the end I was running backwards as fast as I possibly could and the bird just kept coming. It didn't seem aggressively predisposed but I wasn't keen to confirm this and I was particularly relieved when it ran off the track and into the forest. There were no such hair-raising incidents this time, and after unsuccessfully searching the tracks I headed back to the car to reconsider my options. There at the carpark was a male cassowary and his half-grown stripy chick wandering down the entrance road. Bird number 599 under the belt.

At the mangroves near the town of Cardwell I found bird number 600, a Mangrove Robin, a cute enough little black and white bird, but no Cassowary. Having clocked 600, and with nobody else around, I cut loose and did a little dance around the mangroves. It was not only a dance of joy but one of vindication, for no matter how

I did for the rest of the year, I'd at least made it to this stage. It had taken me twenty-two years to see my first 600 birds in Australia; this year I had reached that tally in just 252 days. Very few people had achieved this in their lifetime, let alone a year, so I afforded myself a moment of feeling satisfied. I only needed thirty-four to break the record and a hundred more for my real goal.

I got back in the car and started the long drive south. I was still pumped but the longer I drove the more it hit home that I didn't have anyone close enough to share the excitement of the moment. As the beautiful green exuberance of the tropics flashed by, I was reminded that when you choose to follow a lone path, you end up alone.

But still I'd seen 600 birds in a little over nine months. That's all that really matters isn't it? Isn't it?

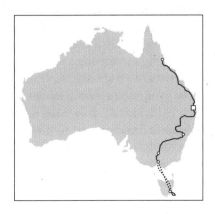

CHAPTER 24

16 September, Lamington National Park, Queensland: *608 species*

Rolling south now, target Tasmania, and the end of my first lap of the continent. As I headed down the east coast it was a matter of picking off the few remaining species I needed. I got Eastern Grass Owl at the Tyto Wetlands on the outskirts of Ingham, courtesy of a John Young tip-off. I arrived at dusk and walked the fifteen minutes to the viewing platform overlooking the area's swampy grasslands in the dark. When I got to the observation deck I was greeted by a glum British twitcher who had been waiting forlornly for over an hour for one of the owls to pop up from the thick grass.

With the typical moroseness of a dipping twitcher he turned to me, looking cynically at my spotlight, and said, 'I don't like your chances, mate.' I replied nonchalantly, 'We'll see about that.' On went the spotlight and in one of those brilliantly serendipitous moments the beam pointed directly at an Eastern Grass Owl in flight. The Brit was gobsmacked. That's how we do it in this country, mate.

For a few days my luck seemed to hold. Pied Monarch at Jourama Falls National Park, Cotton Pygmy-goose at Ross River Dam near Townsville, a detour up onto the Eungella Range near Mackay managed to snare me the little-known Eungella Honeyeater and I finally connected with Mangrove Honeyeater on the outskirts of Brisbane. After five solid days of driving I was winding my way in the dark up to the Lamington Plateau on the border of New South Wales. I love long distance driving – the sense of freedom, being out on the open highway as one landscape folds into the next – but the intense concentration involved in keeping two tonnes of machine on the correct part of the road exacts a demanding mental and physical toll. If I have been driving for five or more hours (which I had for five of the past six days) by the end of the day I am quite shattered.

Arriving at Lamington, one of my favourite places on the planet, would normally have been just the tonic for such exhaustion. The plateau overlooks the high-rise developments of the Gold Coast whose towers from this far away resemble the bones of some beach-washed sea creature bleaching in the sun. Covered in the most wonderful rainforest, and with a surfeit of bubbling creeks, waterfalls and spectacular vistas, Lamington couldn't be further from the crass, commercial world visible in the hazy distance. Within minutes of entering this heavenly green realm I usually sense a feeling of calm wash over me. But I knew what was in store, and the thought of it merely caused my already tense, exhausted body to clench just a little tighter.

If ever I had a bogey bird it was the Rufous Scrub-bird. An ancient relative of the lyrebird, it is only found in the remnant patches of Antarctic Beech that sit on a few remote mountaintops along the east coast. A link with a prehistoric Gondwanaland past, Antarctic Beech forests are straight out of *Lord of the Rings*. The massive trunks of these ancient trees are covered in a thick layer of moss that seems to absorb any sound, creating a cathedral-like atmosphere on the forest floor. Out of the dense fern cover that spreads along the ground you half expect to see a few hobbits and dwarves emerge. There was probably as much likelihood of that happening as there was of me seeing a Rufous Scrub-bird.

The nearest suitable habitat is a six-kilometre hike from the campground. It is actually one of the most beautiful paths you could ever walk but having done it so many times before, it took on the proportions of a forced march. On the first day there I bumped into Geoff Walker, who was also birding his way down the coast after completing the second of the Torres Strait cruises. It is theoretically easier to see Rufous Scrub-bird when there is more than one of you: when a singing bird is located one person secretes themselves away somewhere with a good view of the forest floor while the other sneaks around behind the bird and gradually moves it on. For the beater there is no hope whatsoever of seeing the bird, but for the ensconced observer there is a good chance the scrub-bird will dash past. As Geoff and I didn't even hear so much as a peep from a scrub-bird we were saved the stress and indignity of having to toss to see who would be the beater and who the fortunate observer and after an hour or two Geoff had to head back, leaving me to fruitlessly search for the rest of the day. I remembered talking with Geoff on the first Port Fairy pelagic back in March, when he'd seemed totally flummoxed that I was presumptuous enough to say I was going after seven hundred species for the year.

Later he confessed to me that until that day out on the Lamington track he had not only been sceptical but a little peeved at my attempt, fearing if I did manage to reach seven hundred on my first try it would somehow devalue it for everybody else. But as he left me on the mountain that day feeling quite knackered after his recent birding efforts, his attitude to my quest was turned around. He couldn't believe I was still out there trying to chase this recalcitrant bird down and thought, 'If Sean's going to put that much into it, he's welcome to the record.'

At that moment I couldn't quite believe how much effort I was putting in either. Walking out the next morning at dawn my leg muscles were in agony. I was so tired. At least I had better luck – I actually heard a bird calling. I crouched down behind a log and tried to pish it in. Pishing is the process of either sucking in air to make a kissing sound or blowing it out to make a harsh 'pshh' noise. These sounds are supposed to emulate young birds in distress and are meant to bring in small birds to investigate whatever the threat is. Sometimes it works, often it doesn't – the only guarantee is that you end up looking like a total nerd. Suffice to say the scrub-bird wasn't fooled. Though it kept singing only five metres in front of me, the undergrowth was too dense for me to locate it. It didn't call again for the rest of the day.

Morning three and as I hauled my sorry, aching carcass out along the track I calculated that I would have walked over fifty kilometres for this wretched bird by the time the day was through. The first time I did this trek in the eighties I managed to snub one of Australia's biggest movie stars. They were filming the TV movie *The Riddle of the Stinson* starring Jack Thompson. As I was jogging along the track in the pre-dawn I was startled by a nine-foot monster emerging from rainforest. It was actually the sound recordist holding a boom mic to record some ambient birdsong for the movie. We talked for a while as I explained why I was out before dawn. I later had a scrub-bird scurry between my legs as I sat on a log but it went by in such a brown blur that I couldn't be sure it wasn't a marsupial mouse or a low-flying brown meteor.

Trudging dejectedly back to camp I passed the entire film crew heading out to their location. I got sick of saying g'day to the first twenty people and completely ignored the twenty-first, who happened to be Jack Thompson. Immediately behind him was the sound guy so I stopped for a chat to tell him how I'd gone with the bird. At that stage of his career I don't think Jack was used to being snubbed because he backtracked and introduced himself. Even though he was the most famous person I'd ever met I was too tired to care and Jack slunk off looking quite hurt that I seemed to prefer the sound guy to him. Sorry, Jack, twitching does that to you – turns you into an animal.

On day three I heard a male bird singing. Dispensing with the pishing technique I decided to try and stalk the vocalist. I hit the ferny deck and with careful sloth-like movements began crawling along on my belly toward the singing. For twenty minutes I was down below fern height, among the moss and lichen and leeches, petrified that the bird would stop singing and move off. Eventually I halted, a small clearing just ahead of me as a male Rufous Scrub-bird hopped into view. Oblivious to my presence it continued bouncing along within touching distance, probing in the moss for insects. It was easy to see what an ancient bird this is – no fancy mod cons on this model, just short, stubby wings, plain brown and grey plumage and a basic beak curving simply out of its head. After thirty seconds it was gone, and so was I. I removed myself from the undergrowth and started to dance. I sang and hollered in a victory stomp. At last the bogey was off my back. I couldn't remember ever feeling that relieved. The long trek back to camp that had seemed like such a chore now felt like a skip through the park.

I was still delirious with relief when I arrived at the New South Wales border further down the range at a place called Natural Bridge. There is a house right on the border that looks like it might have been some sort of customs building. As I pulled out the football to kick it across the border, a bloke in the house peered out in utter incomprehension. He even picked up the phone at one stage, and then thought the better of it. After all, who was he going to call? The police? 'Ah yeah, g'day, it's Bert at the customs house. There's a guy here with binoculars filming himself kicking a football. Better send out the tactical response unit. Maybe the drug squad too.'

Two days later my mood was not quite so festive. I was in the Capertee Valley in central New South Wales, the heart of Regent Honeyeater country, and had not had a sniff. Driving down across the Great Divide from Grafton to Armidale to add the New England race of Forest Raven – in case it ever gets split out as a separate species – I rang David Geering, head of the Regent Honeyeater Recovery Team, hoping he would have a few leads. He told me that if I'd rung a week earlier I could have come out with him to Warwick in Queensland where he banded a few. Having just come from Queensland, that was not welcome news. There had been a couple of reports from the Capertee, the core remnant of their range, but due to the dry conditions nothing much had flowered and they'd been pretty thin on the ground there of late.

After a couple of days searching in extremely windy conditions I could confirm they were very thin on the ground indeed. I saw plenty of good birds, including Square-tailed Kite, Speckled Warbler and Turquoise Parrot but no Regents. And no Plum-headed Finch either. Driving here I had probably passed dozens of Plummy sites but had kept ploughing on, confident I would see them in the Capertee. Wrong.

By this stage it was Thursday and I had to be in Tasmania by Saturday. It looked like I'd have to come back for these two stop-outs another time, which could put a serious dent in my schedule. As the business end of the year rapidly approached I could ill afford to keep missing species that I'd have to come back for a second crack at. Prospects didn't seem to be improving when the next day I dipped out yet again on Little Bittern on the swamps near Deniliquin, and by mid afternoon I still didn't have Superb Parrot, the one bird I really needed in the Deniliquin area. To the south of Denny the open plains of the Riverina give way to the largest red gum forest on the planet, centred on the Murray and Edward Rivers. This is the breeding ground of the Superb Parrot and after hours of fruitless searching it looked like I would have to spend the night here, look for the parrots in the morning and head straight to the airport to catch my plane to Tassie. I noted with dismay that there had been a fair bit of logging activity in the vicinity of a known Superb Parrot hot spot. Perhaps this was why I was having trouble getting onto them. Just as I was about to pull the tent out of the back of the car a pair flew overhead and though I only managed a decent look at the duller female, Superb Parrot was on my list.

All that was left for me to do was to kick the footy from New South Wales into Victoria – no mean feat as to do it I had to kick the ball across the Murray River, seventy or eighty metres wide! Then I remembered that the actual border runs right on the edge of the waterline, so I found a log in the river (New South Wales), jumped over to it and kicked the ball back onto shore (Victoria). Now I could finally head home.

After almost three months I finally got to sleep in my own bed. My housemates were out when I got home and I was asleep when they came in so I didn't get to see them until breakfast time.

'Oh, you're back,' said a slightly surprised Nancy.

'Yeah. Gotta go,' I replied.

'Where?'

'Airport. Flying to Hobart. See ya.' And I was out the door.

'You know you're mad,' Nancy yelled after me.

What was mad was that while I was away Collingwood had had their best season in ten years and had made the finals. Andrew Stafford, who'd just arrived from Brisbane, picked me up at Hobart Airport and instead of going birdwatching we found a pub with a telly so that we could watch the Collingwood–Port Adelaide preliminary final. Andrew is a fellow Collingwood tragic and we spent the afternoon annoying the locals as we whooped and cheered those mighty Magpies to victory. We were in the Grand Final! There was no way I'd be anywhere else but Melbourne the following Saturday.

The omens were looking good. The Pies were in the Granny and the boat trip hadn't been cancelled despite some ominous looking weather. If it had been called off again, I think I would have slashed my wrists. This was my last chance for Southern Ocean seabirds and I needed as many as I could get. I figured I had about an even money chance of snaring five, and there was always the possibility of something even more spectacular turning up. Without them my goal of seven hundred was all but kaput.

It was a glorious day out at sea, and with twenty-four species of seabird observed everyone agreed that it was a highly successful trip. Except me. I only got two additions to my list. Finally I had a satisfactory view of Antarctic Prion and late in the day a gorgeous Southern Fulmar snuck up alongside the boat. Andrew and Chris Lester managed to see a Blue Petrel barrelling past for the briefest of moments but sadly it didn't show itself again.

Andrew and I tried to compensate that night by twitching the Masked Owl at the Waterworks Reserve site, only it turned out that Andrew didn't actually have a 'site' as such. When he was last here he just happened to turn his torch on and, as with my Eastern Grass Owl at Ingham, managed to shine it directly at a Masked Owl. We wandered about in the dark with no success until it was time for us to catch our respective planes.

As we took off I could see the snow reflecting the starlight off the surface of Mount Wellington. A little more than a week ago I was in the tropics. A little more than a week ago I thought I had a chance at seven hundred.

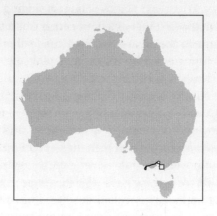

CHAPTER 25

28 September, Melbourne Cricket Ground, Victoria:
611 species

After nine months of constant birding, three months of it on the road, I collapsed in a total heap on arriving home. I was exhausted. I was over it.

To make matters worse, I sat down and reassessed my tally. Taking into account all the birds I had dipped out on, including the five crucial species I was counting on seeing during the now-cancelled Ashmore Reef cruise, I wouldn't even reach seven hundred. Whichever way I looked at it, the maximum total I could reasonably expect to see was 699 species. Mike Carter had been right. Barring a major catastrophe I would easily break the record but the thought of falling short of the magic seven hundred left me in a deep funk.

Not helping things was the fact that the Pies didn't win the flag. I really thought we had a chance. I managed to get standing room tickets to the Grand Final. We were the underdogs against the Brisbane Lions, a clearly superior team, full of champions. But Grand Final day turned out to be very wet. The rain never let up and the ground was soaked, making skilled football difficult, perfect conditions for us. I'd screamed myself hoarse singing the club theme song even before the first ball was bounced. It was a tight, ferocious, magnificent contest, the greatest game of football of my life. Except for the ending. Going down by nine points when we seemed to have the run of play was shattering.

For weeks I was haunted by the loss. Not only because it brought back a flood of memories of sitting bereft in front of the telly as a kid watching another team whip our sorry butts on Grand Final day, but because I saw a parallel with my own predicament. Being a Collingwood supporter had forged my psyche as much as growing up in Seaford. Barracking for the Pies throughout the seventies and eighties inculcated in me that working class doubt that, no matter how hard you try, no matter how worthy you are, you'll never really be quite good enough. Like the Pies I felt I could punch above my weight, put in a good effort, but I would always just fail to bring home the prize. It took me a good couple of weeks to rise above the nihilism of it all.

I only went birdwatching twice, once to the old stomping ground at Seaford, where conditions looked favourable for a very good summer, and once to Port Fairy for a pelagic. While down there we heard that an Eastern Grass Owl had turned up nearby and though it wouldn't be a year tick for me, it would be an addition to my Victorian list. We failed to find it. Similarly, at sea the next day, despite seeing a whole swag of great seabirds in superb conditions, for the first time that year I failed to add a new species on a boat trip. I was feeling about as flat as the muted ocean.

I managed to catch up with friends and family but that only reinforced that once more I was about to head off alone. As much as I enjoy my own company, there is something to be said for having someone to come home to. I was facing almost three months in some of the remotest parts of Australia at the absolutely fiercest, hottest time of the year when I could have been at home in comfort. I didn't much want to leave again, but, though I'm not sure I exactly understand why, I just knew I had to rev up again to play this thing out. There were less than three months of the year left. It was a race against time, against the heat, the monsoon, great distances, and loneliness. But mainly, it was a race against the birds. Or Jack Lemmon, to see which jalopy can make it to Paris first.

No, hang on, it's definitely a race against the birds.

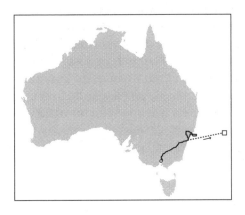

CHAPTER 26

17 October, Lord Howe Island:
616 species

Lord Howe Island has always held great allure for me. The image of Mounts Lidgbird and Gower, great rectangular chunks of rock imposing themselves majestically above a lush green island and sparkling blue lagoon, burned in my brain. That it was also chock-a-block with birds only increased its appeal. For years I'd dreamed that one day I would gaze up at those two sentinels rising dramatically out of the ocean and soak in their magnificence.

Finally I was here. But as I sat looking across the lagoon at the mountains, something wasn't right. The waters weren't sparkling; they were grey and sullen. All but the base of the mountains was completely enshrouded in dense cloud. The wind whipped off the ocean with ceaseless ferocity, bringing with it squalls of stinging rain. This was not the island paradise of my dreams. This was not the inspiring kick-start to the remainder of the year that I had been counting on.

And it had taken me so long to get to here. I actually thought I would be on Lord Howe around Easter to take advantage of the small window when both the summer and winter breeding seabirds are present, but vagrants such as Hudwits and Laughing Gulls had changed my plans. The only other time this overlap occurs is around late September–early October, so I sat down to book a flight on the Internet. Fortunately, as I did I happened to notice that a vacancy had opened up on a pelagic off Newcastle to the north of Sydney. Suddenly an opportunity had arisen for me to have one last crack at the East Coast seabirds I'd missed earlier in the year. A quick rearrangement of plans saw me delay Lord Howe by a couple of days, loading up the truck and heading off.

Thirteen hours later I rolled into Swansea where the boat was to set out the next morning. I slept in the car, and dawn broke with unseemly haste. Still groggy I noticed the first of the birders arriving at the dock. I asked one of my fellow passengers if I'd need wet weather gear for the boat. He started to rave about the catering on board and how the sausage rolls were to die for.

'Sounds good but will I need wet weather gear?'

'Oh no, it's a great boat. Really comfortable. I've never got wet once,' he assured me.

So the plastic pants and anorak stayed on dry land.

We boarded the boat and the bloke I'd spoken to immediately made his way up to the sheltered fly deck from where he didn't move for the whole day. Of course he never got wet as he never set foot outside his dry little cocoon. For me it was another story. The boat was a zippy cabin cruiser used for big game fishing. It went like the clappers, which meant we could get a lot further out from the shelf than a typical pelagic cruise, increasing our chances of turning up something good. But as it was designed for fishing not bird observing, the only place to stand if you wanted a proper view of all the birds was right at the back of the boat, which meant you'd get wet – very, very wet. Within ten minutes I was soaked, and remained that way for the next ten hours.

The long distance strategy suggested by the organizers, Richard Baxter and Phil Hansbro, had paid dividends. They had gone out the day before and managed to see both Gould's and Cook's Petrel, two birds I would have killed to see. Expectations were high. Within a few minutes we started to see our first seabirds. Many on board were relative novices to pelagic birding and there was much excitement and many questions directed at the experts. I could understand why they kept going to Phil for advice – he is a major seabirder who had far more experience than anyone else on board; an ebullient Geordie, Phil cut his teeth in the hectic world of British twitching in the eighties and early nineties and was rapidly closing in on his ambition to see every pelagic species in the world but what was really surprising was that people were also turning to me for advice. I still felt like I had a lot to learn but I did have a recognisable name amongst the birding community now, so people automatically assumed I knew what I was on about. As I attempted to answer a few identification questions I suddenly realised that all these boat trips were paying off, and I almost felt like I really did know what I was talking about.

As we headed out one old boy kept wanting advice on the dark birds that were following the boat. They were Wedge-tailed Shearwaters, the most common shearwater along this part of the coast. Phil and I explained to him how to tell them from other shearwaters, such as Sooty and Flesh-footed. Periodically he would ask one of us, 'Is that a Fleshy-foot?' It was always a Wedge-tailed and we would explain the differences again. After this had happened about five times he approached me with a twinkle in his eye, pointed to the all-dark shearwater flying past the boat and pronounced confidently, 'Wedge-tailed Shearwater.' It was the first Flesh-footed Shearwater of the day. I almost didn't have the heart to tell him.

Some of you might be thinking what does it matter what kind of shearwater it was? If he wanted to call it a Wedge-tailed Shearwater – or a Marzipan Nipple-clamp, for that matter – where's the harm? Well, apart from the innate desire of humans to identify the world around us – the first act Adam carried out according to the Bible was to name all the animals and birds – there is a very good reason for us all to be singing from the same hymnbook: there needs to be a common parlance so that everyone can agree on what they are looking at. A case in point happened just a few minutes later when, at our first stop, Phil called a Buller's Shearwater. This was the first of this New Zealand species to been seen in Australian waters for the entire year so naturally I was very keen to see it. Unfortunately everyone else was crammed down at the aft of the boat and my view was blocked by about a dozen heads with binoculars clamped to their eyes. For a terrifying minute I couldn't find it.

Buller's Shearwater is probably the most handsome of its family. Most shearwaters are a plain dark colour above; Bullers sport a striking design of grey with a dark 'M' pattern across the back. They are pretty distinctive so it was disturbing that I couldn't get onto it.

The bloke standing next to me was having similar trouble when suddenly he exclaimed in delight, 'Ah, there it is, I've got it. Buller's Shearwater.' I followed the direction of his binoculars as he traced a path around the front of the boat towards our side, but I couldn't see anything remotely resembling a Buller's. The guy next to me was oohing and ahhing and saying he'd still got it. I was frantic, almost screaming, 'I can't see it, I can't see it.'

Phil came over and stood next to me, watching. 'What can't you see?'

'The Buller's!'

'I'm not surprised. It's over there,' he said, pointing to a patch of ocean on the port side. I scrambled over from starboard and managed to get onto the Buller's just as it flew off. What would have been a crippling view turned out to be not much more than a fleeting glimpse. I don't know what the guy next to me had been calling a Buller's Shearwater but it certainly wasn't the same bird I eventually saw.

The Buller's was an unexpected and most welcome bonus and the day just got better from there. Well past the shelf break we picked up both Gould's Petrel and Black-bellied Storm-Petrel, two species I had written off for the year. I wouldn't have got the Gould's at all if not for Phil's hawk-like vigilance. After a thirteen-hour drive the day before I was starting to nod off and most of the others had similarly lost interest in proceedings. Not Phil. His cry of Gould's Petrel jolted me from my slumber and got me a bonus bird. Back at Phil's place later that night I mentioned his doggedness in keeping vigil out on the ocean to his girlfriend Nicole, and she rolled her eyes, telling me that when she and the other twitching widows get together she wins the 'my partner is the more fanatical than your partner' competition every time. Phil grinned triumphantly. I'm not sure it's a mantle I'd be happy to accept as there are some extreme freaks out there in the twitching world.

Not that I'm complaining. He got me two extra species for the year. On my last trip to Tasmania I thought I needed five year ticks to have a chance of seven hundred, and I only picked up two. With the three bonuses off Newcastle I was back in the running. Armed with information from Phil and Richard Baxter I spent the next day trying to run down some of the remaining birds that I needed for this part of the country: Spotted Quail-thrush, Common Koel and Little Bittern. I failed on all of them even though they'd all been seen at the sites I visited only days before.

The last time I'd been on the Central Coast was for my grand-mother's funeral. I squeezed in a visit to her and my grandfather's graves. Before you get too impressed by my familial piety, I should probably point out that there was a baser motive for my visit. At the funeral koels constantly called from the bush gully next to the ceme-tery, so I thought it might be worth a shot this time. No luck. If God did exist, surely my grandparents would have had a word in the big fella's ear and convinced Him to send over a koel or two. Or perhaps it was proof of eternal life – my grandparents could just as easily have arranged for the koels to keep silent to pay me back for not vis-iting them sooner.

Sacrilege aside, this was but another example of how twitching had permeated my everyday world. I remember as a child, before I could read, staring at traffic signs and knowing that once I learnt to read I would never not be able to look at that sign without knowing what it said. (I was a far more profound child than I am an adult.) Birding had become like that for me. It is a language that, once learnt, I have been unable to unlearn. Everywhere I go I am auto-matically birding in my head whether I am conscious of it or not. Everywhere I go I am tallying up a bird list for that location. I went to a friend's wedding in the Solomons, held in the grounds of the Honiara Botanic Gardens. In every single photograph of me in the congregation during the outdoor ceremony my head is craned skyward, looking for birds.

On Lord Howe my birding was anything but subconscious. I did nothing but look at birds. It truly is a magnificent place for wildlife. The tragedy is that it was once so much better. By the end of the nineteenth century hunting pressures from the first settlers and visiting whalers had seen larger birds such as the Lord Howe Swamphen, Parakeet and Pigeon become extinct, but the forests were still alive with a whole suite of smaller birds. Then, on 14 June 1918, the steamer *Makambo* ran aground just offshore, liberating rats on the hitherto predator-free island. Within five years at least five species of bird had become extinct. Wherever I went on Lord Howe I was haunted by a line from a local naturalist quoted in Ian Hutton's book on Lord Howe Island, written only two years after the rats' arrival: 'the quiet of death reigns where all was melody'.

My accommodation turned out to be next door to Ian Hutton's house. Though he was down with a serious flu he was still happy to chat about his beloved island. Ian came to birding a bit differently to most in that he first fell in love with Lord Howe and then with its birds. After many visits he eventually moved here and now knows more about the island's birds than anyone else. He suggested that I should try the area around Little Island for the one remaining endemic, the Lord Howe Woodhen.

The story of the woodhen is one outstanding conservation triumph in a plethora of tragedy. Probably too big to be much affected by rats (which are now subject to a major control effort), the woodhen was hit hard by a number of other factors: mainly hunting for the pot by the early settlers and competition with and destruction by the animals they introduced, including goats, cats and pigs. By the late 1970s fewer than forty birds survived on the inaccessible slopes of Mounts Gower and Lidgbird. A concerted pest eradication effort and captive breeding program have brought the Lord Howe Woodhen back from the brink and it is now estimated around two hundred birds roam the island.

They even turn up in the main settlement. Indeed, while I was out looking for them at Little Island one wandered out onto the lawn of the lodge where I was staying. It spent half an hour parading in front of Gloria and Leslie, two older birders I had met who were also staying at the lodge. They had decided to take it easy rather than bust a gut going all the way out to Little Beach, and they took great delight in telling me all about it when, all hot and bothered, I got back.

For the first hour or so it looked like I'd pulled the wrong rein with Little Island. There was simply no sign of the birds. Apparently they are very curious and are attracted by any loud noise, such as the banging together of two rocks. I was clanking rocks together until they crumbled to sand, and not a peep. I began to suspect that the whole rock-banging thing was just a ploy by the locals to create fresh topsoil for the island. I remembered reading an account by an early hunter who attracted the curious birds to their doom with ridiculous ease simply by producing noises the birds had never heard before. I decided to do an experiment to see which modern noise a woodhen who had spent its entire life on a small South Pacific island would never have heard.

I thought I'd give hip-hop music a try. Sadly, no success with the impromptu rap stylings of MC Doolio. Perhaps another form of music? I tried a bit of James Brown, followed by everything from Monty Python to Kylie, but nothing seemed to work. Apart from Neil Diamond. Not just any part of Neil Diamond, but the bit at the end of the musical intro to 'Crunchy Granola Suite' where Neil proclaims, 'Good Lord!' As soon as I uttered those words (in the style of Neil Diamond, of course) a pair of woodhens came running. They were ridiculously tame birds so every time I hit them with a 'Good Lord!' they would respond with up to ten seconds of shrieking. If you are ever on Lord Howe and woodhens are proving elusive then a bit of 'Crunchy Granola' might not go astray.

No matter how loudly you sang Neil Diamond, the White-bellied Storm-Petrel couldn't hear it. An easy target for the rats, they only nest on inaccessible offshore islets so the only way to see them is to take a boat out into the deep offshore waters where they feed. As soon as I arrived I'd inquired about getting out on a boat. I'd been given the name of a skipper, Jack Shick, who had a reputation of being birder friendly and would go out in all but the roughest of weather. Instead I had been railroaded by the owner of the lodge I was staying at to join a group going out with another skipper called

Bondy two days later. The weather was perfect until, naturally, the day we were meant to go out.

As I sat forlornly looking out at the angry white caps of the stormy ocean, Bondy came down and joined me briefly to check out conditions. Maybe I learnt something from my Norfolk Island experience; in any case I'd begun to assert myself more, letting nothing get in the way of seeing a new bird. Taking pity on me Bondy swore he would get me out to sea before I left on Saturday.

To take my mind off things I headed out to Ned's Beach on the other side of the island to watch the spectacle of the Flesh-footed Shearwaters coming in to their nesting burrows for the evening. This is one of the more dangerous pastimes in the birding world as the birds don't seem to have any kind of braking mechanism. They just barrel in at great speed and seem to crash-land on the edge of the forest, whereupon they emit a triumphant, chipmunk-like 'Yippee!' Several times careening birds missed me by a matter of inches.

Ian Hutton told me I was not guaranteed Little Shearwater out at sea and promised he would take me out one night to visit the new colony he had recently found, the first Little Shearwaters to breed on the main island since the arrival of the rats: a sure sign that the eradication program was already bringing results. On the designated night he looked dreadful, wracked with flu, but he insisted on taking me out. There are few cars on Lord Howe; everyone gets about on bikes. So in the teeth of a howling gale Ian rose from his deathbed and we cycled into the night across the island. The rain was so thick I lost sight of him as soon as he got ten metres ahead. We arrived at the breeding ground thoroughly sodden but managed to find a couple of adults and a healthy, fat Little Shearwater chick which looked as close to a penguin as anything can get without actually being a penguin. Very cute.

The next day dawned with slightly improved weather but it was still grim. Bondy assured me we'd get out that afternoon regardless. We gathered at noon. The wind had eased somewhat but the waves beyond the lagoon were still capped with foam. Three people took one look at the conditions and immediately pulled out. Seven of us decided to risk our luck. The only other birder was Leslie; she was spending her retirement travelling the world and, having recently been to Antarctica, these conditions weren't going to put her off. I was worried about the others though. The aim of the trip was to get out to Ball's Pyramid, twenty-three kilometres to the south of the main island. Between the two is a deep oceanic trench, a favoured feeding ground of storm-petrels. I needed to get out to this spot for a shot at the bird.

As soon as we passed out of the lee of the island I could see most of the non-birders starting to turn green. I had taken a pill and felt totally confident about the conditions but I estimated the first person might start chucking in a matter of minutes. If they did so before we got out into deep water, Bondy might feel compelled to bring the boat back in and I'd dip. For the next half-hour I kept a tense vigil, one eye scanning for storm-petrels, the other watching for the first signs of heaving on board. It was a neck and neck race. Right at the halfway point I saw the first of about eight White-bellied Storm-Petrels. Exactly one minute later, the first of the passengers lost their lunch over the side.

When I left the island the next morning, I looked back from the plane and the sun broke though the clouds shining exactly as it had in my dreams all those years.

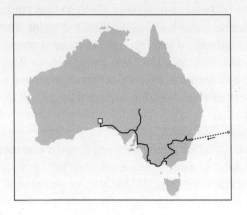

CHAPTER 27

1 November, Nullarbor Plain, South Australia:
625 species

Sighting the Australian landmass as the plane from Lord Howe approached Sydney, I was struck with the daunting reality that in the next few weeks I'd be crossing that vast expanse, and then some. But before I did there were still a couple of birds from the southeast corner of the continent that I hadn't connected with and I wasn't going to leave until I did.

I drove straight to the Capertee Valley for my last ditch attempt at Regent Honeyeater. Heading up over the Blue Mountains, the precipitous range that had hemmed in European settlement for twenty-five years, I encountered the first bushfires for the season. These were not merely prescriptive burn-offs, they were full on, out of control wildfires. In a typical season you might expect a couple of these conflagrations in December or January, but in mid October? After years of below average rainfall the bush was so dry that we were in for one hell of a fire season.

The drought was responsible for the extreme difficulty I'd had finding Regent Honeyeater throughout the year. The few surviving

Regents had had to go even further afield to find sufficient food as the trees failed to blossom in district after district. There were still meant to be a couple of Regents lurking around the Capertee. One or two had even been seen attempting to build a nest but when I arrived the entire area was even drier than it had been only a month earlier. Any tree that had been promising to flower in early September had been chastened by a month of hot, dry weather, joining the wilted throng.

Even the grasses had failed to seed, meaning there was little food around for my other target species, the Plum-headed Finch. I didn't even know where to start looking for it. Several times small birds flew up from the side of the road as I drove past but every time I went back to check up on them they always turned out not to be Plum-heads. Towards the late afternoon a group of four birds flew up from a ditch I had driven past half a dozen times already. I almost didn't stop but, with a sigh of resignation, I turned the car around for another look. Sure enough, four Plum-headed Finches popped their heads up; the only time I'd see this species for the year.

With only an hour of light left I made my way back down to the bridge over the dry river bed, the last reported place Regent Honeyeater had been seen and the only spot in the entire valley where anything was in flower. Not that it was much, just a bit of mistletoe in some of the streamside River Oaks. In a drought of this magnitude in the past, the Regents would vacate the valley for somewhere within their vast range where there were pockets of habitat that could support at least part of the population. This survival strategy was perfectly suitable when there were vast tracts of Box-Ironbark and other types of woodland available for them to move about in. They were like the touring cars of the bird world. They would move through the country using certain areas as refuelling stops. When one of these filling stations had no fuel available, they would use their extensive knowledge of the network to make their way to the next stop. Today those tracts are just not there and most of the filling stations in the chain are missing. So when their core refuge areas such as the Capertee Valley fail to produce, they have to travel a hell of a long way to the next station, running on empty.

And by this stage, having been at it since 5 am, I was as stuffed as a Regent Honeyeater. I was out of energy and ideas, the sun was sinking and nothing was calling. I packed up to leave but thought the better of it. I figured I might as well wait another half an hour – I had very little hope of seeing a Regent, but if I was travelling out of the valley in the car I'd have no hope at all. So I just stooged around, soaking in the peace of a bush sunset.

I wandered back down to the bridge and as I did a largish honeyeater flew up into the top of a lone tree in the paddock to have a good look around. Without much expectation I put my bins up to it and there was a Regent Honeyeater. At a casual glance the Regent Honeyeater appears rather ugly – predominantly scaly black and white markings with a pink, warty face. It is an aggressive little mongrel, constantly interrupting its feeding to chase away any other bird that dares go within a sniff of its feeding tree. Not much to recommend it, really. But then it opens its wings and what has been just a hint of yellow explodes into a glorious display of rich gold, particularly striking in this instance where its luminescence was highlighted by the glowing rays of the setting sun. Like so much of Australia's wildlife, it is stunningly beautiful once you look beyond a seemingly drab exterior.

As with the Rufous Scrub-bird I was ecstatic but it was a poignant joy. After the bird flew off I stood on the bridge looking along the river in the enveloping darkness contemplating the fate of this quintessentially Australian species. How long will its call continue to ring through this valley? If I was to do another Big Twitch in thirty years time (I think it will take me that long to recover from this one) Regent Honeyeater would be the bird I would most expect to no longer exist in the wild. I could be wrong. There is a massive effort being undertaken to help this species recover but I wonder if it is a case of too little too late. Perhaps it is the pessimism borne of spending an entire day out in the parched landscape, but as I turned back to the car I realised twilight had merged into night and I was astonished to find that I was crying. As I said, it had been a very long day.

And it was but the first of many such long days. Following a tip-off from Sydney birder Dion Hobcroft I altered my course by a couple of hundred kilometres to pick up Black Honeyeater near West Wyalong. Having travelled through Central Australia I should already have seen this desert species but the drought had so disrupted the normal patterns that nothing was certain anymore. I made my way back down to the Chiltern area where Barry Trail had recently seen Spotted Quail-thrush. BJ was celebrating the declaration of the new national parks after years of campaigning and had treated himself to a three-day bushwalk through the Barambogie Ranges, soon to be combined with the Chiltern Box-Ironbark National Park. That's how environmentalists celebrate for fun – deprive themselves of creature comforts.

BJ cautioned that in three days of walking this was the only pair he had seen. Undeterred I headed up into the range and at the first likely patch of suitable woodland with a tussocky understorey I pulled up and within ten minutes had located a pair showing very well indeed. After dipping on this bird all year I seemed to get them with ridiculous ease. I earmarked this spot for future reference but it didn't do me much good as three months later this site was completely obliterated in the devastating bushfires that engulfed much of this part of the world.

I returned home for a couple of days to refresh my supplies and prepare for my final onslaught. Nancy was away and when she returned I was just about to leave.

She seemed slightly taken aback: 'Well, it's been nice knowing you, I guess.' By the time I got back in the New Year, Nancy had bought a house of her own and moved out. Even though we shared a house for almost a year I can't recall having had more than a dozen conversations with her.

I took the coastal route out of Victoria, managing to dip on Little Bittern at Cranbourne, Masked Owl at Lorne, Cape Gannet at Portland and Sanderling at several coastal sites. Not a promising start.

Once I reached South Australia I headed inland in order to seek the only two birds in all of southeastern Australia I still needed. The first of these, Red-lored Whistler, I was rather surprised to pick up at Comet Bore in Ngarkat Conservation Park. This site used to be a great spot for Red-loreds but a major fire went through a few years ago destroying most of the suitable habitat. I wasn't really expecting anything, but it made a convenient camping site. While on a walk the next morning I found what looked like a patch of old growth habitat – perhaps somewhere the fires had missed – and to my astonishment saw a female Red-lored Whistler accompanied by an immature. A couple of weeks later the area was again destroyed by fire.

The other bird I needed was Malleefowl. After failing to find it at what I was assured to be a 'dead cert' site at Pooginook Conservation Park I was thinking of heading out to Gluepot for the third time and not moving until one of the bloody birds showed up. Then I heard of a place called Eromophila Park, a working wheat farm that had retained substantial patches of mallee. Stella Mack, the amazing woman who runs the property has been throwing grain to the local Malleefowls for over thirty years and they have become quite tame. At one point she had up to seven birds coming in for a feed and there were as many as seventeen of these rare birds in the general area. Many of the surrounding properties, however, cleared their mallee blocks to make way for more wheat paddocks and the Malleefowl have nearly all died off. Currently in the grip of drought, those cleared paddocks stand denuded of cover, their precious top-soil lying heaped against the roadside fence-lines whilst the Eromophila Park, with much of its original vegetation still intact, seems to be in much better shape.

Now in her seventies, Stella took me out the next morning to meet her favourite pair of Malleefowl. They were working on their nesting mound and approached her like domestic chooks for a handout. Normally these birds are extremely cagey but here they went about their business totally oblivious to our presence. At one point the male bird started displaying to the hen. He raised a small crest on his head (I had no idea they even possessed a crest), stuck his head between his legs and made a deep, resonant booming sound. Very impressive. I must remember that move.

And that was it for the southeast. After three hundred days I had seen everything I wanted in this corner of the country. Anything I'd missed I could see further west or north, so that's where I was headed. It's all part of Australia but in so many ways it is a different country altogether. For starters the next town is rarely less than a hundred kilometres away and at that time of year there is substantially less traffic on the road. It is too hot. Many tourist places close down, especially up north where there is no business over the monsoon season. The locals try to keep out of the heat or find reasons to do business down south in the cities. It is truly a lonely road.

Especially at places like the Birdsville Track. No-one wants to be out there at this time of year, not even me. But after consulting Dave Harper on my way through Adelaide (where one of his daughters gave up their bed for me to sleep in – stealing a child's bed, how low can this twitcher go?) I decided it was worth the 1200-kilometre detour to the start of the Birdsville as he had seen Inland Dotterel there after we had gone our separate ways back in August. It was a long way to go for a long shot but the only other site I had was out on the Nullarbor and if I missed it there it was seriously unlikely I would fluke across it anywhere else.

I arrived at the dusty outpost of Marree at the start of the Birdsville Track right on dark. As I was heading into the pub for a meal a bunch of women called raucously from the balcony of the old brick hotel, insisting I come up and have a drink with them. I felt like John Wayne rolling into some town in the Old West, but instead of showgirls with a heart of gold these ladies turned out to be a Kiwi nurse and her aunties…with hearts of gold. The niece had been working in an Outback hospital further north and was heading home to New Zealand. Her aunties, who lived in Australia, had decided they would go up and drive her down to Adelaide, giving them all a holiday.

They certainly were festive and within seconds had thrust a cold beer into my hand. When I told them what I was up to they thought I was pulling their leg. I had come all this way to look for just one bird? No, there had to be another reason. Perhaps I was on the run from the law. I had to bring up my bird books and spotlight to show them I seriously was going to head out onto the Birdsville Track to spotlight for the dotterel. They asked me where I planned to spend the night. Out on the track, most likely. They wouldn't stand for it and the niece kindly offered for me to sleep in her room. I graciously declined but they were very insistent. As I finally dragged myself away, one of the aunties took hold of my arm and said, nodding knowingly, 'You really should stay the night here with my niece. Look at her, you'd be mad not to.' I laughed it off and left them to their merriment.

I drove along the Birdsville for about an hour, unsuccessfully scanning the gibber plains for any signs of life. I was quite exhausted and pulled over by a creek to sleep for the night. As I was laying my sleeping bag out in the back seat of the car I thought, 'What are you doing, Dooley? You've had an offer to spend the night with a buxom nurse. It would be discourteous to turn down her hospitality.'

I arrived back in Marree and the party on the balcony had broken up. I snuck up to the nurse's room and knocked. I could hear her snoring. I knocked louder. She stirred. As I stood there waiting for her to get to the door, the manager of the pub came up the stairs.

'What the hell do you think you're doing?' he demanded.

'Oh, I'm just visiting my friend,' I stammered. 'She asked me to come up.'

Thankfully the door opens and there was my saviour, my refuge. She looked at me blearily and said, 'Who are you?'

Two evenings later I was out on the Nullarbor Plain looking for Inland Dotterel. This is extraordinary country. Totally flat for hundreds of miles, no stick of vegetation rising taller than knee height. I doubt there is anywhere else in the world where you can be in such an open space – even the remotest ocean has waves with their peaks and troughs. It is an astonishing place, made all the more so by the fact that creatures actually thrive here. The only other time I'd been here was driving back from Perth with Groober in 1987. With us was one of my mate's mates who needed a ride back to Melbourne. We were trying to do the run nonstop in two days.

About the only place we did stop was out here in order to see the Nullarbor race of the Cinnamon Quail-thrush, which back then was considered a full species. Arriving a couple of hours before dark Groober and I raced out across the heat of the plain trying to track them down, leaving the mate's mate to cool his heels in the car. Once it got too dark to see we returned hot and dejected only to find the mate's mate asking about a bird that he'd seen feeding around the car. The description he gave fitted the Nullarbor Quail-thrush perfectly. They still haven't found his body.

This time round I did see the quail-thrush, now that it didn't count as a full species. Typical. I stopped to look for it anyway as maybe one day it would be split out again and I could add it to the official Big Twitch list. As I got out of the car I was greeted with a blast of furnace-like air so fierce that it seared the soft membranes inside my nose, and every morning for the rest of the year I woke up to find my nose clogged with dried blood.

As I headed further into the Nullarbor a massive thunderstorm hit. I later heard on the radio that scientists estimate lightning struck the ground in South Australia two hundred thousand times that day. I don't know how they worked that out but it felt like half those strikes were around me. In those conditions sitting in a metal box in the middle of a vast plain where nothing else around you for miles is taller than a few inches is not exactly my idea of fun. Later someone told me about the Faraday Cage, a physics principle that claims you won't be struck by lighting if you are in a moving vehicle. That reassurance would have come in handy at the time and by the time I made it to the tiny railway siding of Cook on the Trans-Australian Railway, I was quite rattled.

Cook was once home to quite a community of railway fettlers but today all the labour is brought in from further afield and Cook has become a virtual ghost town. I saw out the storm with a bunch of railway workers waiting for their changeover with the Western Australian crew. They'd been waiting a long time as the wind had blown live wires across the carriages of the goods train they were supposed to be crewing. We chatted for a couple of hours and I gained a little insight into this fascinating world. I felt like I'd been cast back into a Charles Chauvel film of the 1940s.

The front eventually passed and I tentatively headed out onto the plain once more. In all that time not a drop of rain had fallen. And not an Inland Dotterel was to be found either, even out at the airstrip where they are supposedly relatively easy to see. I was, however, treated to the most extraordinary sunset, not just for the intensity of colours but because there is nothing to interrupt the panorama. The sense of scale was unrivalled by anything I had seen before.

Not having seen even a hint of an Inland Dotterel on the drive in, heading back the hundred kilometres to Highway One at night my biggest problem was not running them over. I almost hit at least twenty. They must have all been there as I barrelled past, yet not one of the buggers had deigned to show itself. Now they were everywhere. By the time I reached the bitumen I'd quite had my fill of this bird I had been yearning to see for so long. I pulled off the road, trying to keep out of sight of any passing psychopath cruising the highway looking for fresh meat – not an easy task when there is no vegetation to obscure your vehicle. In the end I didn't care because I was absolutely buggered. Two and a half thousand kilometres in three days. Tomorrow I'd have to do it all again. Oh God.

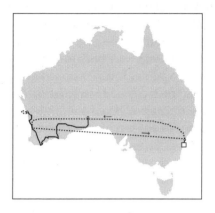

CHAPTER 28

7 November, Shoalhaven Heads, New South Wales:
632 species

When you hit the Western Australia border after crossing the Nullarbor Plain, there are still another 1400 kilometres to go before you reach the outskirts of Perth. That's why Esperance, the first major town you hit if you choose the coastal route, seems like such a great little town. After thirteen and a half hours of driving – with virtually no stopping – it felt like heaven to me. Well, I did make one exception and stopped at the border to kick the footy across. With the difference in time zones I was able to defy the laws of physics and kick the ball two and a half hours into the past, when I booted it into Western Australia, then two and a half hours into the future, by kicking it back into South Australia. Spooky but true.

Equally spooky was my arrival in Esperance. It was the Dick Smith at Innamincka scenario all over again as I drove into town to be greeted by the shenanigans of the local 'Festival of the Winds' carnival. After days spent alone I was now surrounded by throngs of families and platoons of street performers. Seeking refuge I entered the pub to book a room and was greeted by a giant mascot that looked for all the world like the Capital City Goofball from the Simpsons. I'm sure all those people were having a great time, but they were freaking me out.

By the next night things were back to normal and I was sleeping in the car alone once again, this time camped in the backyard of the ranger's residence at the Fitzgerald River National Park. On the Perth pelagic back in June, Peter Wilkins, one of the park's rangers, had told me that he sees Western Whipbirds virtually from his kitchen window and that if ever I was coming through, I should drop by and check them out. Foolish words, really. Wisely Peter and his family had gone to a cricket club function in Jerramungup, the nearest town. Arriving at his place just before sunset I searched the scrub for the whipbird, hearing one distantly but not getting anywhere near it. By the time the Wilkins family returned from Jerramungup I was bedded down and, only half awake, could hear kids saying, 'Daddy, there's a man asleep in our backyard.' Or maybe I dreamt it. Next morning I was up at dawn which, due to the recalcitrance of the Sandgropers, who refuse to move to daylight savings, meant that was around four thirty. After a couple of hours' searching in the scrub I'd still had no luck and Peter took pity on me. Though quite hungover he chipped in to try and get me the bird.

There is a bit of a trick to seeing Western Whipbird. Not only are they very reluctant to show themselves, preferring to remain hidden in the densest scrub, they only call on average once every half-hour or so. This can make for a hell of a time trying to track one down. The key to success, Peter assured me, is to not pussyfoot around but move as quickly and quietly when you hear the bird start to call. While it calls it is less likely to hear you approach and you may have a chance. We tried this a couple of times with no luck whatsoever, partly because whipbirds are notoriously ventriloquial and we could never agree on where the call was coming from.

Eventually we got onto a male calling halfway up a small mallee tree. In the books this bird looks particularly drab, a kind of dull olive. In the flesh I think it looks damn sexy, though I may be biased, having wanted to see this bird for fifteen years. As it called we could see why it is so difficult to pinpoint. When it turned its head even slightly to one side, the call seemed to be thrown metres away in the direction it was looking. Mission accomplished, I left Peter to nurse his hangover and moved further along the coast.

En route I finally managed to get onto a White-winged Triller, ten months after first hearing one back at Chiltern. I was filled with as much relief over this relatively common species as I had been over the whipbird because if I had failed to see the triller this year I would never be able to show my face at the bird club ever again. Then again, maybe that wouldn't be such a bad thing…

The Noisy Scrub-bird is reputedly even harder to see than its Rufous counterpart. Thought to be extinct within a couple of decades of its discovery by John Gilbert in the 1840s, it wasn't until 1961 that it was confirmed to still exist. At that time Two Peoples Bay, the only site on which it had survived, was earmarked for a township and a concerted campaign was undertaken to protect the area. One of the scrub-birds' greatest supporters was Prince Philip. There is a plaque at Two Peoples commemorating his visit to the site a few years later, though it turns out he dipped on seeing the bird. I guess I am a bit of a republican at heart but I would love to be introduced to the Prince just to be able to grip him off about seeing the Noisy Scrub-bird. It did take me an hour crawling around in the undergrowth, not at Two Peoples Bay but at Cheynes Beach, where there is a translocated population, but I did see it. The Noisy Scrub-bird is aptly named because its main call of several sweet notes is ear-piercingly loud. For twenty minutes it called within five metres of me but the scrub was so dense and the bird so wily I couldn't see it, even though it felt like my ears were bleeding. Eventually it popped up onto a branch just above my head and stared at me with its head cocked for a full five seconds, as if to say, 'Are you happy now?' Then it was gone. Take that, Prince Philip.

With a few hours of daylight left, I realised that I had enough time to get to Two Peoples Bay for the last of the skulking triumvirate, the Western Bristlebird. Back in 1987 this was the easiest of the three to find and as I pulled up at the carpark at Little Beach things were looking pretty good. I saw what was probably a bristlebird dive from the top of a bush into the dense coastal heath. It would only be a matter of minutes before another one showed itself.

Minutes turned to hours and I had nothing. As is often the case with birding, the easy becomes difficult and the difficult easy. Then, just as the sun sank behind the granite hills that surround this most picturesque stretch of coastline, a Western Bristlebird popped back up onto the same bush and I had done it – three of the most infuriatingly hard to see birds in Australia all on the same day. How good did I feel?

I took a motel room in Albany and planned my next step. In the morning I'd look for Rock Parrot and then, having seen all the southwestern specialties, I'd head north where I'd break the record somewhere in the Pilbara in a few days' time. I plugged in the laptop to catch up on emails and check out Birding-aus. A Canada Goose had turned up near Sydney.

I called Mike Carter, who of course had already gone for it and ticked it off. He and most of the Sydney twitchers I subsequently talked to were all of the opinion that it was a genuine wild bird and not some escapee from a collection. They all urged that this was one I should definitely not miss out on. It seemed ridiculous to fly across the country for a bird that I might not even see (it had first been reported a week earlier), but there was something so deliciously perverse about the concept that I couldn't resist using up the last of my frequent flyer points to go for it.

No matter where I looked around Albany I simply could not find Rock Parrot. I wasn't sure if they were all that common around Perth, but that is where I'd now have to look after I got back from Sydney. It would be incredible to miss out on this bird and yet pick up a Canada Goose, a vagrant from New Zealand where English colonists had brought it following its introduction from North America to England in the seventeenth century.

Driving up to Perth I listened to an emotional Damien Oliver give his speech after just riding the winner of the Melbourne Cup. His brother, also a jockey, had died in a race fall not long before. It got me thinking about all the Melbourne Cups I worked at with my dad over the years. Dad was a bookie and writing down bets for him was the job that got me through my long stint at uni. For most the Melbourne Cup is the racing event of the year. For me it was a total pain. It was crowded, and I spent the day working my butt off while drunken yobbos around me were having a good time. And that was just Dad and my other co-workers – you should have seen the punters! Mainly I hated working at the Cup because it meant I could never take the holiday long weekend to go birding. Ironically, here I was twitching on Melbourne Cup day and would have given anything to be back there working with Dad again.

I began the next day looking out over the Indian Ocean and ended it facing the Pacific. I had been told that the goose was easy to find – I just had to head down to the river at Shoalhaven Heads and look for the Black Swans. The estuary of the Shoalhaven is particularly huge and I spent the rest of the following day searching it without seeing a single swan, let alone a goose. By five o'clock I was back where I'd started and resigned myself to coming back the next day. I set up the scope one last time and forlornly scanned the estuary. There in the middle, was the Canada Goose swimming about five hundred metres offshore, and not a swan in sight.

Seeing the goose saved me having to spend the night at Shoalhaven and I made my way back to Sydney where there was a bit of a twitchers' shindig at a city pub. Who would have thought it, twitchers actually capable of socialising? Oh well, being Sydney they must all have been pumped up on some sort of love drug or something. It's not natural, I tells ya.

The next day I was back in Perth and, unexpectedly, two birds closer to the record total, having also seen Common Koel in Sydney. I hadn't been able to get onto this chook of a bird all year and then on the one day I saw seven. Sometimes I wonder whether the birds have meetings, devising schedules to mess with twitchers' minds. I now needed just one bird to equal the record, two to break it. I dipped out on Little Bittern at Herdsman Lake, a fantastic wetland just north of the city, and headed for another site, this time a little further north at Joondalup. As soon as I got out of the car I could hear a bittern booming. I saw a dirty big black Tiger Snake in the grass next to me, but the bittern remained hidden. Probably creeping out the neighbours, I hung around until it got dark then, armed with a spotlight and tape player, I headed off into the swamp determined to finally nail this sucker. Come sunset the bird started calling almost continually. Not that it made itself any more obvious.

There was nothing for it but to enter the murky water and head off into the reed beds to try and get up close and personal. The stinking water got deeper and deeper until it was over the top of my gumboots. Still the bittern boomed. I went in deeper. Eventually the black water reached to that critical point that every male swimmer knows – where your testicles can contract no further. I started playing the tape – bugger the bird's sensibilities. By this stage, particularly after I'd extracted a two-inch leech from my bleeding leg (God, I hope Tiger Snakes aren't attracted by blood) I was more than happy to disrupt this bird's routine – hell, I was tempted to burn the reed bed down. For about an hour there was a bizarre Mexican standoff between me and the bittern. I played the tape. It answered. I could see the top of the reed the bird was on swaying in the moonlight every time it called, and though it was almost within touching distance, still the bird wouldn't show. Eventually my spotlight battery ran out before the booming bittern did and I retreated to the car defeated.

The next day up the coast at Lancelin, about as far north as Rock Parrots go, I was standing down by the windswept beach almost being decapitated by kite surfers. Fit, tanned and muscular, the kite surfers looked askance at this figure in mismatching shorts, shirt and stupid hat scanning the offshore island with binoculars, not taking the slightest bit of notice as they primped and preened and struted their stuff. I've only got eyes for Rock Parrots, not rock-hard abs. As I arrived a couple of parrots flew across to the island but I couldn't be sure they weren't Elegant Parrots. So I waited and scanned, scanned and waited. In calmer weather I would have swum over to the island. I even contemplated hitching a ride with one of the kite surfers. Instead, after a couple of fruitless hours I drove down to a beach south of the town where there is another island just offshore that looked suitable. Here I was able to drive onto the beach and get as close as I dared to the water's edge. The binoculars revealed nothing. Using the window for stability I peered through my telescope. The first place I looked there was a Rock

Parrot sitting unobtrusively on a rock ledge. Bird number 633. I had equalled the record. It was 10 November. Every bird I saw from then on would be the new record.

Lesser Noddy was next on my list and the only place you can find it in Australia is near its breeding grounds on the Abrolhos Islands, sixty kilometres off the coast of Geraldton. To get there I'd have to find a dive boat, but after ringing around the news was not great: the next boat wasn't going out for another two days and would be spending two full days out at the islands. There used to be a hydroplane that would land in the lagoon next to one of the breeding islands. I gave them a call and they told me they'd taken the skis off the plane and didn't do those trips anymore. They were happy to fly me out to the island though with no airstrip we wouldn't be able to land.

In a normal year the wet season doesn't really kick in until December but it can start as early as November – if it kicked in before I got up north it would cut off access to several species of birds and I'd have blown the whole timing of my run. I simply couldn't afford four days to look for the Lesser Noddy so I forked out the money for a flight and on the morning of 12 November we took off in a light plane from Geraldton Airport. Half an hour later the green lagoons of the Abrolhos loomed out of the deep blue of the ocean and we set a course for the cay where the Lesser Noddies breed.

I instructed the pilot to circle the island rather than fly over it – the last thing I wanted to do was disturb the birds from their nests. Very quickly I found that when we circled low enough to get a close view we were travelling too fast for the birds to remain in view for long enough. When we swept higher the view was steadier but the birds were too far off to adequately identify. Finding a happy medium was extremely difficult. I opened the window and was kind of half hanging out of it as we circled a few more times. I almost had enough on the birds – a dark, almost black body colour contrasting with a strong white cap, fine, delicate wings; the fact that I knew this was the Lesser Noddy colony below me – but not quite enough to prove I wasn't looking at the similar, larger Black Noddy. Then I saw a group of four Common Noddies. They looked bulky and massive, approaching twice the size of the other birds. There was no way a Black Noddy could have looked that small in comparison. Lesser Noddy, bird number 634. The record is mine.

The pilot congratulated me and as we swung back to the mainland I finally started to get a sense of real satisfaction. Crossing over the coastline the mix of cooler sea air and the warm mass coming off the dry, hot continent created a band of turbulence that sent my head crashing into the ceiling of the plane. 'Great,' I thought, 'I live to hold the record for a full half an hour.' We landed without mishap and I allowed myself to pump the air in triumph, making a goal signal like an AFL umpire and breathing a huge sigh of relief. In the grand scheme of things it was only a pointless, trivial record but geez I was glad to have done it.

But it was not over yet.

CHAPTER 29

16 November, Broome, Western Australia:
638 species

I sat in my car at Geraldton Airport, watching the pilot move the plane back into the hangar, and considered my options. It was 12 November, with fifty days remaining till the end of the year. Ahead lay the entire sweep of northern Australia: the Pilbara, the Kimberley, the Top End, Cape York – some of the toughest and most remote roads in the country at the hottest, most dangerous time of year. It was going to be lonely. There was no guarantee I wouldn't be cut off by cyclones. My money was starting to run short. Maybe if I got back to Melbourne I'd be able to give a certain woman a ring and see if we had a future. To call it quits now was no disgrace; I had the record, after all. I started the engine and pulled out of the airfield. The next intersection would dictate my life's path: turn right towards Perth and I'd be home in a week; turn left towards the furnace of an Outback summer and I wouldn't see Melbourne until the New Year.

I planted my foot down and headed into the blazing interior. Hitting the mulga belt near Mount Magnet for the second time that year I was struck by the difference the heat made. Back in June it was quite pleasant to be out in the scrub in the middle of the day. Now even the Emus were doing it tough, and at every stop the bush was deathly silent. I set up camp in The Granites just north of Mount Magnet, having failed yet again to find the Chestnut-breasted Quail-thrush. This, the Chiming Wedgebill and Spinifexbird were the last three species found in the southern half of Australia that I had yet to tick off and I was determined not to leave this part of the country until I'd nailed them all.

It was a warm night and I took advantage of this to sleep out naked under the stars. The further north I headed the further into mosquito country I'd go, so I savoured the moment. Staring up at the incandescent Milky Way, sucking back an ice-cold stubbie courtesy of the car fridge I picked up in Perth, life seemed pretty good.

Next morning I was greeted by a dawn chorus of deafening silence. Barely a bird and definitely none of my target species greeted the morning so I cut my losses and headed north through the staggeringly vast emptiness of the Outback. This was still marginal pastoral country so every ten or so kilometres I whizzed past a startled bunch of raggedy sheep that kicked up little clouds of red dust as they scrambled away into the scrub. It was hard to believe anybody could make a living out here, yet in each remote town magnificent civic buildings and private residences stand, though often empty – evidence of a more optimistic time when it was thought that human endeavour could conquer all.

Just outside Cue, one such creaking, dusty town, I headed into the desolate scrub to search for the quail-thrush. This is one of Frank O'Connor's favoured sites for this bird but after an hour kicking my way across the stony ground I was beginning to have my doubts. It wasn't yet seven in the morning and already the plains were heating up. A brisk hot wind carried away any of the thin peeps the quail-thrush might have been making. Things were not looking promising. But then I spied movement a hundred metres ahead of me and cautiously approached. Expecting a lizard or a rabbit, I was amazed to see a female Chestnut-breasted Quail-thrush huddling beneath a small acacia. Finally, after all those days in western Queensland, this last of the quail-thrush, those surprising little jewels of birds, was accounted for.

And that turned out to be the birding highlight of the day. Enormous distances were driven. A lot of dry country rushed past the window, every stop hotter than the last, each with fewer and fewer birds. Nowhere could I find a Chiming Wedgebill. They were meant to be all through this country, but not wherever I stopped.

The other species I was after was the Spinifexbird. This is the little bastard of a thing that had me scrambling up every spiky, spinifex-covered ridge within two hundred kilometres of Alice Springs for no reward other than an improved fitness level and thighs as hard as roadhouse pasties. Rolling into the mining town of Newman about an hour before dusk, having been on the road for twelve hours, I was finally back in Spinifexbird habitat. Behind the caravan park was a spinifex-covered ridge that looked promising. Within minutes a medium-sized brownish bird with a distinctly longish tail hopped up onto a distant bush and started singing. This had to be Spinifexbird. I continued tracking it as the light began to fade until eventually I got close enough to identify it not as a Spinifexbird but the Pilbara race of Striated Grasswren. While happy to see it – this is a seriously cute bird, a distinct race that few birders have caught up with and which might one day be split out to a full species – it was still not a Spinifexbird.

By this time it was almost dark and I trudged back to my car disconsolate and tired. I was out before dawn again the next morning and finally, after just fifteen minutes, I was within touching distance of a Spinifexbird. After all the anguish I'd suffered, this bird seemed ridiculously obliging. I wished the same could have been said for the wedgebill. As I trundled on through the Pilbara I was almost oblivious to its harsh beauty, focused as I was on this one stupid plain brown bird.

I came out the other side of the Pilbara near Whittenoom, site of one of Australia's most shameful industrial tragedies. The town was established for the workers at the asbestos mine in the nearby Whittenoom Gorge. No-one from the company told the miners or their families that the dust being carried from the mine on the scorching wind was laden with blue asbestos fibres that would lodge in their lungs and, years later, leave them dying an unspeakably horrific death from asbestosis and mesothelioma. The mine is now closed, yet a handful of people obstinately cling on. They said that since the clean-up there was no longer a health threat but I found the place creepy nonetheless. There is always a sadness associated with ghost towns, but at Whittenoom it resonates far more ominously, and I felt compelled to get out of there.

This feeling of doom was compounded when I checked my references at Whittenoom and realised that I had actually driven out of the territory of the Chiming Wedgebill. If I wanted to see the bird I would either have to backtrack through country where I'd already dipped, or head to the west and then south again, a detour that would cost me hundreds of kilometres. This was the last bird I needed from the southern half of Australia. I could easily have forgotten about it and headed north, where a whole swag of tropical species awaited, but I just couldn't let this one go. To miss out on a clean sweep felt like a failure, so I was determined to complete the set.

Another entire day driving. It is absolutely impressive, stark country out here, made more so by the spectacular storm that swept in. One minute I was driving through a searing, parched landscape that looked like it had never seen rain, the next I was in the midst of a blinding torrential downpour that brought roos and Perenties (lizards second only in size to the Komodo Dragon) out onto the road for a drink, and I had to swerve all over the place to avoid colliding with them. I made my way back down through the Pilbara, past the stunning, twisted rock formations of the Hammersley Gorge, past the sweltering iron ore town of Tom Price and hit the coast at Onslow, a mere five hundred kilometres in the wrong direction.

Onslow is the cyclone capital of Australia. It has been knocked down more times than the narrator of that Chumbawamba song but like those idiots in Hurricane Alley in the US Midwest, people keep rebuilding. Tonight all was calm and the sunset over the Indian Ocean idyllic, but I couldn't really enjoy it, afflicted as I was with the agitation of wedgebill fever. The references I had said that Onslow is the northern extremity of its range but the habitat didn't quite look right – too flat and open for my liking. This was borne out the next morning when, again rising before dawn, I searched the surrounding country with no luck. There was nothing for it but to head south.

And south. And even further south, all the time getting further from where I wanted to go. My first Oriental Plover for the year was a slight compensation but there was not a chime from the wedgebill. I actually began to hate this bird. To loathe it. The very thought of it made my blood boil. I should have been in in Broome by now but here I was dipping back below the Tropic of Capricorn, stopping at every likely desolate patch of clapped-out scrub for a bird I couldn't stand.

As I was nearing Carnavon, almost four hundred kilometres south of where I started, I noticed a subtle change in the vegetation: it seemed a little taller, a little thicker. It was past two o'clock in the arvo and I was feeling like shit. Then in the distance came that call. It's a staccato tune that has been described by some as sweet and by others as like a squeaky wheel. To me it sounded like the pulsing of the strings in Edith Piaf's *Non, Je Ne Regrette Rien* played through a tin whistle. It is an unforgettable sound and it had me hurdling the wire fence and chasing the source into the scrub. And finally there it was, sitting halfway up a tree calling its heart out – a Chiming Wedgebill, bird number 638.

It took at least an hour after swinging the car back onto the road and heading north again before my black mood began to lift. This was the last of the southern birds out of the way. I might well miss many of the tropical species but after eleven months I had tri-umphed over the south. By the time I got into Karratha at 10 pm my anger had long gone and I was feeling well satisfied. I had been on the road for seventeen hours and was completely knackered. Pulling in to the quietest side street I could find – no easy task in a mining town on a Friday night – I was all set for a well-earned sleep.

It was the first time all day I had been in mobile range so I checked my messages. There were two from Adrian Boyle, my con-tact in Broome. He was very excited: 'Dools! I know you're in this neck of the woods somewhere, but wherever you are, you've got to get your arse up here. There's a Blue-and-white Flycatcher out at the observatory!'

A Blue-and-white Flycatcher – the first live record for Australia – was serious news. His second message, left just after he had seen the bird, was even more insistent: 'You have to see this thing, it's amazing. WHERE ARE YOU?!'

I immediately rang Adrian. He was out celebrating. Establishing that I was in Karratha he insisted I should immediately head up to Broome, a mere ten-hour drive away. I protested that I couldn't possibly make the journey as I had already been on the road for seventeen hours. His response was simply, 'You do not want to miss out on this bird!'

I hung up and smiled to myself. There was no way I could possibly drive for another ten hours. I was wiped out. As I sat thinking a drunken domestic row started up in the house opposite where I was parked. Better move off, I decided, in case the cops were called and they checked up on me. And while I was at it I might as well head to the roadhouse at the edge of town to grab a bite. It was the only thing open. By the time I got there I realised I was so adrenalised by Adrian's call that I wouldn't be able to sleep. Maybe I could drive on to Roebourne or Wickham, maybe even Port Headland? Oh bugger it, who was I kidding – Broome it was. The only thing vaguely edible at the roadhouse was a dodgy looking pie. I bought it, loaded up on fuel and energy drinks, and took to the road.

About an hour out of Port Headland I realised I was going to hit the wall soon, and I'd rather that wall not be the grill of an oncoming road train. I pulled over and allowed myself two hours' sleep. I woke at 4 am, not exactly refreshed, and set off again. A pink dawn began to form over the Great Sandy Desert as I pulled in to the Sandfire Roadhouse for yet another hideous pie. I was still hours away from Broome. Eventually, after 1700 kilometres of driving since the previous morning with only two hours' sleep, I arrived at the Broome Bird Observatory around ten. Please let it still be here.

I stumbled out of the vehicle and staggered down to the communal shelter where a group of birders was sitting around under the shadecloth. It was already in the mid-thirties. These people weren't twitchers who had flown in specifically for the Blue-and-white Flycatcher but had been assembling here for the last couple of days before they headed off on a wader banding expedition and had just lucked upon this mega rarity. Frank O'Connor was amongst them. I asked him whether the bird had been around. He replied in the affirmative and pointed to the birdbath, saying it had taken a drink there that morning. Barely able to string two words together I asked what time that morning. He looked blank, as did the others, before deciding no-one had seen it for about two hours.

Two hours? The exact amount of time I'd spent sleeping by the roadside. This live bird first for Australia – an absolute stunner – had been here a mere two hours ago, shamelessly displaying for all and sundry? This bonus bird would have put me back on target for a theoretical seven hundred. And I'd missed it by two lousy fucking hours.

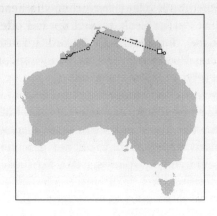

CHAPTER 30

21 November, Mount Carbine, Queensland:
661 species

I trudged back to the car totally shattered, ostensibly to get my camera gear in case the Blue-and-white Flycatcher did re-emerge, but mainly so I was out of earshot of the others as I repeated the f word eight thousand times. Oh well, at least I hadn't killed myself in the mad dash to get here and I was in Broome at last. All I needed was a good sleep and I'd be having the time of my life.

Suddenly Frank was upon me, yelling, 'Sean, it's back, it's back!'

I rushed down and there was the Blue-and-white Flycatcher, sitting right beside the shelter. A male in full breeding plumage, the rich blue of his back shimmered in the tropical sun, contrasting spectacularly with his clean white front. As I excited as I was, I did feel sorry for him as I watched his wings spread slightly and mouth open panting, trying to dissipate some heat. Not only had this thing flown an extra couple of thousand kilometres past its usual wintering grounds, when it finally made it to land it was hit with the furnace of northwestern Australia in November. It was not yet midday and the temperature was already around thirty-eight degrees.

Having had my fill of the flycatcher, the heat and tiredness began to kick in. Adrian Boyle turned up and offered his lounge room floor for me to crash on. He shared a house with another birder, Chris Hassell, and between them they ran Turnstone Nature Discovery Tours. They couldn't be more contrasting in appearance, Adrian a nuggety ball of energy from the South Australian bush, Chris a tall and sinewy Pom, but together they make a great team sharing an incredible passion for and knowledge of the birds and wildlife of the Broome region. As I was soon to find out.

As I was setting up my sleeping gear at their place, Adrian excitedly told me what was about in Broome. It sounded tremendous but I was absolutely wiped out from the drive and couldn't possibly tackle anything until the next day. Suddenly a massive storm hit. Where moments before it had been full sun and almost forty degrees, now there was a torrential downpour with fierce hail. I was watching the blanket of raindrops (as big as a Collingwood supporter's tears) when Adrian snapped into action: 'Come on, we have to go. This rain's not good news for you, Sean. If this sets in all the birds around town will head for the plains and then you'll never get them!' And with that he dragged me away from my sleeping bag and into the car.

Broome sits on Roebuck Bay, the rich mudflats of which are one of the world's major wader destinations. When the nearby Roebuck Plains fill after wet season rains, they become an equally good habitat for thousands of freshwater waders. After arriving from Asia, many of these birds congregate around the coast at Broome, waiting for the inland plains to fill. Adrian was convinced that if this storm marked the beginning of the wet, all the birds he had lined up for me would disperse, which was why we had to see them *now*.

And so began possibly the greatest forty-eight hours of birding in my life. The Blue-and-white Flycatcher alone would have made the trip worthwhile but in just over twenty-four hours we saw such sensational rarities as Yellow Wagtail, Long-toed Stint and Swinhoe's Snipe at the sewage works; and Common Redshank and Asian Dowitcher out on the mudflats of the bay. In the mangroves we ticked off such little-seen species as Dusky Gerygone, Mangrove Grey Fantail and White-breasted Whistler. The whistler is a surprisingly cute bird – the field guides don't really capture how striking it is with its chestnut collar that looks remarkably like a velvet stole.

By late the next morning I had everything I was after and then some, with the exception of Yellow Chat, the first bird that we hadn't got almost instantly when we'd looked for it. As we unsuccessfully searched the saltmarsh that these extremely enigmatic and little-known birds are supposed to frequent, I felt that at last Adrian's genius for finding rarities was tarnished. Undeterred, he was saying we'd keep searching the plains for them when, about five hundred metres away, some small birds flew up onto a fence and, sure enough, they turned out to be Yellow Chats.

For twenty years I had wanted to visit Broome, but even my dreams had never anticipated this reality. After less than two days I had added sixteen new birds to my list, which was all the more remarkable considering how far advanced my list was. The last time the list had kicked along so quickly was when I first hit the tropical coast of Queensland back in August. It had been a truly sensational two days. But now there was nothing more to see, I had to push on.

I arrived somewhat dazed at Derby, the next town up the track. The dream run I'd had seemed too extraordinary to be true, like winning best actor, best director and best picture when all you'd been nominated for was best short animation. But the astonishing birding was not done with yet as news filtered through that an Isabelline Wheatear had turned up in Mount Carbine, North Queensland. Apart from having one of the most arcane of all the bird names, the Isabelline Wheatear was an extraordinary sighting because it breeds in central Russia and migrates to Africa, Arabia and northwestern India. The closest it had ever previously come to Australia was a single record from Burma, over six thousand kilometres away.

Even though Mount Carbine was on the other side of the country, I simply had to go for this bird. I couldn't get a flight immediately so I had a little over a day to sweat it out around Derby. And sweat was in profusion in Derby at this time of year. (Derby, by the way, is pronounced to rhyme with 'Herbie' not 'Barbie', a little tip that will help avoid infuriating the locals as I kept doing. I'm sure the people of Derby are lovely souls but in this heat it is very hard not to be just a little cranky.) Not only was it unbearably hot but the town itself is not situated on the most prepossessing stretch of land, surrounded as it is on three sides by desolate saltpans. It was as if the air itself was too hot and bothered to move and just hung indolently around the saltpans choking the life out of everything.

Still, the surrounding area was surprisingly good for birds. Great-billed Heron down by the wharf where some of the largest tides in the world flood in every day, Ruff and many other good waders down on the overflow basin at the sewage works. The former can be exceedingly difficult to find, the latter I had all but given up hope of seeing. My run of luck seemed to be continuing.

Another long shot on my list was the relatively rare Garganey, a type of small duck. Over the last couple of years hardly any had been turning up, but Adrian told me that George Swann, another bird guide operating out of Broome, had seen a Garganey up on the Gibb River Road in the Kimberley, near Mount Barnett Station. I'd be travelling up the Gibb when I got back from the Isabelline twitch but I figured I might as well use the time to go check it out as Mount Barnett is only three hundred kilometres up the road, a mere trifle of a distance up here.

As much of the track wasn't sealed, it took quite a few hours to get to Mount Barnett and by the time I arrived it was almost dark. The only wetland I could find was not much more than a large puddle by the side of the road containing only three ducks. One of them turned out to be the Garganey. The three ducks took flight and I marvelled at how close this one had come to getting away. The Garganey was my seven hundredth bird for my Australian list – cause for minor celebration, I thought, so I danced a little jig in honour of the milestone. You can do daggy things like this out here because no-one's around to ridicule you, and even if they were, this part of the world attracts so many eccentrics that a guy with binoculars jiving around a puddle would seem relatively tame. Five days later, when I came this way again, the Garganey was nowhere to be seen. If I had waited I would have been dancing in despair.

I spent the night in the deserted campground at Windjana Gorge, tourist season being over, and mulled on the fact that while the forthcoming three-day detour to Queensland might snare me the bonus of the wheatear, it might also cost me Black Grasswren, Gouldian Finch and potentially half a dozen others if the wet broke early. But the dice was rolled: following the edict of one former Prime Minister, from now on it was 'crash through or crash'. And following the lead of another Prime Minister, I lost my trousers and headed for a skinny dip. Then I saw the Freshwater Crocodiles floating nearby and thought better of it. I know the Freshies aren't supposed to attack humans, as they prefer smaller prey, but I wasn't willing to risk them mistaking certain appendages for that small prey.

As I was queuing to board the plane the next day, the disembarking passengers streamed past, Mike Carter amongst them. He was on a major twitch, having flown from Melbourne to Cairns for the wheatear and now heading over to Broome for the flycatcher. He laughed when he saw me: 'I thought I might see you here.' Then became instantly serious: 'Is it still there?'

'It was still there yesterday, I haven't heard since. What about the wheatear?'

'It was there this morning.' And he was gone.

'What a freak,' I thought to myself. 'Imagine flying all that way just for a bird. It's a bit sad, really.' And then I got on the plane that would take me to Cairns via Kununurra and Darwin. (Even sadder, the flycatcher failed to ever be seen again, and Mike dipped out.)

My plane arrived in Cairns just after dawn and as I pushed the hire car up towards Mount Carbine I prayed that the wheatear would still be hanging around. Given this bird had half the world to choose from, it is beyond comprehension why it chose to land where it did. It was first seen on what's officially called a sports oval, although there was just as little grass and just as many cow pats on the 'oval' as on the adjacent dust bowl of a paddock next door. After expending so much effort to get here it was rather disheartening, especially when, after twenty minutes, I still couldn't locate the bird. There was a dilapidated toilet block on the site and, needing to answer nature's call, I made my way over to it. The Isabelline Wheatear flew up a couple of metres away from the outhouse.

As a rarity the wheatear is everything the Blue-and-white

Flycatcher isn't. It is neither colourful nor spunky – in fact it was hard to tell this little brown job from the other brown jobs lying about on the ground. But it was a new bird for Australia and one I'd never have dreamed would make it onto my list. A couple of local birders turned up and took me to a nearby dam to see some Freckled Ducks, a rare occurrence in this part of the world.

Having seen the wheatear within an hour of arriving, I had almost two full days to kill before I flew back to Broome. Fortunately, Mount Carbine is just a stone-curlew's throw from Kingfisher Park and I was forced to stay there. Isn't life tough? Also there was Chris Tzaros, the Threatened Birds Officer from Birds Australia's Melbourne office, on holiday with his girlfriend Julie. It was Chris's first time up north and he was absolutely buzzing with all the new ticks he was getting. Jules was doing her best to share his excitement, but after Chris dragged her through the mangrove boardwalk at Cairns, where she was attacked by hundreds of sandflies, she was battling the infuriating itch of dozens of swollen red bites. She looked like she had a bad case of chickenpox, but it wasn't enough to stop her joining us on a search for Rufous Owl half an hour up the road.

Julie was typical of the partners of many of the birders I encountered that year. I always used to buy the stereotype of bird-watchers being nerdy losers who could never hope to have a girlfriend. It gave me solace during the many years I was single. I'm a twitcher – being alone comes with the territory. But so many of the really good twitchers, particularly the younger ones, had simply stunning partners. Almost without exception they were smart, attractive and actually seemed to be interested in their partner's ridiculous hobby. It is totally counter-intuitive. How do these uber-nerds get the cute girls? Is it the ultimate triumph of the Bill Gates era, in which geek is the new cool?

When I think about it, though, a surprising number of full-on twitchers are actually quite charismatic. I guess if their childhood experience was anything like mine, they either developed a very thick hide or were so sure of their sense of self that they were prepared to pursue their passion regardless of what others thought. I guess within that 'I don't give a toss what you think of me' are the seeds of cool. If you have passion in one area of your life, you are probably capable of passion in other areas too.

Not that 'cool' would have been the first word to pop into your head if you'd been watching Chris sight his first Pheasant Coucal. The largest member of the Australian cuckoos, the Pheasant Coucal looks more like an archaeopteryx than the birdie that pops out of a clock, so it is quite an impressive bird. One flapped across the road as we were driving and Chris slammed on the brakes and was out stalking it with such concentration that Jules and I were in hysterics. His sheer delight at seeing it reminded me of the thrill of discovery that got me into birding in the first place. I shouldn't really have been laughing at all because my Rufous Scrub-bird victory dance looked like something out of Moulin Rouge compared to Chris's Pheasant Coucal jig. And when Chris's persistence and sharp eye netted us the Rufous Owl hidden amongst the thick creekside vegetation, I was very tempted to start dancing again. I had a pair of these grand birds lined up for the Darwin Botanic Gardens, but in birding nothing is certain so I happily took this species then.

Before I headed back down to Cairns I had a chinwag with Ron Stannard, the owner of Kingfisher Park. I hadn't seen much of Ron when I was through here in September as he was down with Ross River fever. Even now he wasn't quite back to full strength. Filling him in on my progress I lamented that I'd have to wait until I was back around Christmas to get Blue-faced Parrot-Finch and Buff-breasted Paradise-Kingfisher. Ron was as surprised as all the other birders had been seeing the finches up on Mount Lewis. All the others except me, who dipped on this species yet again. He also told me that a pair of kingfishers had been hanging around the orchard for about a week. A quick trip there was enough for an encounter with this exceptionally cute little kingfisher.

Ron also mentioned that Dion Hobcroft had flown up from Sydney and was out at the wheatear site. I decided to say g'day to Dion, who had put me up during my lightning visit to Sydney for the Canada Goose, but when I got there there was no sign of the bird or of Dion. Once I was back in Western Australia I discovered he'd been over at the Freckled Duck dam finding not only them, but also a Grey

Wagtail, yet another bird I hadn't included on my initial list. It hurt. It hurt bad.

Is it human nature in general or the mindset of the twitcher in particular that makes it almost impossible for me to think about that mad dash across the country without grieving for what I missed out on? I got to see one of the most remarkable records in Australian birding history – and am, in fact, the only birder to have both the wheatear and the Blue-and-white Flycatcher –but whenever I think of that time the spectre of the missed Grey Wagtail haunts me. Maybe it's just me. Even though Collingwood won a premiership in 1990, I still ache over the 1970 Grand Final loss to Carlton, and I was barely two at the time. I'm sure that's the attitude that makes a twitcher – moments after seeing a new bird, they are thinking about the next one.

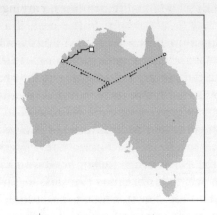

CHAPTER 31

29 November, Kununurra, Western Australia: *674 species*

They call it the build-up. After a long dry season the heat builds and builds. So does the humidity. For weeks, if not months, it is unrelenting. To be outside for more than a few minutes is totally enervating. The whole atmosphere is tense, waiting for something to break as each night fierce electrical storms gather and blast out across the country. Some years it feels like the monsoon will never come.

Also known as suicide season, this is the time of year when the people living in this oppressive environment reflect the tension in the atmosphere and start to 'go troppo'. It is an annual race to see who will crack first, the weather or the people. And it is into this cauldron that I return for the final long leg of the Big Twitch.

On the plane on the way back to Broome I sat next to a bloke who I studied law with. I suppose if I had actually turned up to lectures I would have remembered his face. His name is Tom Cannon and, unlike me, he actually went on and did something useful with his law degree. After working for the Aboriginal Legal Service in the Kimberley he went into private practice representing mainly

Aboriginal clients in personal injury cases, earning him the nick-name 'Smash and Bash Cannon'. In the past, if a Blackfella was injured in an accident that wasn't their fault they would be bandaged up and sent on their way, very rarely getting any of the compensation a Whitefella would expect to receive as a matter of course. Tom's role in enlightening the local Aborigines to the full extent of their rights had not made him the most popular boy in town.

By the time we landed he had roped me into videoing evidence for him in a case where one of his clients had injured himself in a fall. The business owner whose negligence had created the condi-tions for the fall had been dismissive of the injured man's claims. But when 'Smash and Bash' the big city lawyer turned up with me carry-ing a broadcast-quality camera to film witness statements and the site of the incident, you could see him almost wetting himself in the realisation that this thing could no longer be swept under the carpet. At least my camera had come in useful for something.

Eventually I was off, and heading back up the Gibb River Road, reputed to be the worst road in Australia at absolutely the most hor-rid time to travel it. There are a lot of good birds in the Kimberley; it is, after all, one of the last great frontiers, a vast expanse of virtually untouched woodland the size of many European countries. And there is one species of bird that is only found here and nowhere else, the Black Grasswren, and only one regular, accessible location for this species: Mitchell Falls. When I say accessible, it lies almost three hundred kilometres from the Gibb River Road.

All year I had worried that this was where my strategy would fall apart. When I arrived at the turnoff the road was looking good, but there was a roadblock and a sign saying the road was closed as of 1 November. What I hadn't counted on was that the authorities, sick of rescuing stranded tourists cut off by the arrival of the wet, had put a blanket ban on travel along the road without a permit. I could have made a run for it, hoping I wouldn't get caught and fined, but there was always the chance the rains would really kick in and leave me stranded without anybody knowing I was there. On top of that, it was a 750-kilometre round trip from the nearest fuel stop. Though my long-range fuel tanks usually provided me with around a thousand kilometres, I'd be engaging four-wheel drive for most of the journey and that might use more juice than normal. I'd be playing Russian roulette as to whether I'd make it out. In conditions where the mercury reaches forty degrees and the humidity eighty-five per cent, this was not somewhere I wanted to break down by myself.

My only option for Black Grasswren was to try Mount Elizabeth Station where they had occasionally been recorded before. Peter Lacey, the owner of the property, said I was welcome to try but added that nobody had been out looking for them over the past few years. It is a fifty-kilometre drive along a very rough track from the Laceys' homestead to the outlying sandstone escarpment where the birds are meant to reside. For two days I scrambled across the rocky outcrops, unshielded from the fierce tropical sun. I don't think I've ever worked as hard for a bird. After hauling myself up yet another rocky escarpment I wiped my hands over my face to clear away the sweat and in my cupped hands lay a pool of perspiration half an inch deep. I was going through water at the rate of three litres an hour. Thank Godwit I'd bought that refrigerator unit for the car as I could return to savour a cold drink every couple of hours.

It might have been hot but there were still birds about, mainly in the relative cool of the morning. Unlike me, they're not idiots and they mostly shut up shop by about eight o'clock. I still managed to add some nice birds to the list here: White-quilled Rock-Pigeon, White-lined Honeyeater, Sandstone Shrike-thrush and Green-backed Gerygone. But no Black Grasswren. At one point in the middle of the day I paused to rest on a rocky outcrop. From the clump of spinifex next to me I swear I heard a grasswren give its high-pitched call but after waiting with baited breath for another half an hour there was not another peep. Perhaps I was in the first throes of heatstroke and suffering auditory hallucinations.

I had told the folks at Mount Elizabeth that I would only be out for two days and even though I was sorely tempted to stay out in that furnace to have another crack at the grasswrens, I didn't want to be responsible for having a search party organised unnecessarily. For the first time in the year it looked like I had definitely been defeated by a bird.

By the time I arrived in Kununurra a couple of days later, however, I'd hatched a fresh plan. Having consulted Tony Palliser, who with another birder had taken similar action ten years earlier, I started to ring around the air charter companies. My plan was to hire a light plane to fly me out to the nearest airstrip to Mitchell Falls, walk the sixteen kilometres up to the plateau where the grasswrens are, tick them off then walk back down to be picked up the next day. Sure, in such searing temperatures and humidity there was a chance I might die in the attempt, but it was the only way I could possibly see this species now.

The hitch in the plan was the cost. When Tony did it ten years earlier it had cost him and his mate about five hundred dollars all up. The cheapest I was quoted was two thousand. If the trip didn't kill me it was going to make me bankrupt. I just couldn't afford to blow the last of my budget on the one bird. As much as it stuck in my craw, I had to draw a line through any hope of seeing Black Grasswren.

At Kununurra I receive another, more welcome piece of news with the announcement of the birth of Tahlia Ann Dooley, my brother's first child. Oh, how the tables had turned in our family dynamic. I was always the sensible one, Warwick the black sheep, always on the verge of some sort of trouble. As he lay dying my father said to me, 'Do me a favour, Sean. Keep an eye out for your brother after I'm gone. Make sure he doesn't piss his inheritance up against a wall.' Warwick had since got a nice house, car and job, met a lovely woman and now had a beautiful daughter. Me, the supposedly sensible one, was off gallivanting around the country pissing his inheritance up against any wall he could find. I think Dad might have spoken to the wrong son about who needed keeping an eye on.

Not only were the finances tight but so too the window of opportunity for some of the birds I was after. The other critical species I needed to get before the wet season kicked in was the Gouldian Finch. Much reduced in numbers, they were very thinly spread across the vast area of their former range and encounters with them in the bush were very rare, though there was a far greater chance of seeing them in the dry season when they come in to drink at their favoured watering holes. One such hole was at the Wyndham Caravan Park but too much rain had already fallen and there were no finches of any persuasion at the caravan park.

I did find plenty of finches, including Yellow-rumped Mannikins on the irrigated agricultural plains just out of Kununurra. The town owes its existence to the Ord River Irrigation Scheme, one of those 'nation building' projects begun in the 1960s. Northern Australia's answer to the Snowy River Scheme, the damming of the Ord River to create the massive Lake Argyle was the first step in a grand vision to turn the deserts green. This is a concept that is back in vogue, particularly with certain Sydney radio announcers and their mates, but it is interesting to note that after thirty years of government money being pumped into it, the Ord Scheme, though impressive, still hasn't paid for itself.

While the inundation of such a vast area was probably not a plus for much of the local wildlife, it has been beneficial for a select few species, including my old nemesis the Little Bittern. Frank O'Connor assured me he had *the* spot for Little Bittern at Kununurra. He scribbled out a mud map for me when we were on the Torres Strait cruise but after four attempts at dusk and dawn I yet again had no luck. I was seriously regretting not going for it in Brisbane in February as I was running out of ideas for this species.

Frank had drawn me another mud map but there was no label on it telling me which species could be found there and after three months I couldn't for the life of me remember what bird we'd been talking about but I decided I might as well check it out anyway. It was a patch of open woodland much like the surrounding hundred kilometres of open woodland. Perhaps Frank had seen Gouldian Finches, or maybe Pictorella Mannikin, another dry country finch. For all I knew Frank might have lost his keys here. I wandered tentatively about the area, and after about ten minutes a female Red-chested Button-quail flushed from below my feet, staying airborne a remarkably long time and allowing me a good look. To be honest I'd had no real idea where I was going to find this species so I was particularly grateful to Frank's mud map. Then I notice on the ground a keyring with Frank's initials. Turns out they weren't his.

Actually that last bit's not true. But the Red-chested Button-quail certainly is and I was so stoked that I pumped my fist in the air too emphatically and managed to throw out my back. I spent the rest of my time in Kununurra hobbling around like a binocular-carrying hunchback. Strangely, I seemed to fit right in.

Having had no luck anywhere with the Pictorella Mannikin I followed some advice from Tony Palliser, who said he'd seen them in drier country out near the Northern Territory border. I stopped for some finches that turned out to be Long-tailed Finch, and watched a male Spinifex Pigeon presenting his courtship display to a female who seemed mightily impressed with all that chest puffing. I was about to get back in the car when a slight movement further down the road caught my eye. Probably the Long-taileds. Then I heard what might have been mannikins calling further up the road. I was about to turn and chase them when I remembered that 'bird in the hand' saying and turned back to confirm the Long-taileds.

The image that focused in my bins was a male red-headed Gouldian Finch. It was joined by a female red-head and a black-headed male. I'd forgotten just how stunning these critters are in the flesh. One of the most incongruously beautiful birds going round, the colours are extraordinary: glorious greens, purples and yellows that manage to be exquisite without being gaudy. I say incongruous because they contrast wildly with the stark ochre colours of the harsh environment they live in. They were so beautiful it almost made me weep. Or perhaps that was from the sheer relief of happening across a bird I had all but written off. It never happens this way, just fluking on Gouldians. It had to be my lucky day. And to top it off, a few kilometres down the track I lucked onto some Pictorella Mannikins as well.

As I kicked the footy over another state border I couldn't help but wonder how long my luck could hold. I might get as many as 705 if I saw everything possible. This was contingent on the weather as much as anything else. As I drove into the Northern Territory I passed all the waterholes where I had been planning to look for Gouldian Finch. With so much water lying about there was no way they would have been coming into drink at these places. The sheer improbability of my chance encounter with them near Kununurra seemed all the more miraculous.

It was the last day of November. One month, twenty-six species to go. Easy…Yeah, right.

CHAPTER 32

3 December, Kakadu National Park, Northern Territory:
680 species

As I was driving through the Top End I heard on an ABC radio bulletin some news that rocked my world to its very foundation – Midnight Oil had split up. For twenty years the Oils had provided the soundtrack to my birdwatching life. One of the reasons I kept at birdwatching through my teen years (aside from an inherent nerdiness that just couldn't be suppressed) was that twitching was about the most punk thing I had ever been involved in. Perhaps not quite as rebellious as growing a mohawk, putting a spike in your arm or throwing bottles at the police, but it was more exciting than anything else in my teenage world. While I could have spent the weekends hanging around in sub-urban lounge rooms drinking rocket fuel or smoking bongs and listening to bands like the Dead Kennedys, the Birthday Party and the Violent Femmes, it seemed to me far more radical and exciting to be out on road trips chasing rare birds and listening to the Dead Kennedys, the Birthday Party and the Violent Femmes.

And of all the bands that fuelled those all-night twitches across the countryside, the Oils were king. I guess it helped that they were one of the few bands with an environmental sensibility but, more importantly, they played some kick-arse rock'n'roll. A shared passion for the Oils had cemented my friendship with Puke and Groober as much as our mutual passion for birds. We tried to combine the two wherever possible. The first day I saw Regent Honeyeater at Chiltern was also the first time I heard the 'Bird Noises' EP on the crappy tape deck in Puke's old Valiant. We commandeered Puke's cousin's farmhouse at Chiltern that hot January night to watch a live telecast of one of their concerts. I don't know what his country cousins made of these young idiots spazzing it up around their lounge room in emulation of Peter Garrett's epileptic dancing style. I think their parents used it as a cautionary tale of what happens to you when you go to the big smoke.

The Oils did an outdoor gig at Portarlington on the coast south of Melbourne. After a spot of wader watching on the way down we threw ourselves into the thick of the mosh pit during the gig. On the way home we stopped, bruised and sweat encrusted, at a dodgy hamburger joint in Geelong, and we realised we were standing next to then Midnight Oil bassist Peter Gifford buying junk food while Garrett himself waited in the car. It was the first time I ever recall being star struck, apart from the day I met Roy Wheeler.

I remember being disappointed with their best-known album, *Diesel and Dust*, when I first heard it back in 1987 – too many acoustic guitars for my liking. It was only when I travelled through the Outback that I realised what genius that album showed. The red soil reverberated in every note. If you want an understanding of the Outback's essence, drive the road from Coober Pedy to Marla with 'Beds Are Burning' cranked up loud and you'll know what I am talking about.

The only song that betters anything else in terms of evoking a quintessentially Australian spirit is the Triffids' 'Wide Open Road'. Coming from Perth this band must have made the long haul across the Nullarbor to the east coast commercial centres innumerable times, and that song captures so brilliantly the essence of travelling across the Australian landscape, both physical and emotional – I hardly need to explain why it was easily my song of the year, though it wasn't the song I heard most throughout the year. Unfortunately Kasey Chambers' 'Am I Not Pretty Enough' won that gong. Every time I turned on a commercial radio station anywhere outside the cities that song would be playing. I just couldn't get it out of my head. It drove me crazy. Possibly literally. Stocking up on supplies in the supermarket at Kununurra I found myself in the checkout queue singing about whether my heart was too broken – at full volume judging by the looks I got.

While in the supermarket I bumped into a British couple who were twitching their way around the country. They were travelling in the opposite direction to me so I was eager to hear how they'd gone with the Purple-crowned Fairy-wren at Victoria River Crossing. I'd seen it there before and hadn't factored in a back-up location. They grumbled that they'd spent two full days there without a sniff, a response that threw me into a mild panic.

I arrived at the crossing minutes before dark and headed straight from the roadhouse down toward the long grass near the river's edge where the wrens should have been. It was very humid, with thick clouds encroaching overhead and a light drizzle starting to fall. Not exactly great conditions. Within ten seconds of entering the habitat I had a party of these beautiful birds around me, the male with his striking lilac-striped head coming to within a metre. It was hard to believe those Brits had had such difficulty. No wonder the Poms were doing so poorly at cricket – they seem to miss everything.

The birds just kept falling into place. Out in the woodlands near the small town of Pine Creek in the gathering ominous gloom of afternoon storm clouds I managed to find a pair of Chestnut-backed Button-Quail, a bird I had missed out on every time I'd been up this way. I was so worried about finding it that I'd budgeted a couple of days for this one and the Hooded Parrot, which I got onto first thing the next morning. How long could this run continue?

Not that I was complaining as it gave me more time in Kakadu. Kakadu is simply phenomenal. I'm not sure I'm a particularly spiritual person but there is something about the place that made me feel I was in the presence of a higher spiritual force. It is not just the spectacular scenery – you could arguably find more spectacular sandstone cliffs within an hour of Sydney. Perhaps it is the scale, or the abundance of wildlife. Perhaps the fact that it is home to a living culture that has been connected to the place for tens of thousands of years.

My visit would be tragically brief, though, as there were very few new birds left for me. Driving to my first destination I ticked off the first of these, a Partridge Pigeon, beside the road into Gunlom. Gunlom is a waterfall made famous by the first Crocodile Dundee movie. It is also known as Waterfall Creek but I prefer an earlier European name, UDP Falls. UDP stands for Uranium Development Project and it's a lovely reminder of the past (and current) history of the area. The powers that be think the name might be something of a turnoff for tourists. I love the name and fewer tourists mean fewer disturbances to the White-throated Grasswren for which Gunlom is *the* spot. The grasswrens live atop the massive escarpment amongst a myriad of boulders, spinifex bushes and crevices into which they can disappear at a moment's notice. This is what makes them so difficult to see. In 1988 I totally dipped despite three attempts. Then in 1998 I saw them easily. I suspect that by the time most birders make it up the hot, steep climb they are huffing so hard the grasswrens can hear them a mile off.

I hadn't been planning to do this climb late in the morning but as I had cleaned up at Pine Creek I found myself here a day or so early. Rather than set up camp I figured I should have a crack at these things. By the time I reached the top of the escarpment I was covered in sweat. There were plenty of birds about – White-lined Honeyeater, Sandstone Shrike-thrush, Helmeted Friarbird – but no grasswrens. I stopped to rest on a large boulder from where I could see both the interior of the plateau with its massive sandstone tors and rock formations, and the endless wooded plains below. Once I'd got my breath back and my heart rate down to normal, I could actually take the time to appreciate what a brilliant place this is.

As I gazed slack jawed at the landscape around me, I noticed some movement in the rocks below. In a rush of adrenaline I lifted my binoculars: Variegated Fairy-wrens. Damn. But hang on, there was something else, much bigger and darker. They instantly disappeared into the rock crevices below. They had the advantage: a quick flight down a rock-face takes them a few seconds; it took me at least five minutes to clamber up, down and around the piles of rocks. After leading me a merry dance they finally relented and a pair of White-throated Grasswrens deigned to show themselves, giving me surprisingly good views. Perhaps they were rewarding me for effort. They are exceptionally handsome birds: quite large, almost blackbird-sized, and strikingly patterned with rich chestnut, black and bold white streaks.

Seeing these birds made me feel great. Top birds, stunning backdrop, now I could get out of this sweatbox. I stopped at the pool above the falls and celebrated my sighting with a welcome skinny dip. The water was deep, cool and soothing, and I was lost in the utter delights of the sensation when a tourist party loomed over the ridge, sending me scrambling for my clothes and cutting short my Blue Lagoon moment.

It was only when I was back down from the escarpment that I realised I had seen neither Banded Fruit-Dove nor the Chestnut-quilled Rock-Pigeon up there. The fruit-dove didn't surprise me but the rock-pigeon was a worry – every other time I'd been up on the escarpment I'd almost been kicking them out of the way while searching for the grasswrens. They were probably easier to see first thing in the morning, spending much of the heat of the day sensibly sheltering in the shadows of rock overhangs.

I'd heard of a place called Stag Creek not far from Gunlom that was supposed to be good for Banded Fruit-Dove. I'd never been able to find it before and when I did this time, with the help of a guide-book, I was not impressed. The book mentioned that it was an old mining site but what it failed to mention was that there were signs everywhere warning that the area was radioactive because this was an old uranium mine site. Here was a dilemma I'd never encountered before. Continue on and I risked radiation exposure. Turn away and I might dip out on a new species. The choice was clear. I pushed my way past the sign and looked for the bird. After an hour and a half all I had to show for it was a series of bites from potentially radioactive ants and boots stained with a worryingly bright orange mud – oh, and that third testicle was coming along quite nicely.

Next day I was out at Nourlangie Rock where both species were known to occur. Nourlangie also happens to be home to one of the finest examples of Aboriginal rock art in existence. Though I spent a day and a half with my neck craned skywards scanning for pigeons, even I couldn't help but be moved by the rock galleries filled with images going back thousands of years. At this time of year there are hardly any tourists so for much of the day I had the entire hallowed turf to myself. This is Australia's Sistine Chapel – but after a hot, fruit-less day's searching I was ready to blaspheme in any language. I took one final walk around the circuit. Feeding quietly on the berries of a small rainforest tree growing in the shadow of the main rock was a pair of Banded Fruit-Doves. I wondered whether I'd been oblivious to their gentle presence all day. Still no rock-pigeons, though.

Niven McCrie in Darwin had mentioned a place near the East Alligator River where he regularly saw the pigeons so next morning I was out first thing, pounding the beat on the Bardedjilidji Sandstone Walk (pronounced, I gather, bar-de-jilly) which meanders around a small sandstone outcrop. I didn't find the birds. I did the walk again later when the sun was well up and the still air was starting to really steam. That's when I saw not one, but three Chestnut-quilled Rock-Pigeons. I was naturally very relived and happy to finally get this bird, which I noticed has a ridiculously small head in comparison to the rest of its body. It is a plump, chunky pigeon, almost the size of a city pigeon, but with a head seemingly the size of a marble.

With nothing more to add in Kakadu I had to leave before three days were up. This was the recurring tragedy of the Big Twitch – my quest took me to some of the most amazing, exotic locations imagi-nable and then I'd have to leave as soon as my mission was accomplished. After picking up White-browed Crake at Fogg Dam and Rainbow Pitta (with that gorgeous blue shoulder patch) at Howard Springs, I arrived in Darwin with only two or three required species to get. There I picked up Zitting Cisticola on my first attempt (sounds like something you'd hear in a public health campaign, doesn't it? 'Sean was a happy, healthy young man until he went to

Darwin and picked up Zitting Cisticola. Now he can't show his face in polite society and it really hurts when he pees. And later in life he is at risk of developing cisticular cancer.') At the beginning of the year I imagined I'd be spending at least a couple of weeks based in Darwin, because of its proximity to so many good birds, but all I needed to get now were Oriental Cuckoo, Little Ringed Plover and Chestnut Rail.

The cuckoo proved elusive, as is characteristic of this migratory species. There had been plenty about the week before I arrived but none showed while I was there, though I'd have another chance at this in North Queensland. More disheartening was the disappearance of the Little Ringed Plover. One had been at the sewage works since November – Niven McCrie had seen it the day before I arrived – but we looked both days over the weekend and it had gone, no doubt out onto the local floodplains which were starting to fill as more and more rain fell. The wet season hadn't been officially declared but it was getting very close.

The Chestnut Rail was a very tough proposition – in fact nobody had seen any since late September. I haunted various mangrove habitats around Darwin looking for it. Under the canopy of the mangroves there is no breeze to circulate the air and it became a stultifyingly hot vigil. Luckily I was staying at my friend Sal's place, and though she didn't have air-conditioning she had the next best thing: a swimming pool. If I got too hot during the night I simply donned my togs and went for a midnight swim. It was amazing who you'd bump into in the pool at that time of night.

After five days I was finished. I couldn't keep wasting my time on one bird when between here and North Queensland there were potentially twenty other species I could get. I was packed and ready to leave but as the tide was just right on my final morning, I figured it was worth one last shot, so I headed for a patch of mangroves next to a new canal development. (On one side of the retaining wall were the dank, wonderful mangroves teeming with life; on the other side, sitting on landfill, were modern houses and manicured lawns. Why is it that building the Great Aussie Dream Home invariably involves destroying other creatures' homes?)

Within ten minutes I heard their clattering, braying call. I played the tape and – oh so casually for a bird that had remained steadfastly hidden for so long – a Chestnut Rail sauntered out onto the open mud. For a good five seconds it looked at me imperiously with its red eyes then, realising this was not how the usual script went, it panicked and dashed off madly into the thick of the mangroves.

That was enough for me. The finishing line in Queensland beckoned. A hundred kilometres south at Adelaide River the rain was pounding so hard from the black sky I couldn't see more than five metres in front of me. The wet season had just kicked in – I had made it out just in time.

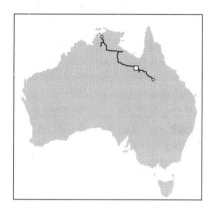

CHAPTER 33

14 December, Mount Isa, Queensland:
687 species

It is hot around Mount Isa, very hot. But the heat is of a different nature to the oppressive humidity of the Top End. Four hundred kilometres from the coast it is much drier and, as strange as it seems, wandering about the bush in thirty-eight degree heat comes as sheer relief. Not that I should still have been there, at least not for the three days I had spent wandering disconsolately around the scrub brushing flies out of my face, swearing even more profusely than I was sweating. The cause of my misery and discomfort? More bloody grasswrens.

I had already tried for Carpentarian Grasswren, a smaller, slightly less impressive version of White-throated Grasswren, at the traditional site for them near the isolated town of Borroloola. This new site I was at, about seventy kilometres from Mount Isa, was apparently far more reliable. Local birdwatcher Bob Forsyth had even built a little stone cairn at the prime location housing a twitchers' visitors' book. Whenever I was back at camp I would torment myself by looking through its dusty pages. It read like a 'Who's Who' of Australian and international twitching, and nearly everyone had eventually scored with the grasswren. As each day passed with no luck it became more and more infuriating to read. 'Him?' I thought. 'He wouldn't recognise a Carpentarian if it came up and bit him on the – Oh, come on, *that* absolute duffer saw four? Impossible.' In the end I had to ban myself from reading it.

Things had been going pretty well up to this point. Sure, I had detoured three hundred kilometres to view a spot where Grey Falcons had been seen, but I'd come to expect that from Grey Falcons because they don't exist. Back on track I was heading south and east, moving out from the tropical woodland of the Top End and onto the open plains of the Barkly Tableland. It was an amazing trip. Every kilometre takes you further into the dry country. The trees start to become more stunted and spread further apart until you are on a virtually treeless plain of staggering proportions. This vast expanse of Mitchell Grass was my last hope for Flock Bronzewing. As the day neared its end I searched the flat horizon for the telltale bulge of a turkey nest dam. The plan was to wait by one until dusk in the hope that the bronzewings would come in to drink. It sounded easy but having missed out on these pigeons in the South Australian deserts I was wary. This wariness turned to major panic when every turkey nest I found turned out to be completely dry. Nothing would be coming in to drink at these.

With the sun hovering low in the sky I spied a windmill about halfway to the horizon and made for it. As I approached, a party of about fifteen plump Flock Bronzewings was circling the dam near the windmill. Sure, it wasn't the forty thousand I could have seen near Birdsville, but I only needed one and these fifteen birds wheeling about in the sunset were one of the most welcome sights of the year.

And then I arrived in hell. Around four o'clock on my first afternoon I managed to hear the squeak of a grasswren. Next morning at the same spot I did a bit better – I saw the tail end of one scamper into a spinifex clump. Over the next two days the situation didn't improve. The bush here is sparse woodland with a spinifex understorey. It all looks the pretty much the same which explains, though not excuses, how I managed to get lost one day despite having GPS and a compass. I climbed to a small ridge under a fiercely blazing sun and sat down under a scraggly gum tree to try and work out my bearings. There was no sign of my camp. All around me was wilderness.

A hazy figure seems to materialise before me. Perhaps it is a fellow lost soul – or perhaps I'd been in the sun too long for it assumed the form of Dick Smith. Prodding his thick prescription glasses up onto the bridge of his nose, he insisted I claim the Carpentarian Grasswren: I replied that I didn't really see it properly.

'Seriously Sean, what else could it be?' Dick demanded testily.

'Female Variegated Fairy-wren?' I postulated.

'Oh come on! It was way too dark. And big. What about the streaking on the back and the thick tail? It had to be a Carp.'

'Yeah, but I didn't see it well enough.'

'You saw the Grey Grasswren for about a half a second longer, yet you're claiming that. What's the difference?'

'I got all the crucial features on the Grey Grasswren. I just don't feel happy about claiming this one – I didn't get the essence of the bird.'

'Oh, who gives a shit about the essence, Dooley!? Just tick the goddam thing. You might not get to seven hundred without it. You won't make King of the Nerds if you don't get to seven hundred!'

As tempting as it was, especially after he added the promise of a lifetime's supply of Dick's True Blue Chest Rub, I decided that to claim the Carpentarian Grasswren would go against everything I wanted to get out of the Big Twitch. Dick Smith wasn't happy and disappeared in a plume of asthma puffer spray. It took me another hour to find my way back to my camp.

To give myself a break from the energy sapping, demoralising patrolling of this uninviting habitat, and to get away from any more creepy visions, I decided to drive into Mount Isa, ostensibly to be within phone range so I could contact Bob Forsyth and find out any local goss from him. Turned out Bob was in Cairns, where I should have been that very minute. While in Mount Isa I tried for another grasswren, the Kalkadoon, another bird that would be elevated to full species status when the new checklist came out.

I tried a couple of likely looking spinifex-clad hills with no luck. On Bob's advice I also tried Mica Creek to the south of the town.

Eventually I heard the high pitched call typical of a grasswren and was trying to home in on it when a couple of locals turned up riding motorbikes. Their revving, whiny engines echoed through the valley negating any chance of hearing the birds again. I trudged back down to my car and began the long drive to my bush campsite. Realising I needed fuel, I turned back into town again. Too late I realised that I had driven past the servo where I could use a discount fuel coupon. I hung a u-turn at the next lights and was immediately pulled over by a police car.

The officer was one of those typical Queensland cops, big and scary. He asked me why I had made the u-turn. Trying to be polite, I pointed out the service station, saying I was trying to get there and as there was no traffic, I thought it would be safe to make the turn. He informed me that it is illegal to make a u-turn at traffic lights in Queensland. I pleaded that, having only just arrived in his fair state, I was ignorant of this local law. (Later I discovered it is also an offence in Victoria – who'd have thought it?) The cop cut me no slack and smirked as he told me it was an expensive lesson to learn. He took my licence and went to write me a ticket.

Didn't he realise he was dealing with a twitcher who had just spent three days in the heat dipping out on a bird he desperately needed? That's like putting a tasty German tourist in front of a hungry crocodile – the croc is bound to snap. I lost the plot completely. Stupid really when you consider the size of this man-mountain, and I knew he would probably have loved nothing better than to beat the crap out of a weedy greenie agitator. But I went off my head at him. I'm not sure what about exactly, but I let him know I'd had a gutful. Luckily (for me as much as for him) he just handed my licence back and departed. I drove the car the remaining twenty metres to the pumps and got out. The laughing attendant behind the perspex window bellowed at me, 'We close at eight-thirty!' with a delighted sneer in her voice. I looked at the clock. It was eight thirty-eight.

The first time I came through Mount Isa was on a hellish fifty-hour Greyhound bus ride from Townsville to Alice Springs during which I was seated opposite the toilet. We had a dinner break at a pub in Mount Isa. A fight broke out amongst some white mine workers and Aboriginal stockmen. One bloke smashed a pool cue on another bloke's head. I couldn't wait to get out of the joint. Now, fifteen years on, I still felt the same way about the place. I filled up with expensive juice at another servo and headed back out to the Carpentarian site.

Next morning I was defeated yet again by a grasswren. Attempting to compensate with the Kalkadoon, I headed out to Mica Creek once more. This time there were no motorbikes but there were also no Kalkadoons. Eventually I climbed to the top of a spinifex-covered mountain, scrambling across the steep, boulder strewn ridges like a rock wallaby. Right at the top – when I was about at the end of my tether – a Kalkadoon Grasswren hopped out onto a nearby boulder, gave a smirk as it checked me out and hopped away again.

I was free to move on. I looked towards my car in the valley below. I figured the quickest way down was not to backtrack along the tortuous path I'd taken coming up, but to head straight down the steeper slope direct to my car. This plan was working well until I jumped onto a massive boulder that broke loose and started to slide down the slope, carrying me with it. I jumped onto another boulder that also dislodged, and again I was rapidly descending – headfirst this time – towards the sharp rocks below. Pulling a manoeuvre that would have done an Olympic gymnast proud, I somehow managed to do a mid-air 180-degree spin and grab onto the side of the mountain, halting my downward momentum. In doing so I plunged my hands directly into the spikes of a spinifex clump. Days later I was still removing spines.

Before heading to the coast I thought I'd continue the misery by having one last try for Grey Falcon. John Young had seen them at Bladensburg National Park, not far from the Outback town of Winton. It would only add about four hours to the trip so I decided it was worth a shot.

I arrived an hour or so before sunset, which John had assured me is the best time to search as the Grey Falcons make a sweep of the waterholes trying to snatch an unsuspecting bird that has come in to drink. There hadn't been a drop of rain since January, though, and the whole area was totally parched. The ranger told me that only one waterhole in the entire park still had any water so that was where I'd be searching. If I could get away from the ranger, that is. The last visitor must have come around the same time as the last rain, and with his family seven hundred kilometres away on the coast, man, was this bloke eager for a chinwag.

I should have stayed chatting. The waterhole was just a sludgy brown puddle, and apart from a couple of very cautious Common Bronzewings there was hardly a bird to be seen. That was it. I was done with Grey Falcon. I was done with grasswrens. I was done with the deserts. All that was left was the sweltering tropical rainforests of North Queensland in the wet. Bring it on.

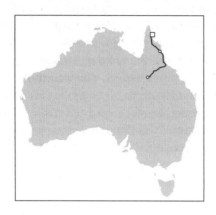

CHAPTER 34

20 December, The Green House, Iron Range, Queensland:
693 species

Once the wet kicks in up north, you can be stranded for months waiting for swollen rivers to subside to a crossable depth, but visiting Cape York at this time of year was unavoidable for me, as the wet season is the only time of year that the Red-bellied Pitta and Black-winged Monarch are present, spending the rest of their time in New Guinea. All along I had factored in the early arrival of the wet and had been planning to fly into and out of Iron Range. Given the heat it would involve an arduous ten-kilometre hike from the Lockhart River airstrip to the camping area, but I was resigned to doing it. There seemed to be no other way.

I thought I had it all worked out but then I hadn't factored in the cost. By the time I arrived in Townsville on the 16th and checked my finances, I realised that my budget had almost dissipated. I didn't have to worry too much, though, as to my amazement the comedy pilot I helped write early in the year had been commissioned by

Channel Nine. I had to be back in Melbourne to start work on 6 January. If I had stayed in Melbourne that year I probably wouldn't have picked up an extra day's work, yet on my return I'd be walking straight into a job that should last a minimum of four months. With that financial buffer I was able to extend my credit card limit by another couple of thousand to cover the flight. Everything seemed to be falling into place perfectly. That had to be a worry.

Remembering that David Harper and his family were in the area for Christmas holidays I gave him a ring. When I told him I was in Townsville, he replied, 'Well I'm at Townsville Common looking at an Oriental Cuckoo as we speak. Do you still need that?'

Did I ever. I raced across town and was standing beside Dave less than fifteen minutes later. The cuckoo, of course, had gone. We headed out there again the next morning and managed not to see it. During our search we bumped into a local birder, Steve Guerrato, who told us there had been a few hanging around Anderson Park in the middle of Townsville. This was like coming home for me as my cousins used to live just around the corner. I saw many of my first tropical birds in these very tame looking gardens. My first ever Great Bowerbird and its bower were still in the same position after twenty years. The entrance to the bower, two avenues of sticks, was festooned with white shells and shards of green glass while the side wall was decorated with the blood red of plastic Coke bottle tops. A feature wall! Even bowerbirds seemed to be watching home renovation shows. A little further on we found a loose group of Oriental Cuckoos. I'd never managed to see this species in more than twenty years of birding, and now I was seeing nine in one shot.

By the time I arrived in Cairns I was all set to book my flight. Then it occurred to me that every local I'd met bemoaned the lack of rain and how, for the second year in a row, the wet might fail. I made a few calls to Cape York and everyone I spoke to said their part of the track was perfectly drivable – in fact all roads were still open. If I drove I'd save hundreds of dollars and could follow my own timetable. Of course if the monsoon kicked in I could be stranded until April. I decided stuff it – it's splash through or splash.

Despite yet another flat tyre before I had even left the bitumen,

I arrived at Iron Range safely. There had been virtually no rain and the creeks were lower than they had been at the height of the dry season. I managed to lock onto a Black-winged Monarch and Green-backed Honeyeater fairly easily, but there was no sign of the pittas. Perhaps they hadn't left their base in New Guinea yet. By walking into the forest with my spotlight that night I was able to track down one of the many Marbled Frogmouths that had been calling frustratingly out of sight. I only needed four more species and I could head back south.

The next day I dropped in on Steve Murphy, whom I'd met back in September. Gathered at his hut were three other PhD students studying various forest creatures. The hut was pretty rudimentary but it did have a generator to run a fridge large enough to keep their home brew cold. In such oppressive heat that is all you need and I welcomed his offer to share a few. We sat on the verandah looking out over to the adjacent rainforest. A young Double-eyed Fig-Parrot poked its head out of a nesting hole just above us and its parents came in at regular intervals to feed it. It was a truly serene and glorious situation.

Steve grilled me on how the twitch was going and I mentioned I still needed Northern Scrub-robin. He replied, deadpan, that it was calling right then. I hadn't even registered what the repetitive piping sound coming from the nearby forest might have been. The bird made its way onto a nearby termite mound and called its heart out for a good two minutes. A cold beer in one hand, binoculars in the other – this is how birding should always be.

Another bird I needed was the Chestnut-breasted Cuckoo. Steve thought I might have needed Gould's Bronze-Cuckoo. I did, and told him I'd have a better chance for it around Cairns. Steve replied that that might be so but as one had just flown into the tree above us, perhaps I wanted to check it out. And he was right – just above our heads sat a Gould's Bronze-Cuckoo. I invoked the names of everything else I needed but sadly the magic wore off and we didn't see any more from the convenience of the verandah. Steve recommended I talk to John Young, who'd recently got the three species I was still after, so I phoned him and it looked like I was all set for the next day.

For the time being I kicked back and stayed for dinner with Steve and his gang. To me this was heaven. I've always had huge admiration for the people I've known involved in field studies. I always thought they were so cool. They often work under extremely difficult conditions and there is never enough funding to go around, but I can't help wondering what if... Sitting out on the verandah under a tropical sky, in company with people who are dynamic and passionate – it really doesn't get any better than this. I seriously could have stayed forever.

Instead I reluctantly dragged myself off so as to be up early to hit the road in pursuit of the last few species left on my ridiculous quest. John Young's gen is pretty spot on because within a couple of hours I have all three targets under the belt: Yellow-legged Flycatcher, Chestnut-breasted Cuckoo and Red-bellied Pitta, the last an exceptionally beautiful bird with shining red plumage emblazoned across its front, contrasting with a dazzling blue back and breast.

And that's all, folks. Apart from Buff-breasted Button-quail, a bird that nobody has sighted for a couple of years, there was nothing left to see at Iron Range. After two days in paradise I was driven out by my own hand. Maybe one day I'll return, buy Steve's hut and sit there on the verandah sucking back a coldie, watching my vanilla beans grow as fig-parrots and scrub-robins and pittas flit about me. For now I had a more pressing dream to fulfil. As I drove the bumpy track back to civilization, I was sitting on six hundred and ninety-six species. Only four to go.

Three after I stopped north of Mount Molloy to check out what looked like suitable habitat for Buff-breasted Button-quail. No button-quail, of course, but I did bump into a pair of Black-throated Finches, one of the most underrated of all the family. Even in photos they appear rather dull but in real life their front is the most delicate peach colour. Hell, as bird number 697 they could have looked like old turds and I still would have got excited.

And so on the evening of 22 December I rolled into Kingfisher Park once more. First on the agenda was Bush-hen, a bird I'd never seen in Australia. It was one of the two birds I missed back in Brisbane in February. During the dry season they are so quiet and seen so infrequently that many think they actually migrate out of the country. In the wet they become a lot more obvious with their loud braying and screaming calls. This wasn't a very good wet, however. There hadn't been enough rain to bring on the Bush-hen's usual breeding season antics, and as a result they were extremely difficult to locate.

Carol from Kingfisher Park told me they'd been seeing Bush-hen down by the river around five every evening. I wandered down at the appropriate time and as I set foot on the bridge I caught something large and black out of the corner of my eye as it flew up from the river bed to my right. I wheeled around expectantly and was disappointed to find a Black Bittern, a bird that normally would have really turned my crank. As I lowered my binoculars I heard a rustle to my left and looked over just in time to catch a Bush-hen erupting from the streamside vegetation to make a desperate flight across the river, giving me bird number 698.

On to 699, the Red-necked Crake. For the past forty years Kingfisher Park has been *the* place to see this secretive inhabitant of the rainforest floor, so like generations of birders before me I made my way down to the pool by the orchard at the back of the park and settled in for my vigil. I waited as dusk fell. And waited. It got darker. Grey-headed Robins come down to drink. The marvellously ridiculous looking Orange-footed Scrubfowl settled noisily into their night-time perches. Not only do they look ridiculous, resembling dinosaurs as much as birds, they also sound ridiculous with their deep maniacal cackle, like a rooster on steroids. But still no crake.

Eventually it was too dark to see properly so I called it stumps. I'd just have to undertake the vigil every evening until I got it. As I disappointedly meandered back through the orchard a Red-necked Crake casually strolled past me in the gloom. If it hadn't almost walked over my feet I wouldn't even have known it was there. Our crossing of paths reminded me of that Warner Brothers cartoon in which the wolf and the sheepdog clocked on for every shift. The Red-necked Crake walked by so nonchalantly that I fully expected it to look up at me and say, 'Morning, Ralph.'

CHAPTER 35

24 December, Mount Lewis, Queensland:
699 species

When, at the start of the year, I mischievously posted on Birding-aus that I was hoping to see seven hundred birds in the one year, I never really thought I would actually get there. I always thought it was achievable – just not by me. Now, almost twelve months later, the seven hundred mark was set to tumble. Only one more, and I knew what I wanted it to be – Blue-faced Parrot-Finch. Over fifteen years I'd made the pilgrimage to Mount Lewis on five separate occasions. Each one had seen me return with an empty space on the checklist. Others had been seeing them recently at the famous clearing but there had only been one or two and they had been very difficult to get onto.

I rose before dawn on the morning of Christmas Eve, determined that this time it would be different. To be honest I was feeling rather sick from lack of sleep – or maybe it was the dodgy noodles I'd cooked the night before, more likely it was from a year's accumulated tension focusing in on this one moment. Bleary eyed I drove up the mountain and parked the car at the concrete causeway where a party of Red-browed Finches were feeding. The parrot-finches will supposedly forage with the Red-broweds, but not this time. Too nervous to risk the sound of the engine scaring off the birds, I tremulously walked the rest of the way to the clearing. Again there were more Red-broweds, again no Blue-faced.

After a couple of minutes I thought I saw something a bit bigger fly down to the base of the grass. I could see one stalk of grass waving about far more wildly than the ones the Red-browed Finches were perched on. This had to be it. Slowly the bird on the grass stem moved up towards the waving seed-head. Like a fisherman who can tell by the strength of the tug on the line that he's got something good, I knew this was the business. Suddenly the bird popped into view. Plump, bright green body, blue face, red rump: a Blue-faced Parrot-Finch, bird number 700.

Rather than dance with elation or pump the air in triumph I was almost taken aback by a sense of anticlimax. Maybe it was because, although the Blue-faced Parrot-Finch sports amazingly bright colours, it was kind of a dopey looking thing. More to the point, I think my muted reaction had more to do with a sense of sheer relief – the pressure was finally off. Suddenly I could empathise with Cathy Freeman after she won the 400 metres at the Sydney Olympics: the weight of a nation's expectations was finally lifted off her shoulders. All right, I didn't have one hundred thousand fans cheering me on, just myself in the rainforest with no-one to share the moment. But as it had been me putting the pressure on myself all year the feeling was, I imagined, somehow analogous…Well, perhaps not quite the same.

Perhaps seeing seven hundred birds in a year is not particularly significant in the grand scheme of things. When you consider everything else going on in the world, the real issues – terrorism, poverty, environmental catastrophe, cancer, relationship break-ups, people texting the wrong number, Brad and Jennifer, hipster jeans – my little achievement doesn't seem terribly relevant. All I know is that as I came down from the mountain, I couldn't wipe the smile off my face.

You'd reckon that after three hundred and fifty-eight days of almost continuous birdwatching I could have afforded to put the bins up and take a well-earned rest. The target that nobody believed achievable had been reached. I didn't need to prove anything more. I could have just kicked back, relaxed and, for once, not had to worry about where the next tick was coming from.

I could have, but I didn't. I decided to celebrate the best way I know how: I went birding.

To this end I headed down to the coast to chase up a report of Red-rumped Swallow. Del Richards, a bird tour operator up this way, had seen one about a week earlier at a place called Newell Beach. On the approach to the town I saw a large group of swallows roosting on some telephone wires above a cane field. Along with the three common species of swallow – the Welcome Swallow and the two species of martin –there were up to fourteen Red-rumped Swallows. This rare Asian migrant wasn't even on the Australian list twenty years earlier. It was on mine now.

On the way back to Kingfisher Park I grabbed a bottle of champagne and shared a celebratory toast with Andrew and Carol. They asked me about my plans for Christmas Day. I hadn't thought about it. There I was, alone, no family, no friends. What to do? Just for a change I thought I might go birding. I decided to do a Big Day and see how many species I could get. I joined Andrew on the morning bird walk and had seventy-five species before I even left Kingfisher Park. Up on Mount Lewis the Blue-faced Parrot-Finches that had eluded me for years now wouldn't leave me alone. I had a pair feeding on the track in front of me and each time I got too close to these supposedly shy birds, they merely flew about ten metres further along the track. This is obviously their true demeanour and they had just been messing with my head for years. My progress was hindered somewhat by the twelfth flat tyre of the year whilst driving down from the mountain and the interminable wait for a Christmas lunch of a prawn sandwich at the only shop open in Port Douglas. Despite not making it out to the drier inland areas I still managed to see 158 species for the day. Best Christmas ever.

On Boxing Day I stooged around the compound at Kingfisher Park, recuperating and just soaking up the delights of the local bird population. That night I joined Andrew and Carol and a local ranger in a spotlighting expedition following up a report of a Greater Glider, a rare mammal this far north. We didn't find the glider but we did flush what turned out to be a Masked Owl from the side of the road. I'd looked for this bird the length and breadth of the country, from the very first night of the year, and here it was unexpectedly on one of the last nights.

The next day I did the dude thing and headed out to the Great Barrier Reef. While the tourists all hit the shallows on Michelmas Cay I spent my time on land marvelling at the cacophony and chaos of the seabird colony. No new bird for the year but plenty to enjoy amongst the screaming terns and noddies. The second half of the boat trip was to an outer reef. I had come out to this reef ten years earlier and was simply blown away by the profusion of colourful life amongst the coral. It was still an incredible experience but there had been coral bleaching as a result of the abnormally high tempera- tures of the ocean (global warming, anyone?), so the snorkelling was a little disappointing.

All good things must pass and if I was to be in Melbourne to start my new non-twitching related job (although in the new series, imaginatively titled *Comedy Inc*, I do manage to slip in my first ever birdwatching sketch involving two bird nerds appearing on the Jerry Springer show), I had to head off. So with something approaching grief I reluctantly left Kingfisher Park and began the long drive home. Two days later I arrived in Brisbane. Collecting Andrew Stafford we headed out to Sherwood Park for one last try for those Little Bitterns. I'd looked for these bastards there before. I'd looked for them in Victoria, New South Wales and Western Australia, and had dipped every single bloody time. As soon as we left the carpark we were greeted by a couple of Bush-hens who put on quite a rau- cous display, giving much better views than I'd had at Julatten. A good sign, perhaps?

You couldn't find a less amenable place than Sherwood for a reclusive species like Little Bittern. The ornamental ponds didn't have a huge amount of suitable habitat, just some rank vegetation fringing the islands in the centre. All around was the noise and hus- tle of humans in leisure mode: people walking dogs, kids playing rugby, a local whose unfenced property lay adjacent to the park starting up his mower and cutting his grass. Incredibly, amidst all this hubbub, a male Little Bittern stood resolutely still, waiting to snatch an unsuspecting water creature as it swam by. Incredibly, after 364 days of birding and 702 prior species, seeing this at number 703 still delivered an enormous adrenaline rush.

Little Bittern was to be my last bird of the Big Twitch. The next day, New Year's Eve, I dropped in on Paul Wallbridge and he calculated that the only possible bird left for me was Streaked Shearwater, which can sometimes be seen from the land, particularly near river mouths. So my last birding moments were spent surrounded by tourists perched above Point Danger on the Queensland–New South Wales border, gazing desperately out to sea through my telescope. No joy.

I made my way down to Byron Bay in New South Wales to watch the year slip away. Jezz and Karen had hired a holiday house there so it was good to spend New Year's Eve with people I care about. And I was relieved that, although I almost cost them their jobs, they welcomed me with open arms, a smile, and a cold beer. We hit the town and I realised with a sinking heart that I was to spend another New Year's Eve in the presence of hippies. Actually, that's a bit unfair as most of the genuine hippies had gone bush. The teeming throng of people milling around us included not just the hippies whose combi vans had broken down, but also masses of drunks, Hare Krishnas, holidaymakers, gangs of teenage boys hoping for a bit of action and a similar number of teenage girls chugging down enough alcoholic soft drinks to ensure at least a few of the boys might succeed in their aim. The countdown clock ticked through to midnight and as the fireworks exploded, people erupted in a frenzy of cheering and drunken pashing.

The Big Twitch was over. I was back in the real world. Looking around this world that I had turned my back on for a year, seeing the manic desperation of those around me to have a good time no matter what, suddenly my quest didn't seem so absurd. In fact it seemed to make more sense than any of the human behaviour I saw around me.

EPILOGUE

13 December, 2004, St Kilda, Victoria:
still no girlfriends

There are a million ways to occupy your time on this planet. They're all pretty much absurd if you analyse them too closely. I chose twitching, one of the more outwardly absurd of them all I suppose but really no more ridiculous than anything else, yet that year of absurdity has had a profound effect on my life since.

Not that being the new Australian birdwatching record holder means terribly much to anyone outside the twitching scene. The opportunity to bring up that fact doesn't pop up in general conversation too often. It took me twelve months of hard slog, almost a hundred and fifty thousand kilometres of travel: eighty thousand by road, sixty thousand by air and two thousand by boat. It cost around forty thousand dollars not including the price of the four wheel drive, video and other equipment, all for seven hundred and three species and a swag of amazing memories. But do you think the woman in the check-out queue cares? You think the guy next to me at the footy gives a toss? And what about the girl with the Rainbow Pitta eyes sitting opposite me at the restaurant table? Does she think, having heard my tale, that I am too much of a weird-arse freak to bother dating a second time?

Not that I can't see how blowing my inheritance to spend a year birdwatching wouldn't come across as a little bit weird. But I know if I had never gone through with it I would not be sitting at this restaurant. The real legacy of the Big Twitch is that for the first time in my life I feel totally comfortable in my own skin. Not because I spent a year birdwatching but because I was able to achieve something I always wanted to do and that has left me deeply satisfied. In the past I doubt I would have been able to ask this woman out for fear of rejection, whereas now I realise that even if the date goes horribly wrong it ultimately doesn't matter because I know I can be by myself, can rely on myself. If I am thrown out of the pack I know I can not only survive, but thrive.

I am happy within myself which is after all, only what my parents ever wanted for me. I reckon they would have thought I was a bloody idiot if I'd told them about my plans but having used their legacy to achieve my goal has somehow lessened the grief I felt at losing them. Before that year I was still raw about their deaths, after it I felt at peace. Sure, it might have been a pretty stupid goal but it was my goal. It was what I really wanted and was able to pound down the demons of self-doubt and loneliness to get out there and actually do it…

This all fell into place for me a few months after I had finished the Big Twitch. I was at a movie premiere. Being a hack comedy writer I hadn't been invited on my own merits but was there as somebody's handbag. It was quite a big occasion, several international names were in attendance along with Melbourne's best and brightest. At one stage I accidentally got caught on the red carpet behind Heath Ledger.

Some screaming fans had yelled for me to turn around so I could sign their autograph books. When I faced the crowd, two fourteen-year-old girls stop screaming and look me up and down disdainfully.

'Who's that?' sniffed one.

'Don't worry, he's nobody,' the other snorted derisively.

It was at that moment that I realised I couldn't disagree with them more whole heartedly. I was who I wanted to be.

My name is Sean and I'm a twitcher. And I don't care who knows it.

Well, that's not quite true. The Big Twitch has made me realise how comfortable I am in my own company but that doesn't mean I want to embrace being alone. I look up at those amazing blue eyes, awaiting a response to my tale. I hold no expectations that she will think my twitching habit is cool but I am desperately hoping that she won't think I am a total freak. She pauses, looks down at the menu and says, 'I suppose we should order before the kitchen closes. They do a great calamari salad here.'

Damn, I thought I was doing so well.

Still, at least she hasn't called a cab just yet.

Official Big Twitch List

1   Sooty Owl, Tyto tenebricosa, Jan 1, Gembrook, VIC
2   Laughing Kookaburra, Dacelo novaeguinaeae, Jan 1, Gembrook, VIC
3   Common Blackbird, Turdus merula, Jan 1, Carlton, VIC
4   Common Starling, Sturnus vulgaris, Jan 1, Carlton, VIC
5   Spotted Turtle-dove, Streptopelia chinensis, Jan 1, Carlton, VIC
6   Little Raven, Corvus mellori, Jan 1, Carlton, VIC
7   Magpie-lark, Grallina cyanoleuca, Jan 1, Carlton, VIC
8   Common Myna, Acridotheres tristis, Jan 1, Carlton, VIC
9   House Sparrow, Passer domesticus, Jan 1, Carlton, VIC
10 White-plumed Honeyeater, Lichenostomus penicillatus, Jan 1, Carlton, VIC
11 Rainbow Lorikeet, Trichoglossus haematodus, Jan 1, Carlton, VIC
12 Tree Sparrow, Passer montanus, Jan 1, Carlton, VIC
13 Feral Pigeon (Rock Dove), Colombia livia, Jan 1, Carlton, VIC
14 European Goldfinch, Carduelis carduelis, Jan 1, Melb.Cemetery, VIC
15 Red Wattlebird, Anthochaera carunculata, Jan 1, Melb.Cemetery, VIC
16 Silvereye, Zosterops lateralis, Jan 1, Melbourne Cemetery, VIC
17 Superb Fairy-wren, Malurus cyaneus, Jan 1, Melbourne Cemetery, VIC
18 Australian Magpie, Gymnorhina tibicen, Jan 1, Melbourne Cemetery, VIC
19 Red-rumped Parrot, Psephotus haematonotus, Jan 1,
    Melbourne Cemetery, VIC
20 European Greenfinch, Carduelis chloris, Jan 1, Melbourne Cemetery, VIC
21 Yellow-rumped Thornbill, Acanthiza chrysorrhoa, Jan 1,
    Melbourne Cemetery, VIC
22 Silver Gull, Larus novaehollandiae, Jan 1, Carlton, VIC
23 Welcome Swallow, Hirundo neoxena, Jan 1, Carlton, VIC
24 Willie Wagtail, Rhipidura leucophrys, Jan 1, Carlton, VIC
25 Musk Lorikeet, Glossopsitta concinna, Jan 1, Carlton, VIC
26 Song Thrush, Turdus philomelos, Jan 2, Northcote, VIC
27 Little Wattlebird, Anthochaera chrysoptera, Jan 2, Royal Botanic Gardens
    Melbourne, VIC
28 Dusky Moorhen, Gallinula tenebrosa, Jan 2, Royal Botanic Gardens
    Melbourne, VIC
29 Pacific Black Duck, Anas surperciliosa, Jan 2, Royal Botanic Gardens
    Melbourne, VIC
30 Black Swan, Cygnus atratus, Jan 2, Royal Botanic Gardens Melbourne, VIC
31 Eurasian Coot, Fulicia atra, Jan 2, Royal Botanic Gardens Melbourne, VIC
32 Hardhead, Aythya australis, Jan 2, Royal Botanic Gardens Melbourne, VIC
33 Galah, Cacatua roseicapilla, Jan 2, Royal Botanic Gardens Melbourne, VIC
34 Bell Miner, Manorina melanophrys, Jan 2, Royal Botanic Gardens
    Melbourne, VIC

35   White-browed Scrubwren, Sericornis frontalis, Jan 2, Royal Botanic Gardens Melbourne, VIC

36   Australian Wood Duck, Chenonetta jubata, Jan 2, Royal Botanic Gardens Melbourne, VIC

37   Nankeen Night Heron, Nycticorax caledonicus, Jan 2, Royal Botanic Gardens Melbourne, VIC

38   Great Cormorant, Phalacrocorax carbo, Jan 2, Royal Botanic Gardens Melbourne, VIC

39   Little Black Cormorant, Phalacrocorax sulcirostris, Jan 2, Royal Botanic Gardens Melbourne, VIC

40   Chestnut Teal, Anas castanea, Jan 2, Royal Botanic Gardens Melbourne, VIC

41   Clamorous Reed-Warbler, Acrocephalus stentoreus, Jan 2, Royal Botanic Gardens Melbourne, VIC

42   Little Pied Cormorant, Phalacrocorax melanoleucos, Jan 2, Royal Botanic Gardens Melbourne, VIC

43   Australian White Ibis, Threskiornis molucca, Jan 3, Laverton, VIC

44   Masked Lapwing, Vanellus miles, Jan 3, Werribee, VIC

45   White-necked Heron, Ardea pacifica, Jan 3, Geelong, VIC

46   White-faced Heron, Ardea novaehollandiae, Jan 3, Geelong, VIC

47   Sulphur-crested Cockatoo, Cacatua galerita, Jan 3, Geelong, VIC

48   Black-shouldered Kite, Elanus axillaris, Jan 3, Geelong, VIC

49   Great Egret, Ardea alba, Jan 3, Winchelsea, VIC

50   Straw-necked Ibis, Threskiornis spinicollis, Jan 3, Winchelsea, VIC

51   Swamp Harrier, Circus approximans, Jan 3, Winchelsea, VIC

52   Yellow-billed Spoonbill, Platalea flavipes, Jan 3, Winchelsea, VIC

53   Royal Spoonbill, Platalea regia, Jan 3, Winchelsea, VIC

54   Purple Swamphen, Porphyrio porphryio, Jan 3, Winchelsea, VIC

55   Wedge-tailed Eagle, Aquila audax, Jan 3, Stoneyford, VIC

56   Grey Butcherbird, Cracticus torquatis, Jan 3, Cobden, VIC

57   Yellow-faced Honeyeater, Lichenostomus frenatus, Jan 3, Ralph Illidge Res, VIC

58   Grey Fantail, Rhipidura fuliginosa, Jan 3, Ralph Illidge Res, VIC

59   Eastern Yellow Robin, Eopsaltria australis, Jan 3, Ralph Illidge Res, VIC

60   Crimson Rosella, Platycercus elegans, Jan 3, Ralph Illidge Res, VIC

61   White-eared Honeyeater, Lichenostomus leucotis, Jan 3, Ralph Illidge Res, VIC

62   New Holland Honeyeater, Phylidonryis novaehollandiae, Jan 3, Ralph Illidge Res, VIC

63   Grey Shrike-thrush, Colluricincla harmonica, Jan 3, Ralph Illidge Res, VIC

64   White-naped Honeyeater, Melithreptus lunatus, Jan 3, Ralph Illidge Res, VIC

65   Brown Falcon, Falco berigora, Jan 3, Port Fairy, VIC

66   Whiskered Tern, Chlidonias hybrida, Jan 3, Port Fairy, VIC

67   Golden-headed Cisticola, Cisticola exilis, Jan 3, Port Fairy, VIC

68   Skylark, Alauda arvensis, Jan 3, Port Fairy, VIC
69   White-fronted Chat, Epthianura albifrons, Jan 3, Port Fairy, VIC
70   Long-billed Corella, Cacatua tenuirostris, Jan 3, Camperdown, VIC
71   Hoary-headed Grebe, Poliocephalus poliocephalus, Jan 3, Stoneyford, VIC
72   Whistling Kite, Milvus sphenurus, Jan 3, Stoneyford, VIC
73   Australian Shelduck, Tadorna tadornoides, Jan 3, Colac, VIC
74   Dusky Woodswallow, Artamus cyanopterus, Jan 4, Seaford Swamp, VIC
75   Brown Thornbill, Acanthiza pusilla, Jan 4, Seaford Swamp, VIC
76   Australian Pelican, Pelacanus conspicillatus, Jan 4, Seaford Swamp, VIC
77   Latham's Snipe, Gallinago hardwickii, Jan 4, Seaford Swamp, VIC
78   Little Grassbird, Megalurus timoriensis, Jan 4, Seaford Swamp, VIC
79   Black-winged Stilt, Himantopus himantopus, Jan 4, Seaford Swamp, VIC
80   Sharp-tailed Sandpiper, Calidris acuminata, Jan 4, Seaford Swamp, VIC
81   Greenshank, Tringa nebularia, Jan 4, Seaford Swamp, VIC
82   Grey Teal, Anas gibberifrons, Jan 4, Seaford Swamp, VIC
83   Curlew Sandpiper, Calidris ferruginea, Jan 4, Seaford Swamp, VIC
84   Red-necked Stint, Calidris ruficollis, Jan 4, Seaford Swamp, VIC
85   Caspian Tern, Sterna caspia, Jan 4, Seaford Swamp, VIC
86   Red-capped Plover, Charadrius ruficapliius, Jan 4, Seaford Swamp, VIC
87   Red-necked Avocet, Recurvirostra novaehollandiae, Jan 4,
      Seaford Swamp, VIC
88   Australian Hobby, Falco longipennis, Jan 4, Seaford Swamp, VIC
89   Black-faced Cuckoo-shrike, Coracina novaehollandiae, Jan 4,
      Seaford Swamp, VIC
90   Eastern Rosella, Platycercus eximmius, Jan 4, Seaford Swamp, VIC
91   Noisy Miner, Manorina melanocephala, Jan 4, Seaford Swamp, VIC
92   Black-fronted Dotterel, Elseyornis melanops, Jan 4, Seaford Swamp, VIC
93   Black Kite, Milvus migrans, Jan 5, Werribee, VIC
94   Fairy Martin, Hirundo ariel, Jan 5, Werribee, VIC
95   Pied Oystercatcher, Haematopus longirostris, Jan 5, Werribee, VIC
96   Black-tailed Native-hen, Gallinula ventralis, Jan 5, Werribee, VIC
97   Musk Duck, Biziura lobata, Jan 5, Werribee, VIC
98   Nankeen Kestrel, Falco cenchroides, Jan 5, Werribee, VIC
99   Banded Stilt, Cladorhynchus leucocephalus, Jan 5, Werribee, VIC
100   Pink-eared Duck, Malocorhynchus membranaceus, Jan 5, Werribee, VIC
101   Australasian Shoveler, Anas rhynchotis, Jan 5, Werribee, VIC
102   Singing Bushlark, Miafra javanica, Jan 5, Werribee, VIC
103   Pied Cormorant, Phalacrocorax varius, Jan 5, Werribee, VIC
104   Horsefield's Bronze-Cuckoo, Chrysococcyx basalis, Jan 5, Werribee, VIC
105   Blue-billed Duck, Oxyura australis, Jan 5, Werribee, VIC
106   Freckled Duck, Stictonetta naevosa, Jan 5, Werribee, VIC
107   Great Crested Grebe, Podiceps cristatus, Jan 5, Werribee, VIC
108   Marsh Sandpiper, Tringa stagnatilis, Jan 5, Werribee, VIC

109 Red-kneed Dotterel, Erythrogonys cinctus, Jan 5, Werribee, VIC
110 Wood Sandpiper, Tringa glareola, Jan 5, Werribee, VIC
111 Darter, Anhinga melanogaster, Jan 6, Kew, VIC
112 Magpie Goose, Anseranas semipalmata, Jan 6, Edithvale Swamp, VIC
113 Buff-banded Rail, Gallirallus philipensis, Jan 6, Edithvale Swamp, VIC
114 Intermediate Egret, Ardea intermedia, Jan 6, Edithvale Swamp, VIC
115 Crested Pigeon, Ocyphaps lophotes, Jan 6, Edithvale Swamp, VIC
116 Spotless Crake, Porzana tabuensis, Jan 6, Edithvale Swamp, VIC
117 Australian Spotted Crake, Porzana fluminea, Jan 6, Edithvale Swamp, VIC
118 Spotted Pardalote, Pardalotus punctatus, Jan 9, Banyule Flats, VIC
119 Little Lorikeet, Glossopsitta pusilla, Jan 9, Banyule Flats, VIC
120 Australasian Grebe, Tachybaptus novaehollandiae, Jan 9, Banyule Flats, VIC
121 Mistletoebird, Dicaeum hirundinaceum, Jan 9, Banyule Flats, VIC
122 Red-browed Finch, Neochmia temporalis, Jan 9, Banyule Flats, VIC
123 Pied Currawong, Strepera graculina, Jan 10, Kew, VIC
124 Brown-headed Honeyeater, Melithreptus brevirostris, Jan 10,
     Langwarrin, VIC
125 Satin Flycatcher, Myiagra cyanoleuca, Jan 10, Langwarrin, VIC
126 Brush Bronzewing, Phaps elegans, Jan 10, Langwarrin, VIC
127 Golden Whistler, Pachycephala pectoralis, Jan 10, Langwarrin, VIC
128 Common Bronzewing, Phaps chalcoptera, Jan 10, Mt. Eliza, VIC
129 Rufous Whistler, Pachycephala rufiventris, Jan 10, Mt. Eliza, VIC
130 Restless Flycatcher, Myiagra inquieta, Jan 11, Chiltern, VIC
131 Yellow-tufted Honeyeater, Lichenostomus melanops, Jan 11, Chiltern, VIC
132 Striated Pardalote, Pardalotus striatus, Jan 11, Chiltern, VIC
133 Rainbow Bee-eater, Merops ornatus, Jan 11, Chiltern, VIC
134 Jacky Winter, Microeca leucophaea, Jan 11, Chiltern, VIC
135 Fuscous Honeyeater, Lichenostomus fuscus, Jan 11, Chiltern, VIC
136 Brown Treecreeper, Climacteris picumnus, Jan 11, Chiltern, VIC
137 Peaceful Dove, Geopelia placida, Jan 12, Chiltern, VIC
138 Black-chinned Honeyeater, Melithreptus gularis, Jan 12, Chiltern, VIC
139 Sacred Kingfisher, Todirhamptus sancta, Jan 12, Chiltern, VIC
140 Turquoise Parrot, Neophema pulchella, Jan 12, Chiltern, VIC
141 Little Eagle, Hieraaetus morphnoides, Jan 12, Chiltern, VIC
142 Striated Thornbill, Acanthiza lineata, Jan 12, Chiltern, VIC
143 White-winged Chough, Corcorax melanorhamphos, Jan 12, Chiltern, VIC
144 Diamond Firetail, Stagonopleura guttata, Jan 12, Chiltern, VIC
145 Tree Martin, Hirundo nigricans, Jan 12, Chiltern, VIC
146 Crested Shrike-tit, Falcunculus frontatus, Jan 12, Chiltern, VIC
147 White-browed Babbler, Pomatostomus superciliosus, Jan 12, Chiltern, VIC
148 Australian Raven, Corvus coronoides , Jan 12, Chiltern, VIC
149 White-bellied Cuckoo-shrike, Coracina papuensis, Jan 13, Chiltern, VIC
150 Collared Sparrowhawk, Accipter cirrhocephalus, Jan 13, Chiltern, VIC

151 White-throated Needletail, Hirundapus caudacutus, Jan 13, Chiltern, VIC
152 Grey-crowned Babbler, Pomatostomus temporalis, Jan 13, Chiltern, VIC
153 Dollarbird, Eurystomus orientalis, Jan 13, Moodemere, VIC
154 Little Friarbird, Philemon citreogularis, Jan 13, Moodemere, VIC
155 Yellow Thornbill, Acanthiza nana, Jan 13, Brimin, VIC
156 Red-capped Robin, Petroica goodenovii, Jan 13, Brimin, VIC
157 Varied Sittella, Daphoenositta chrysoptera, Jan 13, Brimin, VIC
158 White-browed Woodswallow, Artamus superciliosus, Jan 13, Chiltern, VIC
159 White-breasted Woodswallow, Artamus leucorynchus, Jan 13, Chiltern, VIC
160 Tawny Frogmouth, Podargus strigoides, Jan 13, Chiltern, VIC
161 Buff-rumped Thornbill, Acanthiza reguloides, Jan 14, Chiltern, VIC
162 Rufous Songlark, Cincloramphus mathewsi, Jan 14, Chiltern, VIC
163 Weebill, Smicrornis brevirostris, Jan 14, Chiltern, VIC
164 Speckled Warbler, Chthonicola sagittata, Jan 14, Chiltern, VIC
165 Scarlet Robin, Petroica multicolor, Jan 17, Gembrook, VIC
166 Rufous Fantail, Rhipidura rufifrons, Jan 17, Gembrook, VIC
167 Crescent Honeyeater, Phylidonyris pyrrhoptera, Jan 17, Gembrook, VIC
168 Eastern Spinebill, Acanthorhyncus tenuirostris, Jan 17, Gembrook, VIC
169 Rose Robin, Petroica rosea, Jan 17, Gembrook, VIC
170 King Parrot, Alisterus scapularis, Jan 17, Gembrook, VIC
171 Pacific Golden Plover, Pluvialis fulva, Jan 18, Yallock Creek, VIC
172 Eastern Curlew, Numenius madagascariensis, Jan 18, Yallock Creek, VIC
173 Double-banded Plover, Charadrius bicinctus, Jan 18, Yallock Creek, VIC
174 Yellow-tailed Black-Cockatoo, Calyptorhynchus funerus, Jan 19, Gembrook, VIC
175 White-throated Nightjar, Eurostopodus mysticalis, Jan 19, Gembrook, VIC
176 Australian Owlet-nightjar, Aegotheles cristatus, Jan 19, Gembrook, VIC
177 Powerful Owl, Ninox strenua, Jan 19, Gembrook, VIC
178 Cattle Egret, Ardea ibis, Jan 25, Dapto, NSW
179 Red-whiskered Bulbul, Pycnonotus jocosus, Jan 25, Wollongong, NSW
180 Crested Tern, Sterna bergii, Jan 26, Wollongong, NSW
181 Wedge-tailed Shearwater, Puffinus pacificus, Jan 26, Wollongong, NSW
182 Pomarine Jaeger, Stercorarius pomarinus, Jan 26, Wollongong, NSW
183 Fluttering Shearwater, Puffinus gavia, Jan 26, Wollongong, NSW
184 Short-tailed Shearwater, Pufinus tenuirostris, Jan 26, Wollongong, NSW
185 Flesh-footed Shearwater, Puffinus carneipes, Jan 26, Wollongong, NSW
186 Great-winged Petrel, Pterodroma macoptera, Jan 26, Wollongong, NSW
187 Tahiti Petrel, Psuedobulweria rostrata, Jan 26, Wollongong, NSW
188 Brown Booby, Sula leucogaster, Jan 26, Wollongong, NSW
189 Wilson's Storm Petrel, Oceanites oceanicus, Jan 26, Wollongong, NSW
190 Arctic Jaeger, Stercorarius parasiticus, Jan 26, Wollongong, NSW
191 Sooty Shearwater, Puffinus griseus, Jan 26, Wollongong, NSW
192 Kelp Gull, Larus dominicanus, Jan 26, Wollongong, NSW

193　Little Penguin, Eudyptula minor, Jan 26, Wollongong, NSW
194　Lewin's Honeyeater, Meliphaga lewinii, Jan 26, Wollongong, NSW
195　Bar-tailed Godwit, Limosa lapponica, Jan 27, Botany Bay, NSW
196　Little Egret, Ardea garzetta, Jan 27, Botany Bay, NSW
197　Peregrine Falcon, Falco peregrinus, Jan 27, Maroubra, NSW
198　Baillon's Crake, Porzana pusilla, Jan 28, Edithvale, VIC
199　White Tern, Gygis alba, Jan 31, Norfolk Island
200　Red Junglefowl, Gallus gallus, Jan 31, Norfolk Island
201　Black-winged Petrel, Pterodroma nigripennis, Jan 31, Norfolk Island
202　Red-tailed Tropicbird, Phaethon rubricauda, Jan 31, Norfolk Island
203　White-capped Noddy, Anous minutus, Jan 31, Norfolk Island
204　Slender-billed White-eye, Zosterops tenuirostris, Jan 31, Norfolk Island
205　Masked Booby, Sula dactylatra, Jan 31, Norfolk Island
206　Sooty Tern, Sterna fuscata, Jan 31, Norfolk Island
207　Common Noddy, Anous stolidus, Jan 31, Norfolk Island
208　Mallard, Anas platyrhynchos, Jan 31, Norfolk Island
209　Norfolk Island Gerygone, Gerygone modesta, Jan 31, Norfolk Island
210　Emerald Dove, Chalcophaps indica, Jan 31, Norfolk Island
211　Lesser Frigatebird, Fregata ariel, Jan 31, Norfolk Island
212　Whimbrel, Numenius phaeopus, Jan 31, Norfolk Island
213　Ruddy Turnstone, Arenaria interpres, Jan 31, Norfolk Island
214　Grey Ternlet, Procelsterna cerulea, Feb 1, Norfolk Island
215　Wandering Tattler, Heteroscelus inanus, Feb 1, Norfolk Island
216　Masked Woodswallow, Artamus personatus, Feb 1, Norfolk Island
217　California Quail, Callipepla californica, Feb 2, Norfolk Island
218　Kermadec Petrel, Pterodroma neglecta, Feb 2, Norfolk Island
219　Australasian Gannet, Morus serrator, Feb 2, Norfolk Island
220　(Norfolk Island) Red-crowned Parakeet, Cyanoramphus novaezandiae
　　　cookii, Feb 3, Norfolk Island
221　Black-faced Cormorant, Phalacrocorax fuscescens, Feb 3, Pitt Water, TAS
222　Pacific Gull, Larus pacificus, Feb 3, Pitt Water, TAS
223　TASn Scrubwren, Sericornis humilis, Feb 3, Tasman Peninsula, TAS
224　Green Rosella, Platycercus caledonicus, Feb 3, Tasman Peninsula, TAS
225　White-bellied Sea-Eagle, Haliaeetus leucogaster, Feb 3,
　　　Tasman Peninsula, TAS
226　TASn Native-hen, Gallinula mortierii, Feb 3, Tasman Peninsula, TAS
227　Forest Raven, Corvus tasmanicus, Feb 3, Tasman Peninsula, TAS
228　Beautiful Firetail, Stagonopleura bella, Feb 4, Eaglehawk Neck, TAS
229　Shy Albatross, Diomedea cauta, Feb 4, Eaglehawk Pelagic, TAS
230　Buller's Albatross, Diomedea bulleri, Feb 4, Eaglehawk Pelagic, TAS
231　White-headed Petrel, Pterodroma lessonii, Feb 4, Eaglehawk Pelagic, TAS
232　Fairy Prion, Pachyptila turtur, Feb 4, Eaglehawk Pelagic, TAS
233　Yellow-nosed Albatross, Diomeda chlororhynchos, Feb 4, Eaglehawk Pelagic, TAS

234 White-chinned Petrel, Procellaria aequinoctialis, Feb 4,
Eaglehawk Pelagic, TAS
235 Wandering Albatross, Diomedea exulans, Feb 4, Eaglehawk Pelagic, TAS
236 Black-browed Albatross, Diomedea melanophris, Feb 4,
Eaglehawk Pelagic, TAS
237 Striated Heron, Butorides striatus, Feb 5, Narooma, NSW
238 Noisy Friarbird, Philemon corniculatus, Feb 5, Narooma, NSW
239 Azure Kingfisher, Alcedo azurea, Feb 5, Narooma, NSW
240 Leaden Flycatcher, Myiagra rubecula, Feb 5, Narooma, NSW
241 Variegated Fairy-wren, Malurus lamberti, Feb 5, Narooma, NSW
242 Wonga Pigeon, Leucosarica melanoleuca, Feb 5, Mallacoota, VIC
243 Satin Bowerbird, Ptilonorhynchus violaceus, Feb 5, Mallacoota, VIC
244 Brown Gerygone, Gerygone mouki, Feb 5, Mallacoota, VIC
245 Eastern Whipbird, Psophodes olivaceus, Feb 5, Mallacoota, VIC
246 Sooty Oystercatcher, Haematopus fuliginosus, Feb 5, Mallacoota, VIC
247 Glossy Black-Cockatoo, Calyptorhynchus lathami, Feb 5, Mallacoota, VIC
248 Red-browed Treecreeper, Climacteris erythrops, Feb 5, Mallacoota, VIC
249 Scarlet Honeyeater, Myzomela sanguinolenta, Feb 5, Mallacoota, VIC
250 Brush Cuckoo, Cacomantis variolosus, Feb 5, Mallacoota, VIC
251 Little Tern, Sterna albifrons, Feb 5, Marlo, VIC
252 Hooded Plover, Thinornis rubricollis, Feb 5, Marlo, VIC
253 Ringed Plover, Charadrius hiaticula, Feb 5, Marlo, VIC
254 Fairy Tern, Sterna nereis, Feb 6, Marlo,
255 Southern Emu-wren, Stipiturus malachurus, Feb 6, Cape Conran, VIC
256 Gang-gang Cockatoo, Callocephalon fimbriatum, Feb 6, Cape Conran, VIC
257 Pilotbird, Pycnoptilus floccosus, Feb 6, Tarra-Bulga National Park, VIC
258 Grey Currawong, Strepera versicolor, Feb 6, Tarra-Bulga National Park, VIC
259 Superb Lyrebird, Menura novaehollandiae, Feb 6,
Tarra-Bulga National Park, VIC
260 Brown Goshawk, Accipter fasciatus, Feb 6, Mirboo North, VIC
261 Blue-winged Parrot, Neophema chrysostoma, Feb 6, Mirboo North, VIC
262 Red-necked Phalarope, Phalaropus lobatus, Feb 10, Geelong, VIC
263 Blue-faced Honeyeater, Entomyzon cyanotis, Feb 11, Brisbane Botanic
Gardens, QLD
264 Figbird, Sphecotheres viridis, Feb 11, Brisbane Botanic Gardens, QLD
265 Pied Butcherbird, Cracticus nigrogularis, Feb 11, Brisbane Botanic Gardens, QLD
266 Torresian Crow, Corvus orru, Feb 11, Brisbane Botanic Gardens, QLD
267 Australian Brush-turkey, Alectura lathami, Feb 11, Brisbane Botanic
Gardens, QLD
268 Spangled Drongo, Dicrurus bracteatus, Feb 11,
Brisbane Botanic Gardens, QLD
269 Channel-billed Cuckoo, Scythrops novaehollandiae, Feb 11, Brisbane
Botanic Gardens, QLD

270 Chestnut-breasted Mannikin, Lonchura castaneothorax, Feb 12, Hope Island, QLD
271 Common Tern, Sterna hirundo, Feb 12, Brunswick Heads, NSW
272 Little Corella, Cacatua tenuirostris, Feb 12, Brunswick Heads, NSW
273 Bar-shouldered Dove, Geopilia humeralis, Feb 12, Brunswick Heads, NSW
274 Osprey, Pandion haliaetus, Feb 12, Ballina, NSW
275 White-cheeked Honeyeater, Phylidonyris nigra, Feb 12, Evan's Head, NSW
276 Gull-billed Tern, Sterna nilotica, Feb 12, Ballina, NSW
277 Brahminy Kite, Haliastur indus, Feb 12, Ballina, NSW
278 South Island Pied Oystercatcher, Haematopus finschi, Feb 12, Ballina, NSW
279 Tawny Grassbird, Megalurus timoriensis, Feb 13, Samsonvale, QLD
280 Double-barred Finch, Taeniopygia bichenovii, Feb 13, Samsonvale, QLD
281 Olive-backed Oriole, Oriolus sagittatus, Feb 13, Samsonvale, QLD
282 Striped Honeyeater, Plectorhyncha lanceolata, Feb 13, Samsonvale, QLD
283 Pheasant Coucal, Centropus phasianinus, Feb 13, Samsonvale, QLD
284 White-eared Monarch, Monarcha leucotis, Feb 13, Lacey's Creek, QLD
285 Litle Shrike-thrush, Colluricincla megarhynca, Feb 13, Lacey's Creek, QLD
286 Large-billed Scrubwren, Sericornis magnirostris, Feb 13, Lacey's Creek, QLD
287 Spectacled Monarch, Monarcha trivirgatus, Feb 13, Lacey's Creek, QLD
288 Yellow-throated Scrubwren, Sericornis citreogularis, Feb 13, Lacey's Creek, QLD
289 Pacific Baza, Aviceda subcristata, Feb 13, Lacey's Creek, QLD
290 Regent Bowerbird, Sericulus chrysocephalus, Feb 13, Lacey's Creek, QLD
291 Pale-headed Rosella, Platycercus adscitus, Feb 13, Lacey's Creek, QLD
292 King Quail, Coturnix chinensis, Feb 13, Samsonvale, QLD
293 Wandering Whistling-duck, Dendrocygna arcuata, Feb 13, Samsonvale, QLD
294 Wompoo Pigeon, Ptilinopus magnificus, Feb 13, Mt. Nebo, QLD
295 Green Catbird, Ailuroedus crassirostris, Feb 13, Mt. Nebo, QLD
296 Logrunner, Orthonyx temminckii, Feb 13, Mt. Nebo, QLD
297 Brown Quail, Coturnix ypsilophora, Feb 13, Nudgee, QLD
298 Red-backed Fairy-wren, Malurus melanocephalus, Feb 13, Nudgee, QLD
299 Glossy Ibis, Plegadis falcinellus, Feb 14, Hope Island, QLD
300 Richard's Pipit, Anthus novaeseelandiae, Feb 14, Hasting's Point, NSW
301 Painted Snipe, Rostratula benghalensis, Feb 14, Hope Island, QLD
302 Grey-tailed Tattler, Heteroscelus brevipes, Feb 14, Moreton Bay, QLD
303 Terek Sandpiper, Xenus cinerus, Feb 14, Moreton Bay, QLD
304 Brown Honeyeater, Lichmera indistincta, Feb 14, Moreton Bay, QLD
305 Great Knot, Calidris tenuirostris, Feb 14, Moreton Bay, QLD
306 Scaly-breasted Lorikeet, Trichoglossus chlorolepidotus, Feb 14, Moreton Bay, QLD
307 White-headed Pigeon, Columba leucomela, Feb 15, Maleny, QLD
308 Cicadabird, Coracina tenuirostris, Feb 15, Conondales, QLD
309 Paradise Riflebird, Ptiloris paradiseus, Feb 15, Conondales, QLD

310 Dusky Honeyeater, Myzomela obscura, Feb 15, Conondales, QLD
311 Pale Yellow Robin, Tregellasia capito, Feb 15, Conondales, QLD
312 Black-faced Monarch, Monarcha melanopsis, Feb 15, Conondales, QLD
313 Rose-crowned Fruit-Dove, Ptilinopus regina, Feb 15, Conondales, QLD
314 Russet-tailed Thrush, Zoothera heini, Feb 15, Conondales, QLD
315 Comb-crested Jacana, Metopidius gallinacea, Feb 15, Woodford, QLD
316 Brolga, Grus rubicunda, Feb 15, Brisbane, QLD
317 Hutton's Shearwater, Puffinus huttoni, Feb 16, Southport, QLD
318 Plumed Whistling-Duck, Dendrocygna eytoni, Feb 17, Ballina, NSW
319 Black-necked Stork, Ephippiorhynchus asiaticus, Feb 17, Undarra, NSW
320 Lesser Sand-plover, Charadrius mongolus, Feb 17, Taree, NSW
321 Kentish Plover, Charadrius alexandrinus, Feb 17, Taree, NSW
322 Long-tailed Jaeger, Stercorarius longicaudus, Feb 23, Wollongong, NSW
323 Black Petrel, Procellaria parkinsoni, Feb 23, Wollongong, NSW
324 Purple-crowned Lorikeet, Glossopsitta porphyrocephala, Feb 28,
    Gellibrand Hill, VIC
325 Banded Lapwing, Vanellus tricolor, Feb 28, Laverton, VIC
326 White Goshawk, Accipter novaehollandiae, March 2, Glenfyne, VIC
327 Common Diving-petrel, Pelecanoides urinatrix, March 3, Port Fairy, VIC
328 White-faced Storm Petrel, Pelagodroma marina, March 3, Port Fairy, VIC
329 Grey-backed Storm Petrel, Garrodia nereis, March 3, Port Fairy, VIC
330 Sooty Albatross, Phoebetria fusca, March 3, Port Fairy, VIC
331 Southern Boobook, Ninox novaeseelandiae, March 5, Gembrook, VIC
332 Singing Honeyeater, Lichenostomus virescens, March 10, Perth, WA
333 Zebra Finch, Taeniopygia guttata, March 10, Learmonth, WA
334 Green Jungle Fowl, Gallus varius, March 10, Cocos Islands
335 Eastern Reef Egret, Egretta sacra, March 10, Cocos Islands
336 Christmas Frigatebird, Fregata andrewsi, March 10, Christmas Island
337 Christmas Island Imperial Pigeon, Ducula whartoni, March 10,
    Christmas Island
338 Christmas Island White-eye, Zosterops natalis, March 10, Christmas Island
339 Christmas Island Glossy Swiftlet, Collocalia esculenta natalis, March 10,
    Christmas Island
340 Barn Swallow, Hirundo rustica, March 10, Christmas Island
341 Island Thrush, Turdus poliocephalus erythropleurus, March 10,
    Christmas Island
342 White-breasted Waterhen, Amaurornis phoenicurus, March 10,
    Christmas Island
343 Red-footed Booby, Sula sula, March 10, Christmas Island
344 White-tailed Tropicbird, Phaethon lepturus, March 10, Christmas Island
345 Greater Frigatebird, Fregata minor, March 10, Christmas Island
346 White Wagtail, Motacilla alba, March 11, Christmas Island
347 Oriental Pratincole, Glareola maldivarum, March 11, Christmas Island

348 Abbot's Booby, Papasula abbotti, March 11, Christmas Island
349 Common Sandpiper, Tringa hypoleucos, March 11, Christmas Island
350 Java Sparrow, Padda oryzivora, March 11, Christmas Island
351 Black Bittern, Ixobrychus flavicollis, March 12, Christmas Island
352 Christmas Island Hawk-Owl, Ninox natalis, March 12, Christmas Island
353 Pin-tailed Snipe, Gallinago stenura, March 15, Christmas Island
354 Australian Ringneck, Barnardius zonarius, March 18, Perth, WA
355 Laughing Turtle-Dove, Streptopelia senegalensis, March 18, Perth, WA
356 Barn Owl, Tyto alba, March 22, Sea Lake, VIC
357 Spiny-cheeked Honeyeater, Acanthagenys rufogularis, March 22, Merbein South, VIC
358 Yellow-throated Miner, Manorina flavigula, March 22, Merbein South, VIC
359 Emu, Dromaius novaehollandiae, March 22, Cullulleraine, VIC
360 Blue Bonnet, Northiella haematogaster, March 22, Cullulleraine, VIC
361 Southern Whiteface, Aphelocephala leucopsis, March 22, Waikerie, SA
362 Chestnut Quail-thrush, Cinclosoma castanotus, March 22, Gluepot, SA
363 Yellow-plumed Honeyeater, Lichenostomus ornatus, March 22, Gluepot, SA
364 Pied Honeyeater, Certhionyx variegatus, March 22, Gluepot, SA
365 Mulga Parrot, Psephotus varius, March 22, Gluepot, SA
366 Striated Grasswren, Amytornis striatus, March 22, Gluepot, SA
367 Hooded Robin, Melanodryas cucullata, March 22, Gluepot, SA
368 White-fronted Honeyeater, Phylidonyris albifrons, March 22, Gluepot, SA
369 Apostlebird, Struthidea cinerea, March 22, Gluepot, SA
370 Spotted Nightjar, Eurostopodus argus, March 22, Gluepot, SA
371 Chestnut-rumped Thornbill, Acanthiza uropygialis, March 23, Gluepot, SA
372 Regent Parrot, Polytelis anthopeplus, March 23, Gluepot, SA
373 Scarlet-chested Parrot, Neophema splendida, March 23, Gluepot, SA
374 Fork-tailed Swift, Apus pacificus, March 23, Gluepot, SA
375 Southern Scrub-robin, Drymodes brunneopygia, March 23, Gluepot, SA
376 Gilbert's Whistler, Pachycephala inornata, March 23, Gluepot, SA
377 White-winged Fairy-wren, Malurus leucopterus, March 23, Adelaide (Penrice) Saltworks, SA
378 Slender-billed Thornbill, Acanthiza iredalei, March 23, Adelaide (Penrice) Saltworks, SA
379 Red Knot, Calidris canutus, March 23, Adelaide (Penrice) Saltworks, SA
380 Grey Plover, Pluvialis squatarola, March 23, Adelaide (Penrice) Saltworks, SA
381 Black-tailed Godwit, Limosa limosa, March 23, Adelaide (Penrice) Saltworks, SA
382 Hudsonian Godwit, Limosa haemastica, March 23, Adelaide (Penrice) Saltworks, SA
383 Black Falcon, Falco subniger, March 26, Terrick Terrick, VIC
384 Black-faced Woodswallow, Artamus cinereus, March 26, Terrick Terrick, VIC
385 Plains Wanderer, Pedionomus torquatus, March 26, Terrick Terrick, VIC

386   Stubble Quail, Coturnix pectoralis, March 26, Terrick Terrick, VIC
387   Little Button-quail, Turnix velox, March 26, Terrick Terrick, VIC
388   Cape Barren Goose, Cereopsis novaehollandiae, April 1, Werribee, VIC
389   White-winged Black Tern, Chlidonias leucoptera, April 1, Werribee, VIC
390   Mangrove Gerygone, Gerygone laevigaster, April 4, Bribie Island, QLD
391   Laughing Gull, Larus atricilla, April 4, Bribie Island, QLD
392   Broad-billed Sandpiper, Limicola falcinellus, April 4, Toorbul Point, QLD
393   Forest Kingfisher, Todirhamphus macleayii, April 5,
      Sherwood Arboretum, QLD
394   Bush Stone Curlew, Burhinus grallarius, April 5, Uni of QLD, QLD
395   Noisy Pitta, Pitta versicolor, April 5, Mt. Nebo, QLD
396   Spotted Harrier, Circus assimilis, April 5, Lake Samsonvale, QLD
397   Square-tailed Kite, Lophoictinia isura, April 5, Kallangur, QLD
398   Black-breasted Button-quail, Turnix melanogaster, April 6, Inskip Point, QLD
399   Large Sand Plover, Charadrius leschenaultii, April 6, Inskip Point, QLD
400   Flame Robin, Petroica phoenicea, April 9, Seaford Swamp, VIC
401   Striated Fieldwren, Calamanthus fuliginosus, April 21, Werribee, VIC
402   Providence Petrel, Pterodroma solandri, April 28, Wollongong, NSW
403   Bassian Thrush, Zoothera lunulata, April 29, Wollongong, NSW
404   Eastern Bristlebird, Dasyornis brachypterus, April 30, Barren Grounds, NSW
405   Fan-tailed Cuckoo, Cacomantis flabelliformis, April 30,
      Barren Grounds, NSW
406   Ground Parrot, Pezoporus wallicus, May 1, Budderoo National Park, NSW
407   Chestnut-rumped Heathwren, Hylacola pyrrhopygia, May 1, Budderoo
      National Park, NSW
408   Rock Warbler, Origma solitaria, May 1, Bomaderry Creek, NSW
409   Swift Parrot, Lathamus discolor, May 3, Chiltern, VIC
410   Painted Button-quail, Turnix varia, May 3, Chiltern, VIC
411   Royal Albatross, Diomedea epomophora, May 5, Port Fairy, VIC
412   Lewin's Rail, Dryolimnas pectoralis, May 5, Portland, VIC
413   Rufous Bristlebird, Dasyornis broadbenti, May 6, Bay of Islands, VIC
414   Northern Giant Petrel, Macronectes halli, May 11, Port Fairy, VIC
415   Cape Petrel, Daption capense, May 26, Port Fairy, VIC
416   White-fronted Tern, Sterna striata, May 26, Port Fairy, VIC
417   Great Skua, Catharacta skua, June 2, Port Fairy, VIC
418   Slender-billed Prion, Pachyptila belcheri, June 2, Port Fairy, VIC
419   Yellow-throated Honeyeater, Lichenostomus flavicollis, June 6, Melrose, TAS
420   Black-headed Honeyeater, Melithreptus affinis, June 6, Melrose, TAS
421   Strong-billed Honeyeater, Melithreptus validirostris, June 6, Melrose, TAS
422   Dusky Robin, Melanodryas vittata, June 6, Melrose, TAS
423   Black Currawong, Strepera fulingosa, June 6, Cradle Mountain, TAS
424   TASn Thornbill, Acanthiza ewingii, June 6, Cradle Mountain, TAS
425   Pink Robin, Petroica rodinogaster, June 6, Cradle Mountain, TAS

426　Scrubtit, Sericornis magnus, June 6, Cradle Mountain, TAS
427　Forty-spotted Pardalote, Pardalotus quadragintus, June 8, Peter Murrell Reserve, TAS
428　Yellow Wattlebird, Anthochaera carunculata, June 8, Dunalley, TAS
429　Common Pheasant, Phasianus colchicus, June 10, King Island, TAS
430　Common Turkey, Meleagris gallopavo, June 10, King Island, TAS
431　Peafowl, Pavo cristatus, June 10, King Island, TAS
432　Western Thornbill, Acanthiza inornata, June23, Tuart Forest, WA
433　Inland Thornbill, Acanthiza apicalis, June 23, Busselton, WA
434　Western Gerygone, Gerygone fusca, June 24, Tuart Forest, WA
435　Long-billed Black-Cockatoo, Calyptorhynchus baudinii, June 24, Margaret River, WA
436　Red-winged Fairy-wren, Malurus elegans, June 24, Karridale, WA
437　Western Rosella, Platycercus icterotis, June 24, Karridale, WA
438　White-breasted Robin, Eopsaltria georgiana, June 24, Karridale, WA
439　Red-tailed Black-Cockatoo, Calyptorhynchus banksii, June 24, Blackwood River, WA
440　Short-billed Black-Cockatoo, Calyptorhynchus latirostris, June 25, Yanchep NP, WA
441　Roseate Tern, Sterna dougallii, June 26, Geraldton, WA
442　White-backed Swallow, Cheramoeca leucosternum, June 26, Geraldton, WA
443　Pallid Cuckoo, Cuculus pallidus, June 26, Geraldton, WA
444　Western Yellow Robin, Eopsaltria griseogularis, June 27, Kalbarri NP, WA
445　Black-eared Cuckoo, Chrysococcyx osculans, June 27, Kalbarri NP, WA
446　Tawny-crowned Honeyeater, Phylidonyris melanops , June 27, Kalbarri NP, WA
447　Little Woodswallow, Artamus minor, June 27, Kalbarri NP, WA
448　Splendid Fairy-wren, Malurus splendens, June 27, Murchison Crossing, WA
449　Little Crow, Corvus bennetti, June 27, Yalgoo, WA
450　Slaty-backed Thornbill, Acanthiza robustirostris, June 28, Yalgoo, WA
451　Redthroat, Pyrrholaemus brunneus, June 28, Yalgoo, WA
452　Crested Bellbird, Oreoica gutturalis, June 28, Yalgoo, WA
453　Western Bowerbird, Chlamydera guttata, June 28, Mount Magnet, WA
454　Western Corella , Cacatua sanguinea, June 29, Wubin, WA
455　Mute Swan, Cygnus olor, June 29, Northam, WA
456　Rufous Treecreeper, Climacteris picumnus, June 29, Darling Range, WA
457　Southern Giant-Petrel, Macronectes giganteus, June 30, Perth pelagic, WA
458　Soft-plumaged Petrel, Pterodroma mollis, June 30, Perth pelagic, WA
459　Kerguelen Petrel, Lugensa brevirostris, June 30, Perth pelagic, WA
460　Salvin's Prion, Pachyptila salvini, June 30, Perth pelagic, WA
461　Red-capped Parrot, Purpureicephalus spurius, July 1, Wundong Dam, WA
462　Red-eared Firetail, Stagonopleura oculata, July 1, Wundong Dam, WA
463　Western Spinebill, Acanthorhynchus supercilliosus, July 1, Bungendore Park, WA

464   Australasian Bittern, Botaurus poiciloptilus, July 5, Seaford Swamp, VIC

465   Orange-bellied Parrot, Neophema chrysogaster, July 7, Werribee, VIC

466   Barking Owl, Ninox connivens, July 8, Kamarooka, VIC

467   Purple-gaped Honeyeater, Lichenostomus cratitius, July 9, Kamarooka, VIC

468   Shy Heath-wren, Sericornis cautus, July 9, Kamarooka, VIC

469   Chestnut-crowned Babbler, Pomatostomus ruficeps, July 9, Tooleybuc, VIC

470   Mallee Emu-wren, Stipiturus mallee, July 10, Hattah, VIC

471   White-browed Treecreeper, Climacteris affinis, July 10, Yarrara, VIC

472   Black-eared Miner, Manorina melanotis, July 11, Gluepot, SA

473   Grey-fronted Honeyeater, Lichenostomus plumulus, July 12, Gluepot,

474   Chirruping Wedgebill, Psophodes cristatus, July 14, Port Augusta, SA

475   Brown Songlark, Cincloramphus cruralis, July 16, Marla, SA

476   Chestnut-breasted Whiteface, Aphelocephala pectoralis, July 16, Marla, SA

477   Crimson Chat, Ephthianura tricolor, July 16, Marla, SA

478   Grey-headed Honeyeater, Lichenostomus keartlandi, July 17,
      King's Canyon, NT

479   Spinifex Pigeon, Petrophassa plumifera, July 17, King's Canyon, NT

480   Dusky Grasswren, Amytornis purnelli, July 17, King's Canyon, NT

481   Rufous-crowned Emu-wren, Stipiturus ruficeps, July 18, King's Canyon, NT

482   Ground Cuckoo-shrike, Coracina maxima, July 18, King's Canyon, NT

483   Red-browed Pardalote, Pardalotus rubricatus, July 18, King's Canyon, NT

484   Black-breasted Buzzard, Hamirostra melanosternon, July 18,
      King's Canyon, NT

485   Pink Cockatoo, Cacatua leadbeateri, July 19, Luritja Way, NT

486   Bourke's Parrot, Neophema bourkii, July 19, Lasseter Highway, NT

487   Painted Finch, Emblema pictum, July 24, Ellery Creek,, NT

488   Grey Honeyeater, Conopophila whitei, July 26, Kunoth Well, NT

489   Diamond Dove, Geopelia cuneata, July 26, Kunoth Well, NT

490   Franklin's Gull, Larus pipixcan, July 27, Salisbury, SA

491   Elegant Parrot, Neophema elegans, July 27, Tolderol, SA

492   Red-backed Kingfisher, Halcyon pyrrhopygia, July 29, Santa Teresa, NT

493   Cinnamon Quail-thrush, Cinclosoma cinnamomeum, July 29, Andado, NT

494   Banded Whiteface, Aphelocephala nigricincta, July 29, Andado, NT

495   Orange Chat, Ephthianura aurifrons, July 30, Andado, NT

496   Letter-winged Kite, Elanus scriptus, July 30, Mac Clarke Reserve, NT

497   Eyrean Grasswren, Amytornis goyderi, July 30, Andado, NT

498   Gibberbird, Ashbyia lovensis, July 30, Andado, NT

499   Budgerigar, Melopsittacus undulatus, July 30, Finke River Floodout, NT

500   Australian Bustard, Ardeotis australis, July 30, Hugh's Waterhole, SA

501   Thick-billed Grasswren, Amytornis textilis, Aug 4, Lyndhurst, SA

502   Cockatiel, Nymphicus hollandicus, Aug 5, Innamincka, SA

503   Grey Grasswren, Amytornis barbatus, Aug 9, Pyampa, QLD

504   Painted Honeyeater, Grantiella picta, Aug 9, Thargomyndah, QLD

505 Red-winged Parrot, Aprosmictus erythropterus, Aug 10, Eulo Bore, QLD
506 Spotted Bowerbird, Chlamydera maculata, Aug 10, Bowra, QLD
507 Hall's Babbler, Pomatostomus halli, Aug 10, Bowra, QLD
508 Yellow-bellied Sunbird, Nectarinia jugularis, Aug 15, Townsville, QLD
509 White-throated Honeyeater, Melithreptus albogularis, Aug 15, Townsville, QLD
510 Blue-winged Kookaburra, Dacelo leachii, Aug 15, Townsville, QLD
511 Brown-backed Honeyeater, Ramsayornis modestus, Aug 15, Townsville, QLD
512 Nutmeg Mannikin, Lonchura punctulata, Aug 15, Townsville, QLD
513 Rufous-throated Honeyeater, Conopophila rufogularis, Aug 15, Townsville, QLD
514 VIC's Riflebird, Ptilotis victoriae, Aug 15, Paluma, QLD
515 Macleay's Honeyeater, Xanthotis macleayana, Aug 15, Paluma, QLD
516 Grey-headed Robin, Heteromyias albispecularis, Aug 15, Paluma, QLD
517 Spotted Catbird, Ailuroedus melanotis, Aug 15, Paluma, QLD
518 Yellow-breasted Boatbill, Machaerirhyncus flaviventer, Aug 15, Paluma, QLD
519 White-rumped Swiftlet, Collocalia spodiopygius, Aug 15, Ingham, QLD
520 Green Pygmy-Goose, Nettapus pulchellus, Aug 15, Ingham, QLD
521 Helmeted Friarbird, Philemon buceroides, Aug 15, Tully, QLD
522 Crimson Finch, Neochmia phaeton, Aug 15, Innisfail, QLD
523 Shining Starling, Aplonis metallica, Aug 15, Innisfail, QLD
524 Beach Stone-curlew, Esacus neglectus, Aug 15, Cairns, QLD
525 Varied Honeyeater, Lichenostomus versicolor, Aug 16, Cairns, QLD
526 Large-billed Gerygone, Gerygone magnirostris, Aug 16, Cairns, QLD
527 Orange-footed Scrubfowl, Megapodius reinwardt, Aug 16, Cairns, QLD
528 Little Kingfisher, Alcedo pusilla, Aug 16, Cairns, QLD
529 Yellow Honeyeater, Lichenostomus flavus, Aug 18, Windmill Creek, QLD
530 White-throated Gerygone, Gerygone olivacea, Aug 18, Windmill Creek, QLD
531 Black-backed Butcherbird, Cracticus mentalis, Aug 18, Windmill Creek, QLD
532 Silver-crowned Friarbird, Philemon argenticeps, Aug 18, Windmill Creek, QLD
533 Banded Honeyeater, Certhionyx pectoralis, Aug 18, Windmill Creek, QLD
534 Golden-shouldered Parrot, Psephotus chrysopterygius, Aug 18, Windmill Creek, QLD
535 Radjah Shelduck, Tadorna radjah, Aug 18, Weipa, QLD
536 Yellow Oriole, Oriolus flavocinctus, Aug 19, Weipa, QLD
537 Yellow-spotted Honeyeater, Meliphaga notata, Aug 19, Weipa, QLD
538 Great Bowerbird, Chlamydera nuchalis, Aug 19, Weipa, QLD
539 Pied Heron, Ardea picata, Aug 19, Weipa, QLD
540 Lemon-bellied Flycatcher, Microeca flavigaster, Aug 19, Weipa, QLD
541 Torresian Imperial Pigeon, Ducula bicolor, Aug 20, Cairns, QLD
542 Shining Flycatcher, Myiagra alecto, Aug 21, Horn Island, QLD
543 Red-headed Honeyeater, Myzomela erythrocephala, Aug 21, Horn Island, QLD

544 Eclectus Parrot, Eclectus roratus, Aug 22, Dauan Is., QLD
545 Mangrove Golden Whistler, Pachycephala melanura, Aug 22, Dauan Is., QLD
546 Broad-billed Flycatcher, Myiagra ruficollis, Aug 22, Dauan Is., QLD
547 Singing Starling, Aplonis cantoroides, Aug 22, Boigu Is., QLD
548 Australian Pratincole, Stiltia isabella, Aug 22, Boigu Is., QLD
549 Rufous-banded Honeyeater, Conopophila albogularis, Aug 22,
    Boigu Is., QLD
550 Red-backed Button-quail, Turnix maculosa, Aug 22, Boigu Is., QLD
551 Pale White-eye, Zosterops citrinellus, Aug 23, Boigu Is., QLD
552 Tawny-breasted Honeyeater, Xanthotis flaviventer, Aug 23, Boigu Is., QLD
553 Black Butcherbird, Cracticus quoyi, Aug 23, Boigu Is., QLD
554 Northern Fantail, Rhipidura rufiventris, Aug 23, Boigu Is., QLD
555 Spotted Whistling-Duck, Dendrocygna guttata, Aug 23, Boigu Is., QLD
556 Pectoral Sandpiper, Calidris melanotos, Aug 24, Boigu Is., QLD
557 Large-tailed Nightjar, Caprimulgus macrurus, Aug 24, Boigu Is., QLD
558 Collared Imperial Pigeon, Ducula muellerii, Aug 24, Boigu Is., QLD
559 Little Bronze-cuckoo, Chrysococcyx minutillis, Aug 25, Saibai Is., QLD
560 Papuan Flowerpecker, , Aug 26, Saibai Is., QLD
561 Shining Bronze-cuckoo, Chrysococcyx lucidus, Aug 26, Saibai Is., QLD
562 Black-naped Tern, Sterna sumatrana, Aug 29, Dove Islet, QLD
563 Bridled Tern, Sterna anaethetus, Aug 29, Dove Islet, QLD
564 Sarus Crane, Grus antigone, Aug 30, Weipa, QLD
565 Palm Cockatoo, Probosciger aterrimus, Aug 31, Iron Range, QLD
566 Graceful Honeyeater, Meliphaga gracilis, Aug 31, Iron Range, QLD
567 White-faced Robin, Tregellasia leucops, Aug 31, Iron Range, QLD
568 Tropical Scrubwren, Sericornis becarii, Sept 1, Iron Range, QLD
569 Brown Cuckoo-dove, Macropygia amboinensis, Sept 1, Iron Range, QLD
570 Fig Parrot, Cyclopsitta diophthalma, Sept 1, Iron Range, QLD
571 Varied Triller, Lalage leucomela, Sept 1, Iron Range, QLD
572 Superb Fruit-dove, Ptilinopus superbus, Sept 1, Iron Range, QLD
573 Magnificent Riflebird, Ptiloris magnificus, Sept 1, Iron Range, QLD
574 Frilled Monarch, Arses telescophthalmus, Sept 1, Iron Range, QLD
575 Fairy Gerygone, Gerygone palpebrosa, Sept 1, Iron Range, QLD
576 Collared Kingfisher, Todiramphus chloris, Sept 1, Chilli Beach, QLD
577 Grey Whistler, Pachycephala simplex, Sept 1, Iron Range, QLD
578 Lovely Fairy-wren, Malurus amabilis, Sept 1, Iron Range, QLD
579 Papuan Frogmouth, Podargus papuensis, Sept 1, Iron Range, QLD
580 Trumpet Manucode, Manucodia keraundrenii, Sept 2, Iron Range, QLD
581 Yellow-billed Kingfisher, Syma torotoro, Sept 2, Iron Range, QLD
582 Fawn-breasted Bowerbird, Chlamydera cerviniventris, Sept 2,
    Chilli Beach, QLD
583 White-streaked Honeyeater, Trichodere cockerelli, Sept 3, Iron Range, QLD
584 Red-cheeked Parrot, Geoffroyus geoffroyi, Sept 3, Iron Range, QLD

585   Red Goshawk, Erythrotriorchis radiatus, Sept 4, Lakefield, QLD
586   Squatter Pigeon, Geophaps scripta, Sept 4, Mount Carbine, QLD
587   Mountain Thornbill, Acanthiza katherina, Sept 5, Mount Lewis, QLD
588   Atherton Scrubwren, Sericornis keri, Sept 5, Mount Lewis, QLD
589   Golden Bowerbird, Prionodura newtoniana, Sept 5, Mount Lewis, QLD
590   Topknot Pigeon, Lopholaimus antarcticus, Sept 5, Mount Lewis, QLD
591   Bridled Honeyeater, Lichenostomus frenatus, Sept 5, Mount Lewis, QLD
592   Lesser Sooty Owl, Tyto multipunctata, Sept 5, Julatten, QLD
593   Bower's Shrike-thrush, Colluricincla boweri, Sept 7, Mount Lewis, QLD
594   Fernwren, Oreoscopus gutturalis, Sept 7, Mount Lewis, QLD
595   Chowchilla, Orthonyx spaldingii, Sept 7, Mount Lewis, QLD
596   Tooth-billed Bowerbird, Scenopoeetes dentirostris, Sept 7,
      Mount Lewis, QLD
597   Barred Cuckoo-shrike, Coracina lineata, Sept 8, Julatten, QLD
598   White-browed Robin, Poecilodryas superciliosa, Sept 8,
      Big Mitchell Creek, QLD
599   Southern Cassowary, Casuarius casuarius, Sept 9, Mission Beach, QLD
600   Mangrove Robin, Eopsaltria pulverulenta, Sept 9, Cardwell, QLD
601   Eastern Grass Owl, Tyto capensis, Sept 9, Ingham, QLD
602   Pied Monarch, Arses kaupi, Sept 10, Jourama Falls, QLD
603   Cotton Pygmy Goose, Nettapus coromandelianus, Sept 10,
      Ross River Dam, QLD
604   Eungella Honeyeater, Lichenostomus hindwoodi, Sept 11, Eungalla, QLD
605   Mangrove Honeyeater, Lichenostomus fasciogularis, Sept 13,
      Toorbul Point, QLD
606   Albert's Lyrebird, Menura alberti, Sept 14, Lamington, QLD
607   Olive Whistler, Pachycephala olivacea, Sept 14, Lamington, QLD
608   Rufous Scrub-bird, Atrichiornis rufescens, Sept 16, Lamington,
609   Superb Parrot, Polytelis swainsonii, Sept 20, Gulpa, NSW
610   Antarctic Prion, Pachyptila desolata, Sept 22, Eaglehawk Neck, TAS
611   Southern Fulmar, Fulmarus glacialoides, Sept 22, Eaglehawk Neck, TAS
612   Buller's Shearwater, Puffinus bulleri, Oct 13, Newcastle, NSW
613   Black-bellied Storm-Petrel, Fregetta tropica, Oct 13, Newcastle, NSW
614   Gould's Petrel, Pterodroma leucoptera, Oct 13, Newcastle, NSW
615   Lord Howe Woodhen, Gallirallus sylvestris, Oct 16, Lord Howe Island
616   Little Shearwater, Puffinus assimilis, Oct 17, Lord Howe Island
617   White-bellied Storm-Petrel, Fregetta grallaria, Oct 18, Lord Howe Island
618   Plum-headed Finch, Neochmia modesta, Ocober 20, Capertee Valley, NSW
619   Regent Honeyeater, Xanthomyza phrygia, Oct 20, Capertee Valley,
620   Black Honeyeater, Certhionix niger, Oct 21, West Wyalong, NSW
621   Spotted Quail-Thrush, Cinclosma punctatum, Oct 22, Barambogie, VIC
622   Red-lored Whistler, Pachycephala rufogularis, Oct 28, Comet Bore, SA
623   Malleefowl, Leipoa ocellata, Oct 29, Eromophila Park, SA

624 Rufous Field-wren, Calamanthus campestris, Oct 31, Lyndhurst, SA
625 Inland Dotterel, Charadrius australis, Nov 1, Cook, SA
626 Blue-breasted Fairy-wren, Malurus pulcherrimus, Nov 3, Ravensthorpe, WA
627 Western Whipbird, Psophodes nigrogularis, Nov 4, Fitzgerald River, WA
628 White-winged Triller, Lalage sueurii, Nov 4, Boxwood Hill, WA
629 Noisy Scrub-bird, Atrichiornis clamosus, Nov 4, Cheyne's Beach, WA
630 Western Bristlebird, Dasyornis longirostris, Nov 4, Two People's Bay, WA
631 Common Koel, Eudynamys scolopacea, Nov 6, Sydney Airport, NSW
632 Canada Goose, Branta canadensis, Nov 7, Shoalhaven Heads, NSW
633 Rock Parrot, Neophema petrophila, Nov 10, Lancelin, WA
634 Lesser Noddy, Anous tenuirostris, Nov 12, Abrolhos Islands, WA
635 Chestnut-breasted Quail-thrush, Cinclosma castaneothorax, Nov 13, Cue, WA
636 Spinifexbird, Eremiornis carteri, Nov 14, Newman, WA
637 Oriental Plover , Charadius veredus, Nov 15, Old Onslow, WA
638 Chiming Wedgebill, Psophodes occidentalis, Nov 15, 72km North of Carnavon, WA
639 Yellow White-eye, Zosterops luteus, Nov 16, Broome, WA
640 Blue and White Flycatcher, Ficedula cyanomelana, Nov 16, Broome, WA
641 Swinhoe's Snipe, Gallinago megala, Nov 16, Broome, WA
642 Yellow Wagtail, Motacilla flava, Nov 16, Broome, WA
643 Little Curlew, Numenius minutus, Nov 16, Broome, WA
644 Long-toed Stint, Calidris subminuta, Nov 16, Broome, WA
645 Dusky Gerygone, Gerygone tenebrosa, Nov 16, Broome, WA
646 Yellow-tinted Honeyeater, Lichenostomus flavescens, Nov 16, Broome, WA
647 Mangrove Grey Fantail, Rhipidura phasiana, Nov 17, Broome, WA
648 Common Redshank, Tringa totanus, Nov 17, Broome, WA
649 White-breasted Whistler, Pachycephala lanioides, Nov 17, Broome, WA
650 Asian Dowitcher, Limnodromus semipalmatus, Nov 17, Broome, WA
651 Lesser Crested Tern, Sterna bengalensis, Nov 17, Broome, WA
652 Yellow Chat, Epthianura crocea, Nov 17, Broome, WA
653 Sanderling, Calidris alba, Nov 17, Broome, WA
654 Long-tailed Finch, Poephila acuticauda, Nov 17, Broome, WA
655 Ruff, Philomachus pugnax, Nov 19, Derby, WA
656 Great-billed Heron, Ardea sumatrana, Nov 19, Derby, WA
657 Bar-breasted Honeyeater, Ramsayornis fasciatus, Nov 19, Dog Chain Creek, WA
658 Gargeny, Anas querquedula, Nov 19, Mt. Barnett, WA
659 Black-tailed Treecreeper, Climacteris melanura, Nov 19, Mt. Barnett, WA
660 White-gaped Honeyeater, Lichenostomus unicolor, Nov 20, Windjana Gorge, WA
661 Isabelline Wheatear, Oenanthe isabellina, Nov 21, Mount Carbine, QLD
662 Rufous Owl, Ninox rufa, Nov 21, Emerald Creek Falls, QLD

663   Buff-breasted Paradise Kingfisher, Tanysiptera sylvia, Nov 22, Julatten, QLD

664   Northern Rosella, Platycercus venustus, Nov 25, Mount Elizabeth, WA

665   White-quilled Rock-Pigeon, Petrophassa albipennis, Nov 25,
Mount Elizabeth, WA

666   Sandstone Shrike-thrush, Colluricincla woodwardi, Nov 26,
Mount Elizabeth, WA

667   White-lined Honeyeater, Meliphaga albilineata, Nov 26,
Mount Elizabeth, WA

668   Green-backed Gerygone, Gerygone chloronotus, Nov 26,
Mount Elizabeth, WA

669   Masked Finch, Poephila personata, Nov 26, Mount Elizabeth, WA

670   Star Finch, Neochmia ruficauda, Nov 27, Parry's Lagoon, WA

671   Yellow-rumped Mannikin, Lonchura flaviprymna, Nov 27, Kununurra, WA

672   Red-chested Button-quail, Turnix pyrrhothorax, Nov 28, Kununurra, WA

673   Gouldian Finch, Erythrura gouldiae, Nov 29, Kununurra, WA

674   Pictorella Mannikin, Heteromunia pectoralis, Nov 29, Kununurra, WA

675   Purple-crowned Fairy-wren, Malurus coronatus, Nov 30,
VIC River Crossing, NT

676   Chestnut-backed Button-quail, Turnix castanota, Dec 1,
Copperfield Dam, NT

677   Hooded Parrot, Psephotus dissimilis, Dec 2, Umbruwarra Gorge Rd, NT

678   White-throated Grasswren, Amytornis housei, Dec 2, Kakadu, NT

679   Partridge Pigeon, Geophaps smithii, Dec 2, Kakadu, NT

680   Banded Fruit-Dove, Ptilinopus cinctus, Dec 3, Kakadu, NT

681   Chestnut-quilled Rock-Pigeon, Petrophassa rufipennis, Dec 4, Kakadu, NT

682   White-browed Crake, Porzana cinerea, Dec 4, Fogg Dam, NT

683   Rainbow Pitta, Pitta iris, Dec 4, Howard Springs, NT

684   Zitting Cisticola, Cisticola juncidis, Dec 6, Holmes Jungle, NT

685   Chestnut Rail, Eulabeornis castaneoventris, Dec 9, Darwin, NT

686   Varied Lorikeet, Psitteuteles versicolor, Dec 10, Katherine, NT

687   Flock Bronzewing, Phaps histrionica, Dec 11, Brunette Downs, NT

688   Oriental Cuckoo, Cuculus saturatus, Dec 18, Townsville, QLD

689   Marbled Frogmouth, Podargus ocellatus, Dec 19, Iron Range, QLD

690   Green-backed Honeyeater, Glycichaera fallax, Dec 20, Iron Range, QLD

691   Black-winged Monarch, Monarcha frater, Dec 20, Iron Range, QLD

692   Gould's Bronze-Cuckoo, Chrysococcyx russatus, Dec 20, Iron Range, QLD

693   Northern Scrub-robin, Drymodes superciliaris, Dec 20, Iron Range, QLD

694   Yellow-legged Flycatcher, Microeca griseoceps, Dec 21, Iron Range, QLD

695   Chestnut-breasted Cuckoo, Cacomantis castaneiventris, Dec 21,
Iron Range, QLD

696   Red-bellied Pitta, Pitta erythrogaster, Dec 21, Iron Range, QLD

697   Black-throated Finch, Poephila cincta, Dec 22,
67 km North Mount Molloy, QLD

698   Bush-hen, Amaurornis olivaceus, Dec 23, Julatten, QLD
699   Red-necked Crake, Rallina tricolor, Dec 23, Julatten, QLD
700   Blue-faced Parrot-finch, Erythrura trichroa, Dec 24, Mt. Lewis, QLD
701   Red-rumped Swallow, Hirundo daurica, Dec 24, Newell Beach, QLD
702   Masked Owl, Tyto novaehollandiae, Dec 26, Julatten, QLD
703   Little Bittern, Ixobrychus minutus, Dec 30, Sherwood, QLD

Total: 703
Minus all Territories: 668
Plus Torres Strait: 674

ACKNOWLEDGEMENTS

The Big Twitch was initially conceived as a totally solo project – just me against the birds. What soon became apparent was that this was an undertaking impossible to do alone. I am indebted to the bird-watching community for their phenomenal support of my record attempt. In particular I would like to thank Groober, Puke and Mike Carter, not only for their help during the year but for two decades of encouragement, support and friendship.

As I raced around the country there were certain local experts who ensured my efforts didn't run off the rails and I would like to single them out for special thanks: Andrew Stafford and Paul Wallbridge in Queensland; Tony Palliser, Dion Hobcroft and Phil Hansbro in New South Wales; David Harper, John Cox and their families in South Australia; Frank O'Connor and Adrian Boyle in the West and Niven McCrie in the Northern Territory. The Birding-aus website run by Russell Woodford was invaluable for me to plan trips and find out the latest gen on where the rare birds were.

Throughout the year I had the privilege of twitching with innumerable birders who were universally helpful and supportive. The following is by no means an exhaustive list of those I birded with or who helped me out with specific information: Peter Lansley, William Colvin, Eileen Collins, Neville Bartlett, Barry Traill, Susie Duncan, Stuart Cooney, Chris Tzaros, Andrew Silcocks, Lindsay Smith, Peter Milburn, Rod Gardner, Kevin Bartram, Kaye Proudley, Owen Evans, Bill Moorhead, David Stewart, Richard Baxter, Anne Lindsay, David James, Murray Lord, Jo Wieneke, Rohan Clarke, Harry Clarke, Chris Lester, Rosemary Lester, Geoff Walker, Tania Ireton, Paul Peake, Glenn Holmes, Jenny Holmes, Jeff Middleton, Max Orchard, Penny Drake-Brockman, Chris Coleborn, Simon Starr, Bob Way, Bruce Cox, Danny Rogers, Ken Rogers, Trevor Ford, Brendan Neilly, Rob Farnes, Karen Pearson, Frank Mitchell, Greg Hunt, Peter Wilkins, Tony Russell, Colin Rogers, Marco Sacchi, Ross and Marg Betts, Ian and Julie-Lynn McLaren, Fred Smith, Neil Macumber, Bill Watson, Ross Mullholland, Jann Mullholland, Warwick Pickwell, Steve Murphy, Carol Iles, Andrew Iles, Ron Stannard, John Young, David Geering,

Alan Morris, Rob Berry, Gail Berry, Susan Myers, Stuart Dashper, Frank Pierce, David Stickney, Iain Woxvold, Euan Fothergill, Ian May, Stephen Ambrose, Timothy Hyde, Carol Proberts, Leslie Gordon, Gloria Pitts, Peter Bright, Stella Mack, Chris Hassell, George Swann, Peter Lacey, Julie Hennessy, Bob Forsyth, Steve Guerrato, Lloyd Neilson, Greg Roberts.

You are all a magnificent bunch of freaks.

Even more freaky was the fact that the following people with absolutely no interest in birds were also incredibly supportive before, during and after my travels: Indra Kilfoyle, Colin Christmas, Ted Emery, Guy Rundle, Sally Bothroyd, Brendan Sides, Jane Staley, Warwick Dooley, Narelle D'Alton, Anthony Watt, Astrid Briggs, Lorna Hendry, James Shuter, Michael Veitch, Chris and Colleen Diamond, Jeremy Marron, Karen Smith, Rob and Belinda Caldwell, Rob Adams, Anita Punton, Misha Ketchell, Ray Matsen and Tracey Bell. Special thanks are due to Mark O'Toole who twice provided the impetus for the Big Twitch to move from the road to the page and to Jo Colvin who amongst other things introduced me to the term 'birdy-nerdy'.

Much gratitude to the faith in me shown by Allen & Unwin, in particular Andrea McNamara who was foolish enough to believe that a story about an idiot running around the country looking at birds was worth publishing. But then she is a Collingwood supporter so has a natural affinity with hopeless causes.

Finally I would like to thank Eleanor for agreeing to go on a second date despite the whole birdwatching thing.